# TALENT

## DELUXE EDITION

### GOLDEN
### SNIEGOSKI
### AZACETA

| LONDON BOROUGH OF WANDSWORTH | |
|---|---|
| 9030 00004 1070 3 | |
| **Askews & Holts** | 22-Jan-2015 |
| AF | £10.99 |
| | WW14000737 |

ROSS RICHIE CEO & Founder • JACK CUMMINS President • MARK SMYLIE Founder of Archaia • MATT GAGNON Editor-in-Chief • FILIP SABLIK VP of Publishing & Marketing • STEPHEN CHRISTY VP of Development
LANCE KREITER VP of Licensing & Merchandising • PHIL BARBARO VP of Finance • BRYCE CARLSON Managing Editor • MEL CAYLO Marketing Manager • SCOTT NEWMAN Production Design Manager • IRENE BRADISH Operations Manager
DAFNA PLEBAN Editor • SHANNON WATTERS Editor • ERIC HARBURN Editor • REBECCA TAYLOR Editor • IAN BRILL Editor • CHRIS ROSA Assistant Editor • ALEX GALER Assistant Editor • WHITNEY LEOPARD Assistant Editor
JASMINE AMIRI Assistant Editor • CAMERON CHITTOCK Assistant Editor • HANNAH NANCE PARTLOW Production Designer • KELSEY DIETERICH Production Designer • EMI YONEMURA BROWN Production Designer
DEVIN FUNCHES E-Commerce & Inventory Coordinator • ANDY LIEGL Event Coordinator • BRIANNA HART Executive Assistant • AARON FERRARA Operations Assistant • JOSÉ MEZA Sales Assistant • ELIZABETH LOUGHRIDGE Accounting Assistant

TALENT: DELUXE EDITION, July 2014. Published by BOOM! Studios, a division of Boom Entertainment, Inc. Talent is ™ & © 2014 Christopher Golden, Tom Sniegoski, Boom Entertainment, Inc. Originally published in single magazine form as TALENT No. 1-4. ™ & © 2006 Christopher Golden, Tom Sniegoski, Boom Entertainment, Inc. All rights reserved. BOOM! Studios™ and the BOOM! Studios logo are trademarks of Boom Entertainment, Inc., registered in various countries and categories. All characters, events, and institutions depicted herein are fictional. Any similarity between any of the names, characters, persons, events, and/or institutions in this publication to actual names, characters, and persons, whether living or dead, events, and/or institutions is unintended and purely coincidental. BOOM! Studios does not read or accept unsolicited submissions of ideas, stories, or artwork.

A catalog record of this book is available from OCLC and from the BOOM! Studios website, www.boom-studios.com, on the Librarians Page.

BOOM! Studios, 5670 Wilshire Boulevard, Suite 450, Los Angeles, CA 90036-5679. Printed in China. First Printing.
Hardcover ISBN: 978-1-60886-469-0, Softcover ISBN: 978-1-60886-450-8, eISBN: 978-1-61398-304-1

Written by
**CHRISTOPHER GOLDEN
TOM SNIEGOSKI**

Art by
**PAUL AZACETA**

Colors by
**RON RILEY**

Lettering by
**MARSHALL DILLON**

Cover by
**PAUL AZACETA**

Production by
**ED DUKESHIRE**

Original Series
Editor
**MARSHALL DILLON**

Designer
**EMI YONEMURA BROWN**

Deluxe Edition
Editor
**IAN BRILL**

# CHAPTER ONE 1

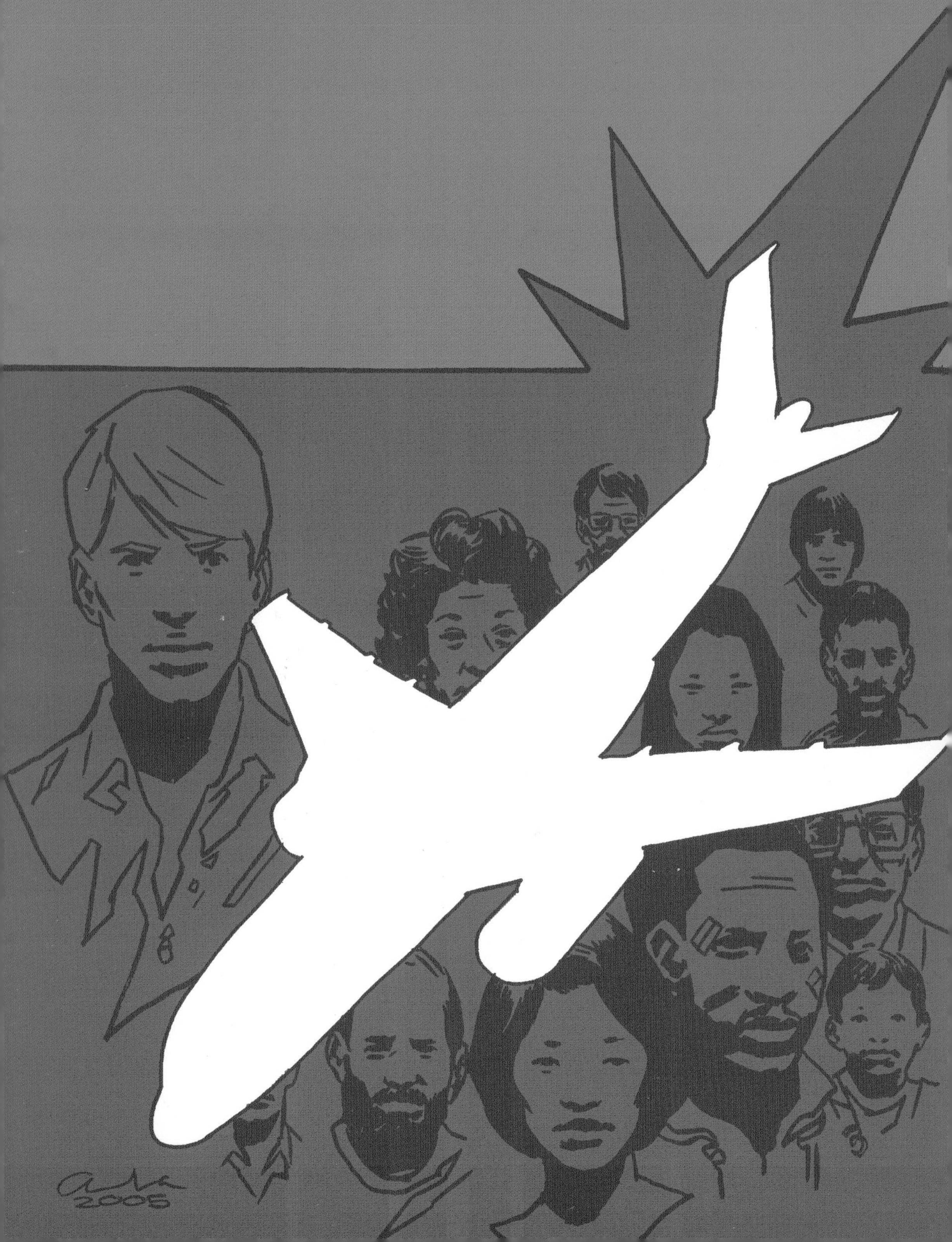

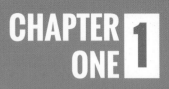

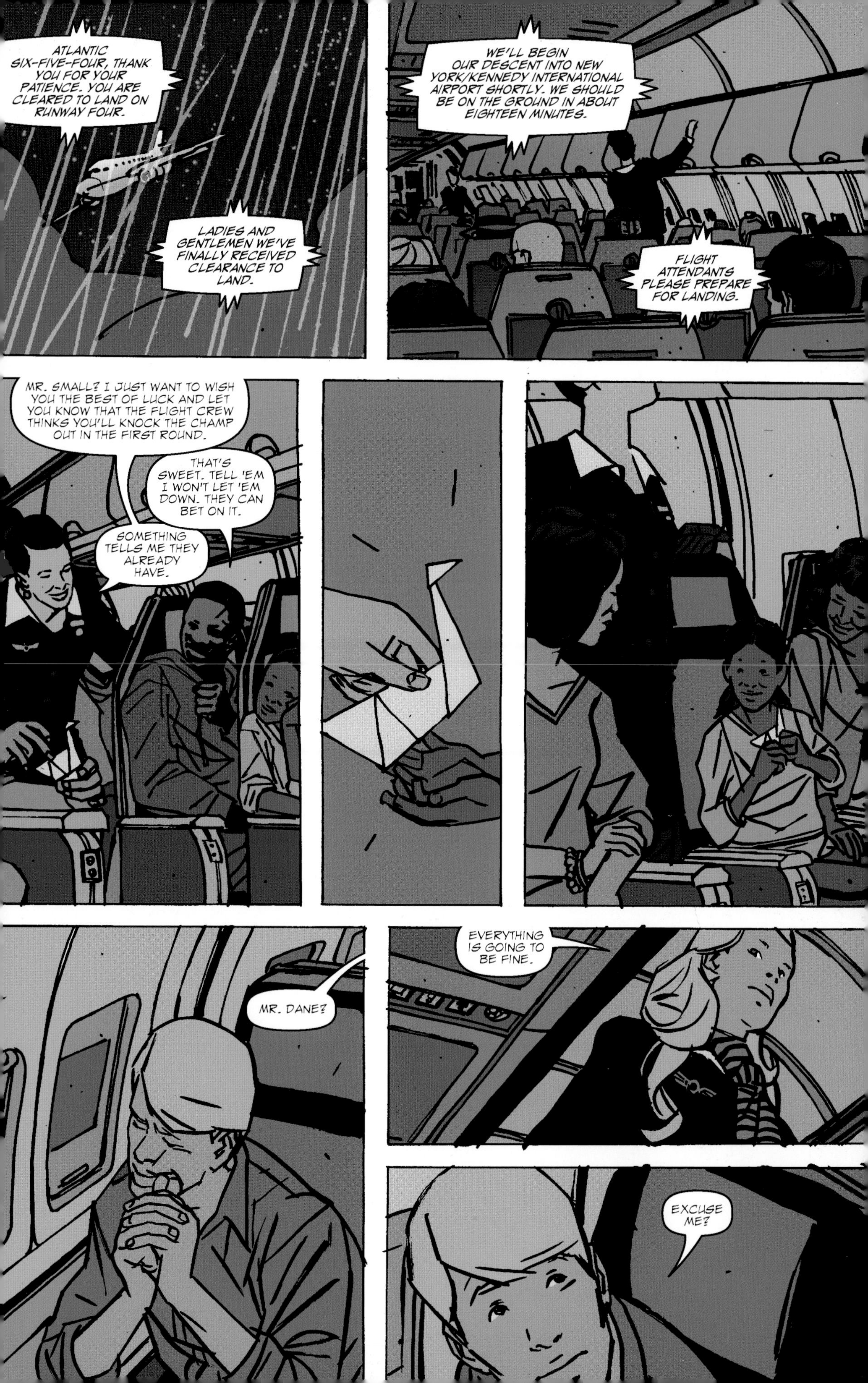
ATLANTIC SIX-FIVE-FOUR, THANK YOU FOR YOUR PATIENCE. YOU ARE CLEARED TO LAND ON RUNWAY FOUR.
LADIES AND GENTLEMEN WE'VE FINALLY RECEIVED CLEARANCE TO LAND.
WE'LL BEGIN OUR DESCENT INTO NEW YORK/KENNEDY INTERNATIONAL AIRPORT SHORTLY. WE SHOULD BE ON THE GROUND IN ABOUT EIGHTEEN MINUTES.
FLIGHT ATTENDANTS PLEASE PREPARE FOR LANDING.
MR. SMALL? I JUST WANT TO WISH YOU THE BEST OF LUCK AND LET YOU KNOW THAT THE FLIGHT CREW THINKS YOU'LL KNOCK THE CHAMP OUT IN THE FIRST ROUND.
THAT'S SWEET. TELL 'EM I WON'T LET 'EM DOWN. THEY CAN BET ON IT.
SOMETHING TELLS ME THEY ALREADY HAVE.
MR. DANE?
EVERYTHING IS GOING TO BE FINE.
EXCUSE ME?

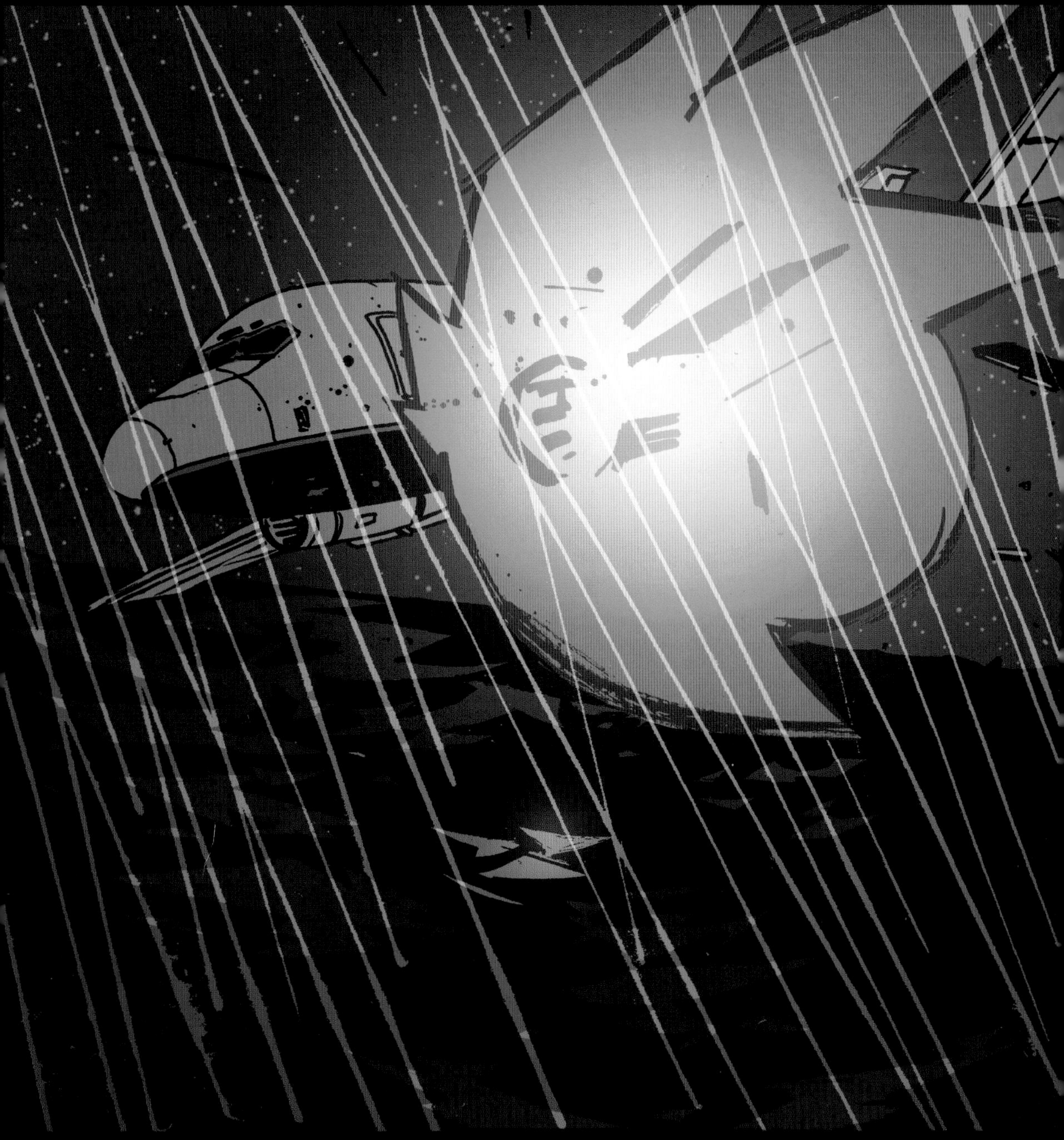

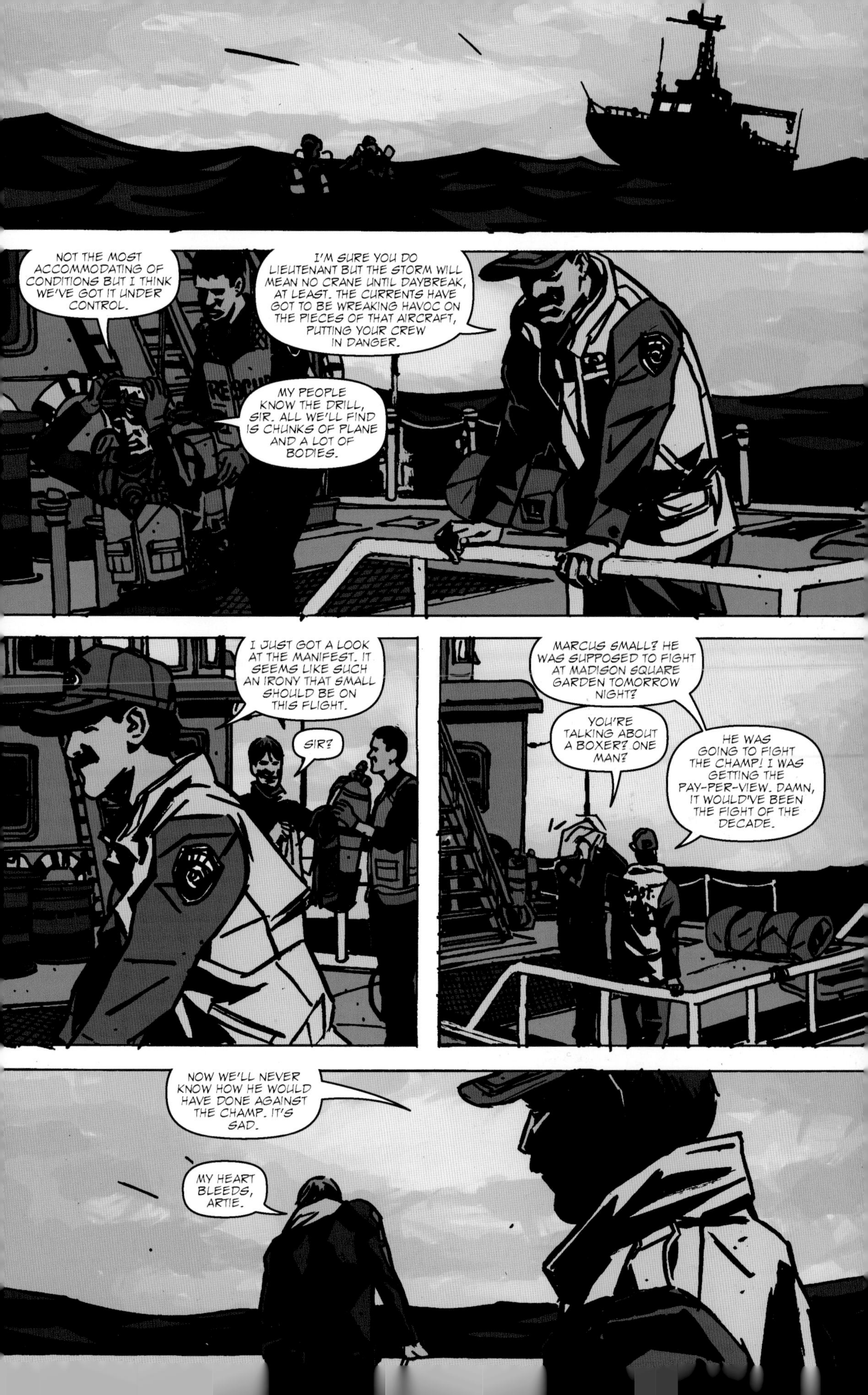
NOT THE MOST ACCOMMODATING OF CONDITIONS BUT I THINK WE'VE GOT IT UNDER CONTROL.
I'M SURE YOU DO LIEUTENANT BUT THE STORM WILL MEAN NO CRANE UNTIL DAYBREAK, AT LEAST. THE CURRENTS HAVE GOT TO BE WREAKING HAVOC ON THE PIECES OF THAT AIRCRAFT, PUTTING YOUR CREW IN DANGER.
MY PEOPLE KNOW THE DRILL, SIR. ALL WE'LL FIND IS CHUNKS OF PLANE AND A LOT OF BODIES.
I JUST GOT A LOOK AT THE MANIFEST. IT SEEMS LIKE SUCH AN IRONY THAT SMALL SHOULD BE ON THIS FLIGHT.
SIR?
MARCUS SMALL? HE WAS SUPPOSED TO FIGHT AT MADISON SQUARE GARDEN TOMORROW NIGHT?
YOU'RE TALKING ABOUT A BOXER? ONE MAN?
HE WAS GOING TO FIGHT THE CHAMP! I WAS GETTING THE PAY-PER-VIEW. DAMN, IT WOULD'VE BEEN THE FIGHT OF THE DECADE.
NOW WE'LL NEVER KNOW HOW HE WOULD HAVE DONE AGAINST THE CHAMP. IT'S SAD.
MY HEART BLEEDS, ARTIE.

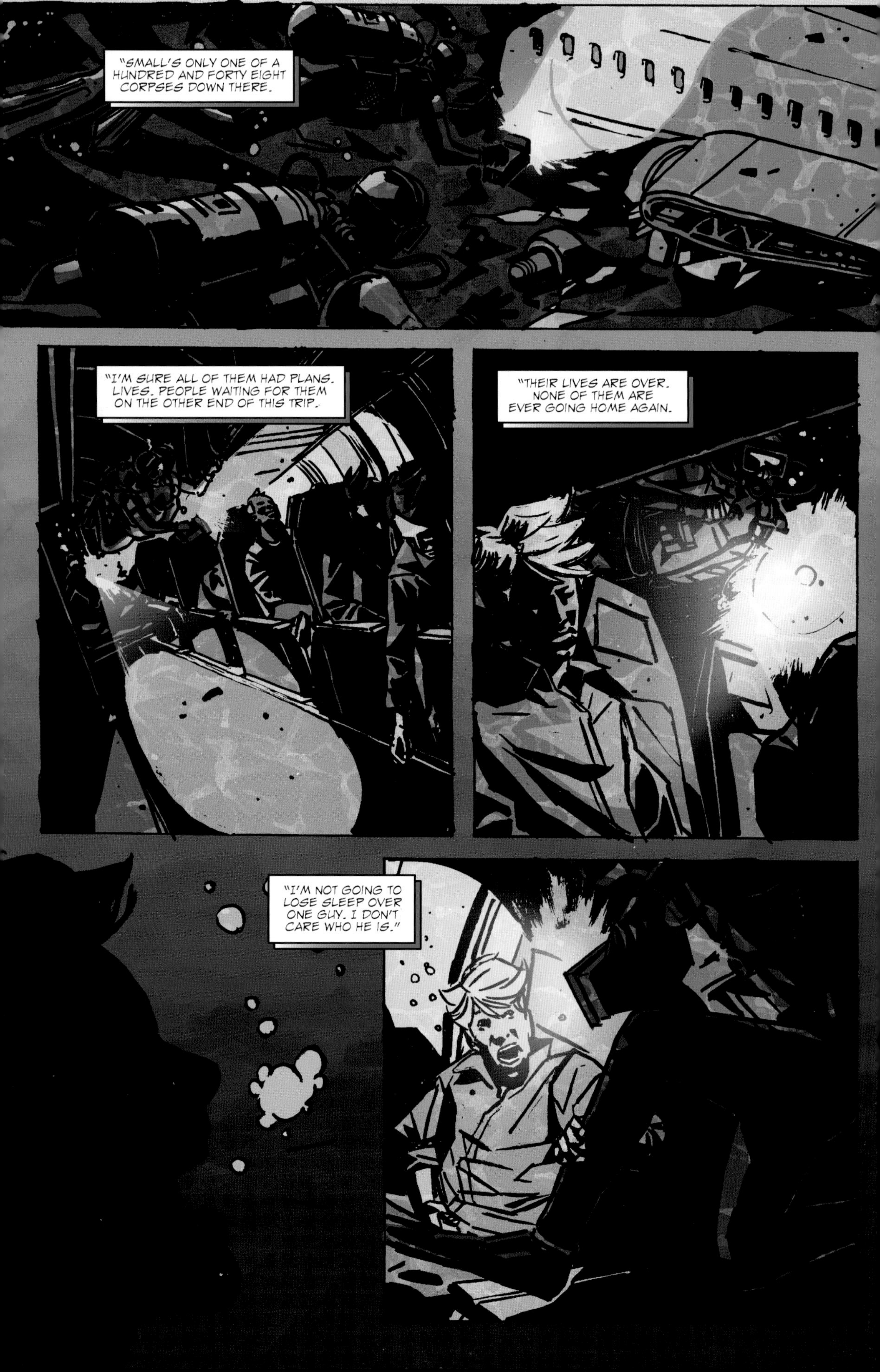
"SMALL'S ONLY ONE OF A HUNDRED AND FORTY EIGHT CORPSES DOWN THERE.
"I'M SURE ALL OF THEM HAD PLANS. LIVES. PEOPLE WAITING FOR THEM ON THE OTHER END OF THIS TRIP.
"THEIR LIVES ARE OVER. NONE OF THEM ARE EVER GOING HOME AGAIN.
"I'M NOT GOING TO LOSE SLEEP OVER ONE GUY. I DON'T CARE WHO HE IS."

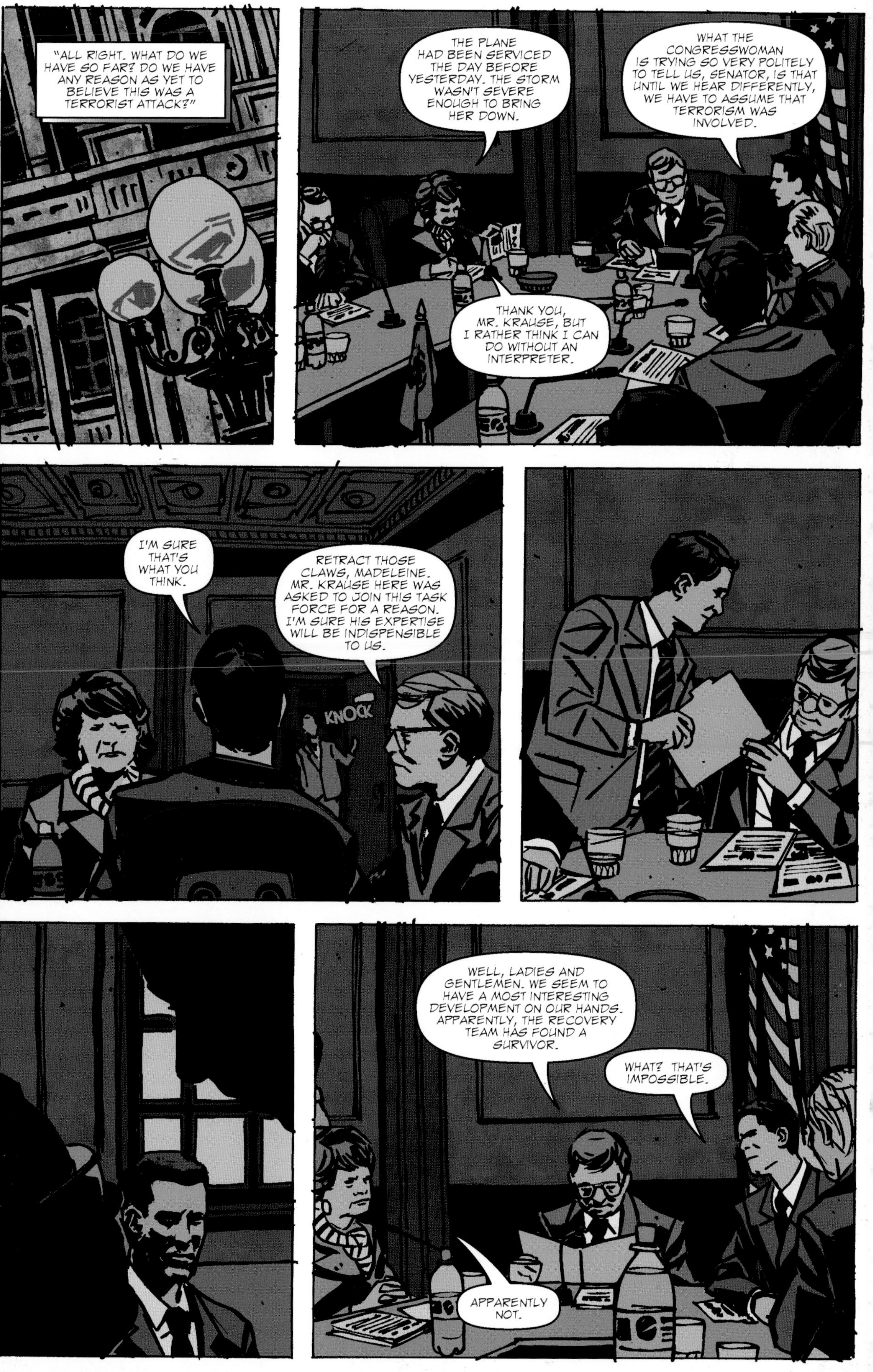
"ALL RIGHT. WHAT DO WE HAVE SO FAR? DO WE HAVE ANY REASON AS YET TO BELIEVE THIS WAS A TERRORIST ATTACK?"
THE PLANE HAD BEEN SERVICED THE DAY BEFORE YESTERDAY. THE STORM WASN'T SEVERE ENOUGH TO BRING HER DOWN.
WHAT THE CONGRESSWOMAN IS TRYING SO VERY POLITELY TO TELL US, SENATOR, IS THAT UNTIL WE HEAR DIFFERENTLY, WE HAVE TO ASSUME THAT TERRORISM WAS INVOLVED.
THANK YOU, MR. KRAUSE, BUT I RATHER THINK I CAN DO WITHOUT AN INTERPRETER.
I'M SURE THAT'S WHAT YOU THINK.
RETRACT THOSE CLAWS, MADELEINE. MR. KRAUSE HERE WAS ASKED TO JOIN THIS TASK FORCE FOR A REASON. I'M SURE HIS EXPERTISE WILL BE INDISPENSIBLE TO US.
KNOCK
WELL, LADIES AND GENTLEMEN. WE SEEM TO HAVE A MOST INTERESTING DEVELOPMENT ON OUR HANDS. APPARENTLY, THE RECOVERY TEAM HAS FOUND A SURVIVOR.
WHAT? THAT'S IMPOSSIBLE.
APPARENTLY NOT.

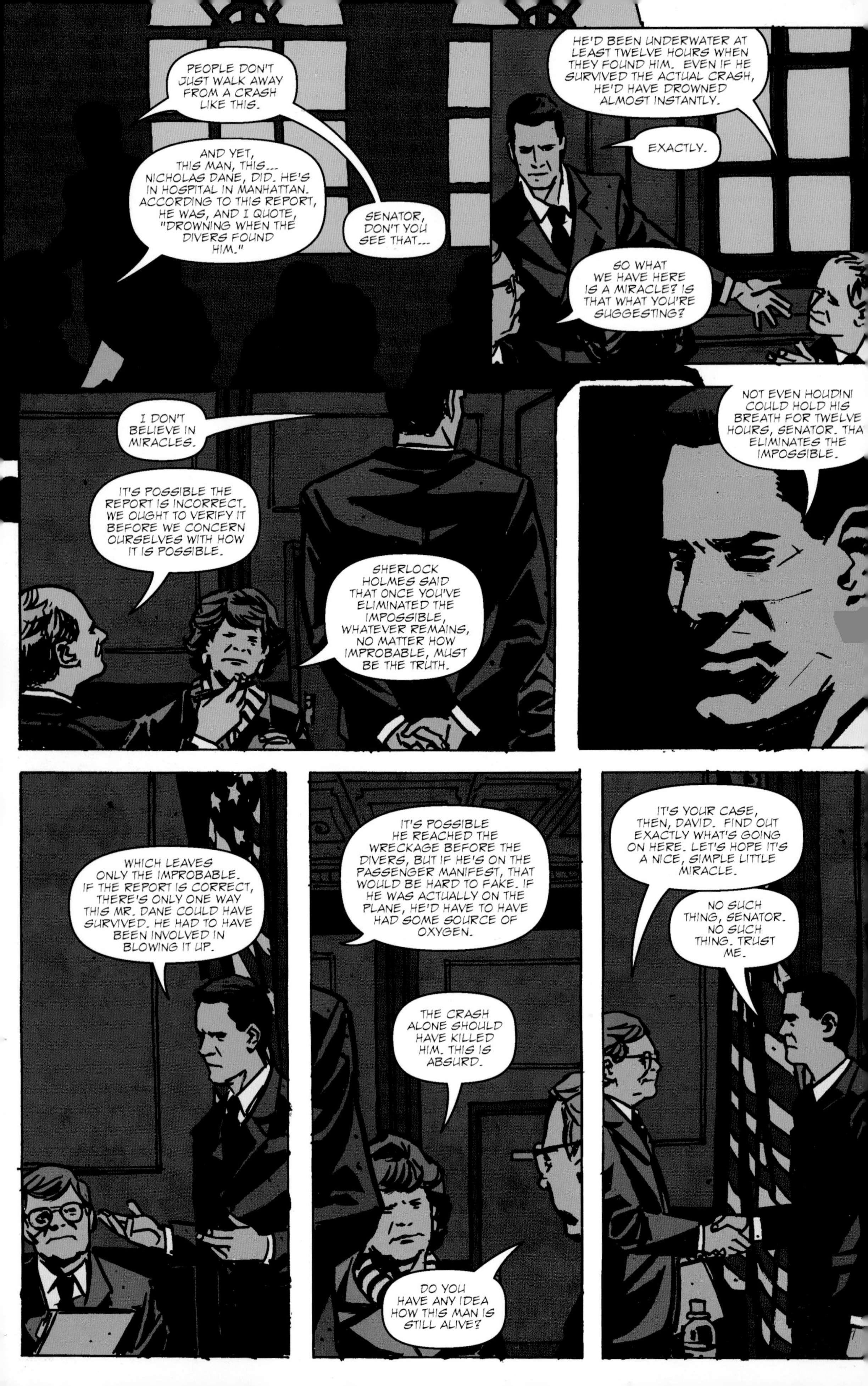
PEOPLE DON'T JUST WALK AWAY FROM A CRASH LIKE THIS.
AND YET, THIS MAN, THIS... NICHOLAS DANE, DID. HE'S IN HOSPITAL IN MANHATTAN. ACCORDING TO THIS REPORT, HE WAS, AND I QUOTE, "DROWNING WHEN THE DIVERS FOUND HIM."
SENATOR, DON'T YOU SEE THAT...
HE'D BEEN UNDERWATER AT LEAST TWELVE HOURS WHEN THEY FOUND HIM. EVEN IF HE SURVIVED THE ACTUAL CRASH, HE'D HAVE DROWNED ALMOST INSTANTLY.
EXACTLY.
SO WHAT WE HAVE HERE IS A MIRACLE? IS THAT WHAT YOU'RE SUGGESTING?
I DON'T BELIEVE IN MIRACLES.
IT'S POSSIBLE THE REPORT IS INCORRECT. WE OUGHT TO VERIFY IT BEFORE WE CONCERN OURSELVES WITH HOW IT IS POSSIBLE.
SHERLOCK HOLMES SAID THAT ONCE YOU'VE ELIMINATED THE IMPOSSIBLE, WHATEVER REMAINS, NO MATTER HOW IMPROBABLE, MUST BE THE TRUTH.
NOT EVEN HOUDINI COULD HOLD HIS BREATH FOR TWELVE HOURS, SENATOR. THA ELIMINATES THE IMPOSSIBLE.
WHICH LEAVES ONLY THE IMPROBABLE. IF THE REPORT IS CORRECT, THERE'S ONLY ONE WAY THIS MR. DANE COULD HAVE SURVIVED. HE HAD TO HAVE BEEN INVOLVED IN BLOWING IT UP.
IT'S POSSIBLE HE REACHED THE WRECKAGE BEFORE THE DIVERS, BUT IF HE'S ON THE PASSENGER MANIFEST, THAT WOULD BE HARD TO FAKE. IF HE WAS ACTUALLY ON THE PLANE, HE'D HAVE TO HAVE HAD SOME SOURCE OF OXYGEN.
THE CRASH ALONE SHOULD HAVE KILLED HIM. THIS IS ABSURD.
DO YOU HAVE ANY IDEA HOW THIS MAN IS STILL ALIVE?
IT'S YOUR CASE, THEN, DAVID. FIND OUT EXACTLY WHAT'S GOING ON HERE. LET'S HOPE IT'S A NICE, SIMPLE LITTLE MIRACLE.
NO SUCH THING, SENATOR. NO SUCH THING. TRUST ME.

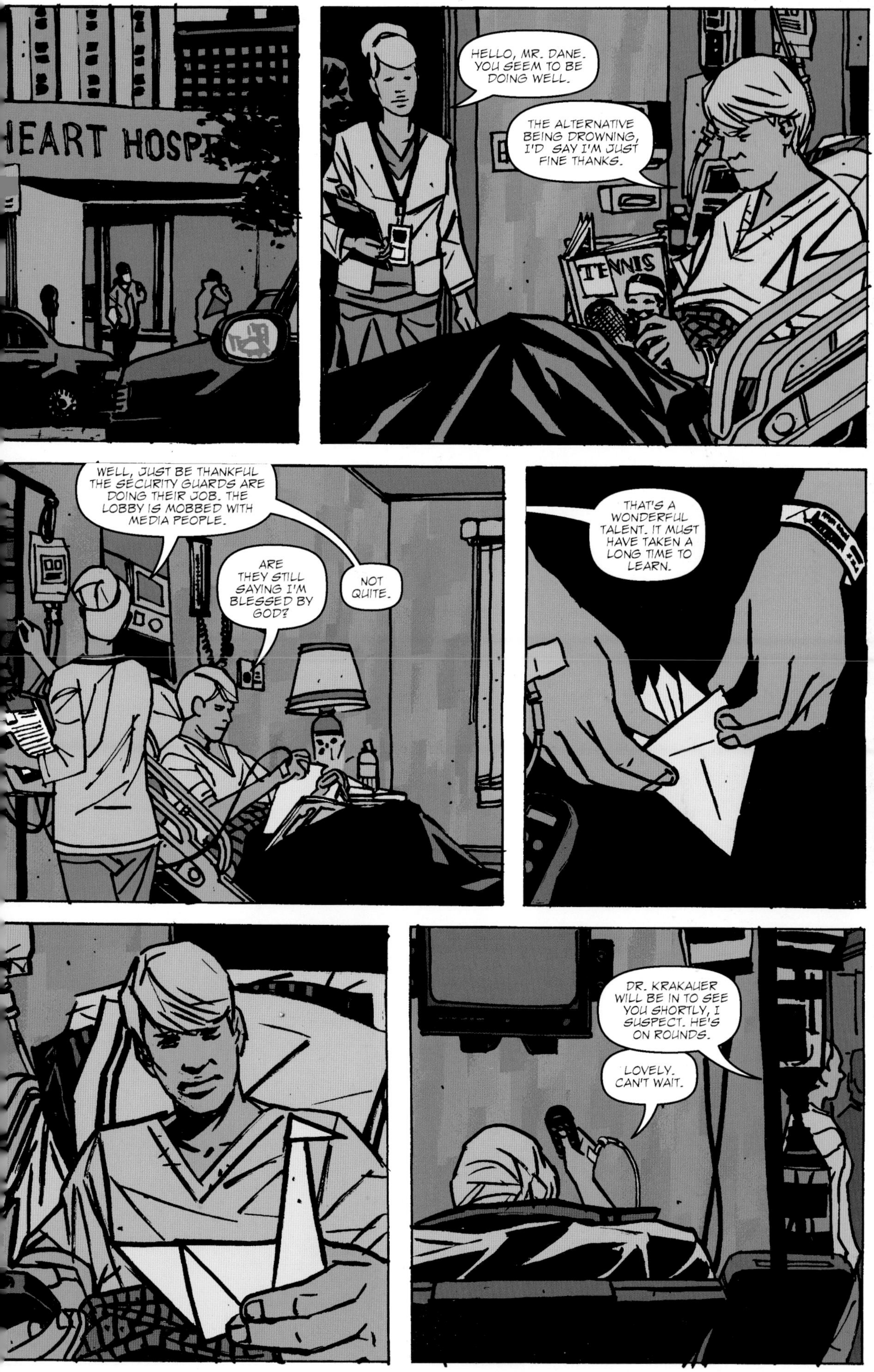
HEART HOSP
HELLO, MR. DANE. YOU SEEM TO BE DOING WELL.
THE ALTERNATIVE BEING DROWNING, I'D SAY I'M JUST FINE THANKS.
TENNIS
WELL, JUST BE THANKFUL THE SECURITY GUARDS ARE DOING THEIR JOB. THE LOBBY IS MOBBED WITH MEDIA PEOPLE.
ARE THEY STILL SAYING I'M BLESSED BY GOD?
NOT QUITE.
THAT'S A WONDERFUL TALENT. IT MUST HAVE TAKEN A LONG TIME TO LEARN.
DR. KRAKAUER WILL BE IN TO SEE YOU SHORTLY, I SUSPECT. HE'S ON ROUNDS.
LOVELY. CAN'T WAIT.

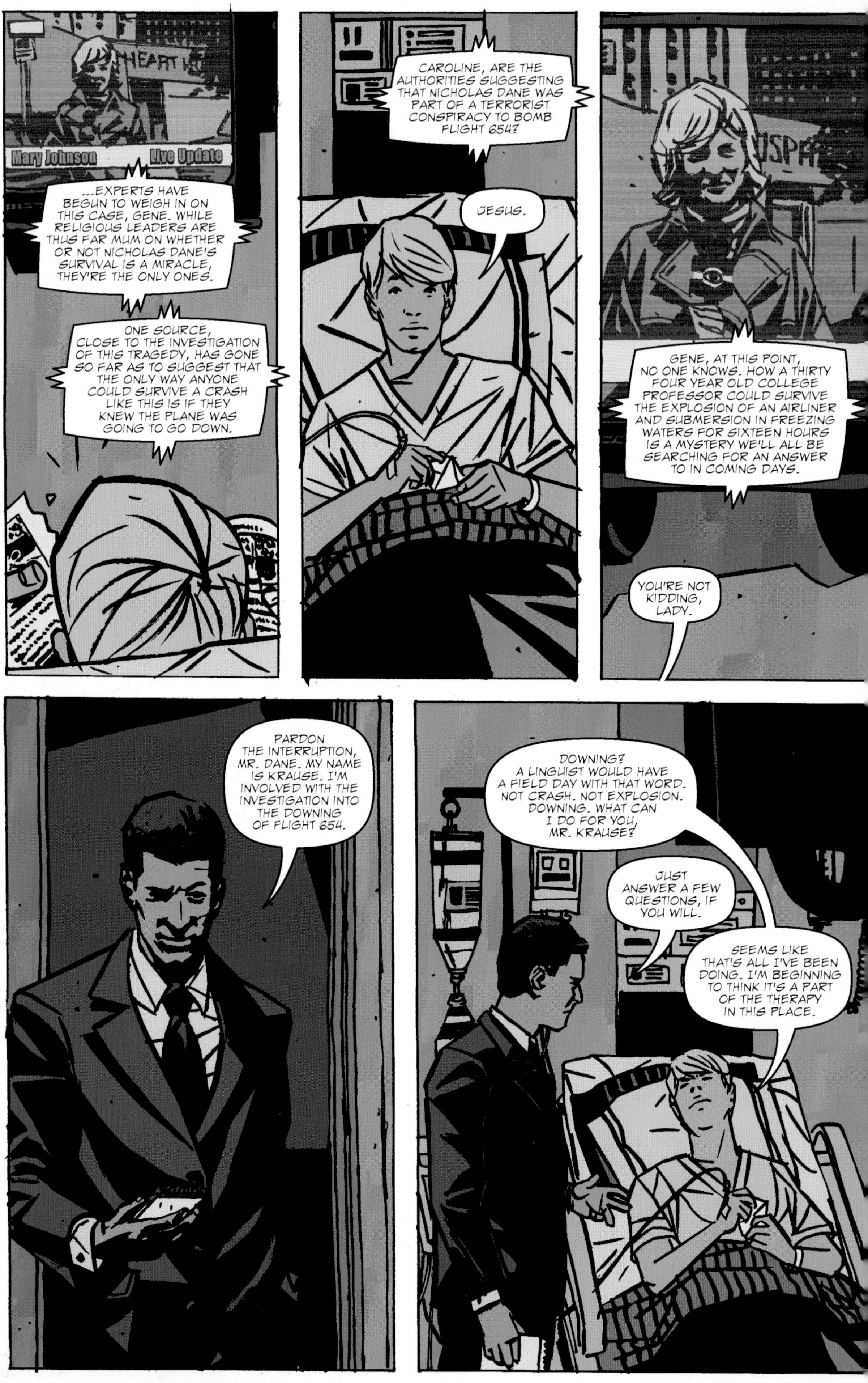
HEART
Mary Johnson
Live Update
...EXPERTS HAVE BEGUN TO WEIGH IN ON THIS CASE, GENE. WHILE RELIGIOUS LEADERS ARE THUS FAR MUM ON WHETHER OR NOT NICHOLAS DANE'S SURVIVAL IS A MIRACLE, THEY'RE THE ONLY ONES.
ONE SOURCE, CLOSE TO THE INVESTIGATION OF THIS TRAGEDY, HAS GONE SO FAR AS TO SUGGEST THAT THE ONLY WAY ANYONE COULD SURVIVE A CRASH LIKE THIS IS IF THEY KNEW THE PLANE WAS GOING TO GO DOWN.
CAROLINE, ARE THE AUTHORITIES SUGGESTING THAT NICHOLAS DANE WAS PART OF A TERRORIST CONSPIRACY TO BOMB FLIGHT 654?
JESUS.
GENE, AT THIS POINT, NO ONE KNOWS. HOW A THIRTY FOUR YEAR OLD COLLEGE PROFESSOR COULD SURVIVE THE EXPLOSION OF AN AIRLINER AND SUBMERSION IN FREEZING WATERS FOR SIXTEEN HOURS IS A MYSTERY WE'LL ALL BE SEARCHING FOR AN ANSWER TO IN COMING DAYS.
YOU'RE NOT KIDDING, LADY.
PARDON THE INTERRUPTION, MR. DANE. MY NAME IS KRAUSE. I'M INVOLVED WITH THE INVESTIGATION INTO THE DOWNING OF FLIGHT 654.
DOWNING? A LINGUIST WOULD HAVE A FIELD DAY WITH THAT WORD. NOT CRASH. NOT EXPLOSION. DOWNING. WHAT CAN I DO FOR YOU, MR. KRAUSE?
JUST ANSWER A FEW QUESTIONS, IF YOU WILL.
SEEMS LIKE THAT'S ALL I'VE BEEN DOING. I'M BEGINNING TO THINK IT'S A PART OF THE THERAPY IN THIS PLACE.

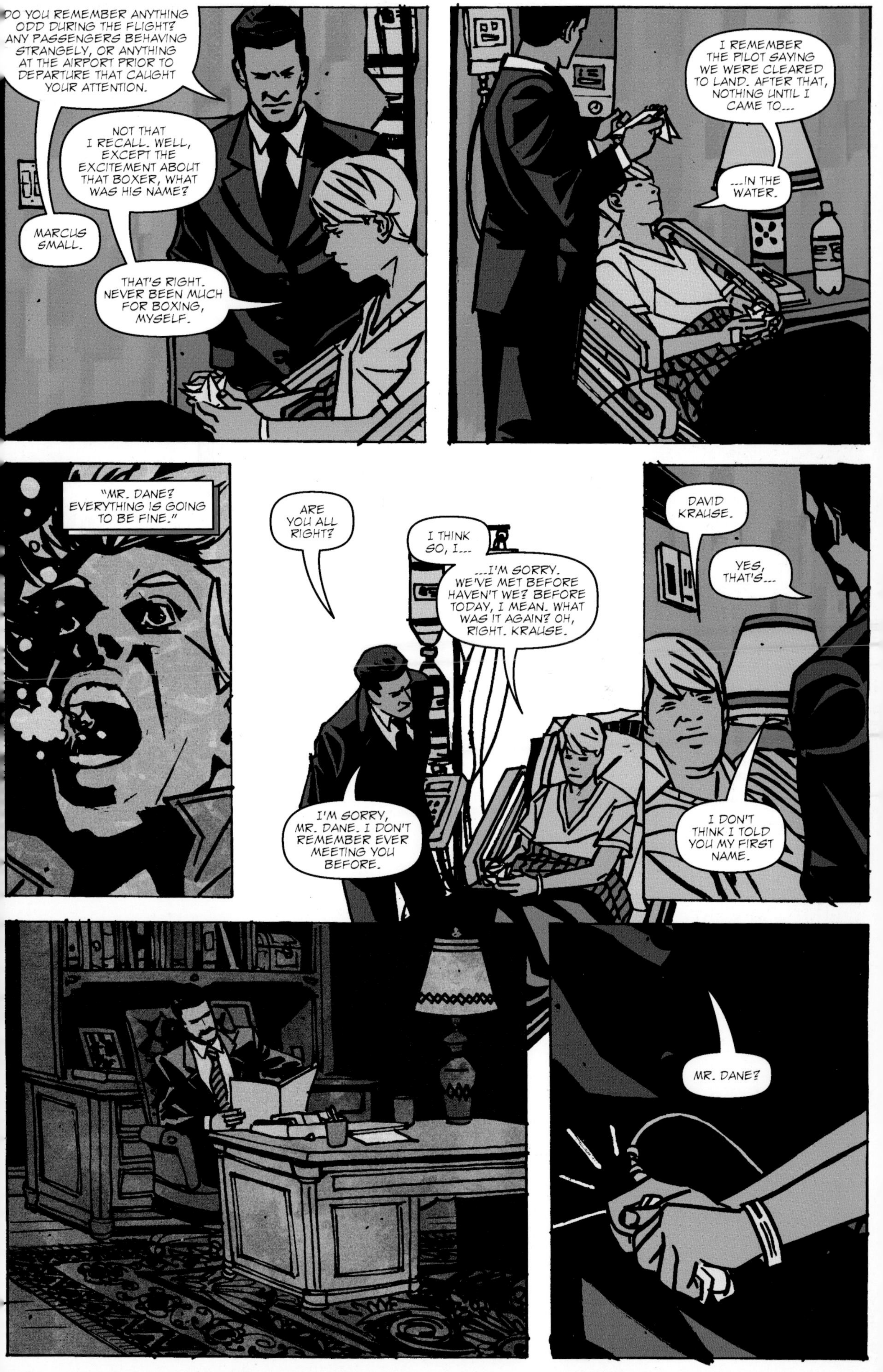
DO YOU REMEMBER ANYTHING ODD DURING THE FLIGHT? ANY PASSENGERS BEHAVING STRANGELY, OR ANYTHING AT THE AIRPORT PRIOR TO DEPARTURE THAT CAUGHT YOUR ATTENTION.
NOT THAT I RECALL. WELL, EXCEPT THE EXCITEMENT ABOUT THAT BOXER, WHAT WAS HIS NAME?
MARCUS SMALL.
THAT'S RIGHT. NEVER BEEN MUCH FOR BOXING, MYSELF.
I REMEMBER THE PILOT SAYING WE WERE CLEARED TO LAND. AFTER THAT, NOTHING UNTIL I CAME TO...
...IN THE WATER.
"MR. DANE? EVERYTHING IS GOING TO BE FINE."
ARE YOU ALL RIGHT?
I THINK SO, I...
...I'M SORRY. WE'VE MET BEFORE HAVEN'T WE? BEFORE TODAY, I MEAN. WHAT WAS IT AGAIN? OH, RIGHT. KRAUSE.
I'M SORRY, MR. DANE. I DON'T REMEMBER EVER MEETING YOU BEFORE.
DAVID KRAUSE.
YES, THAT'S...
I DON'T THINK I TOLD YOU MY FIRST NAME.
MR. DANE?

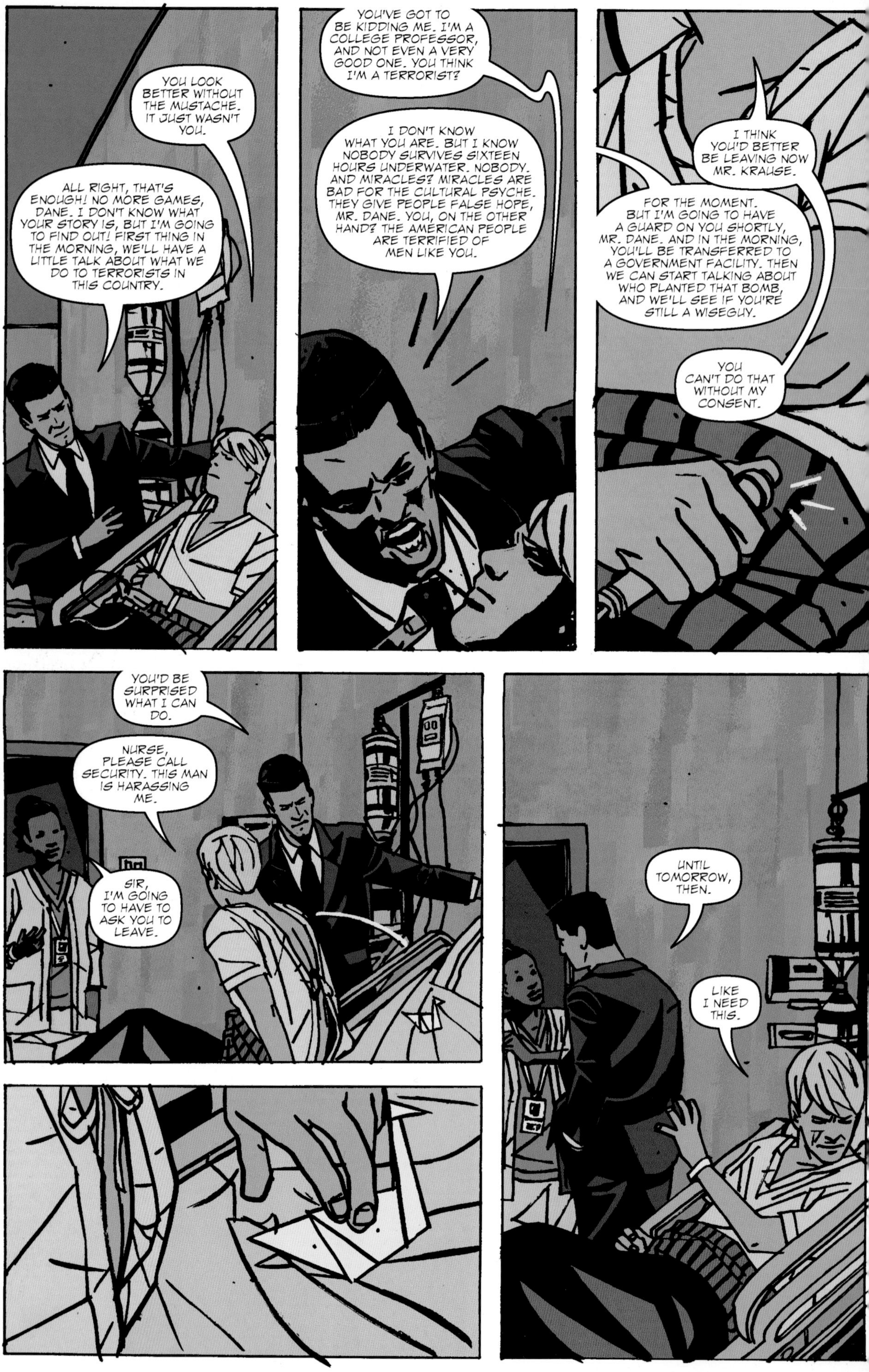
YOU LOOK BETTER WITHOUT THE MUSTACHE. IT JUST WASN'T YOU.
ALL RIGHT, THAT'S ENOUGH! NO MORE GAMES, DANE. I DON'T KNOW WHAT YOUR STORY IS, BUT I'M GOING TO FIND OUT! FIRST THING IN THE MORNING, WE'LL HAVE A LITTLE TALK ABOUT WHAT WE DO TO TERRORISTS IN THIS COUNTRY.
YOU'VE GOT TO BE KIDDING ME. I'M A COLLEGE PROFESSOR, AND NOT EVEN A VERY GOOD ONE. YOU THINK I'M A TERRORIST?
I DON'T KNOW WHAT YOU ARE. BUT I KNOW NOBODY SURVIVES SIXTEEN HOURS UNDERWATER. NOBODY. AND MIRACLES? MIRACLES ARE BAD FOR THE CULTURAL PSYCHE. THEY GIVE PEOPLE FALSE HOPE, MR. DANE. YOU, ON THE OTHER HAND? THE AMERICAN PEOPLE ARE TERRIFIED OF MEN LIKE YOU.
I THINK YOU'D BETTER BE LEAVING NOW MR. KRAUSE.
FOR THE MOMENT. BUT I'M GOING TO HAVE A GUARD ON YOU SHORTLY, MR. DANE. AND IN THE MORNING, YOU'LL BE TRANSFERRED TO A GOVERNMENT FACILITY. THEN WE CAN START TALKING ABOUT WHO PLANTED THAT BOMB, AND WE'LL SEE IF YOU'RE STILL A WISEGUY.
YOU CAN'T DO THAT WITHOUT MY CONSENT.
YOU'D BE SURPRISED WHAT I CAN DO.
NURSE, PLEASE CALL SECURITY. THIS MAN IS HARASSING ME.
SIR, I'M GOING TO HAVE TO ASK YOU TO LEAVE.
UNTIL TOMORROW, THEN.
LIKE I NEED THIS.

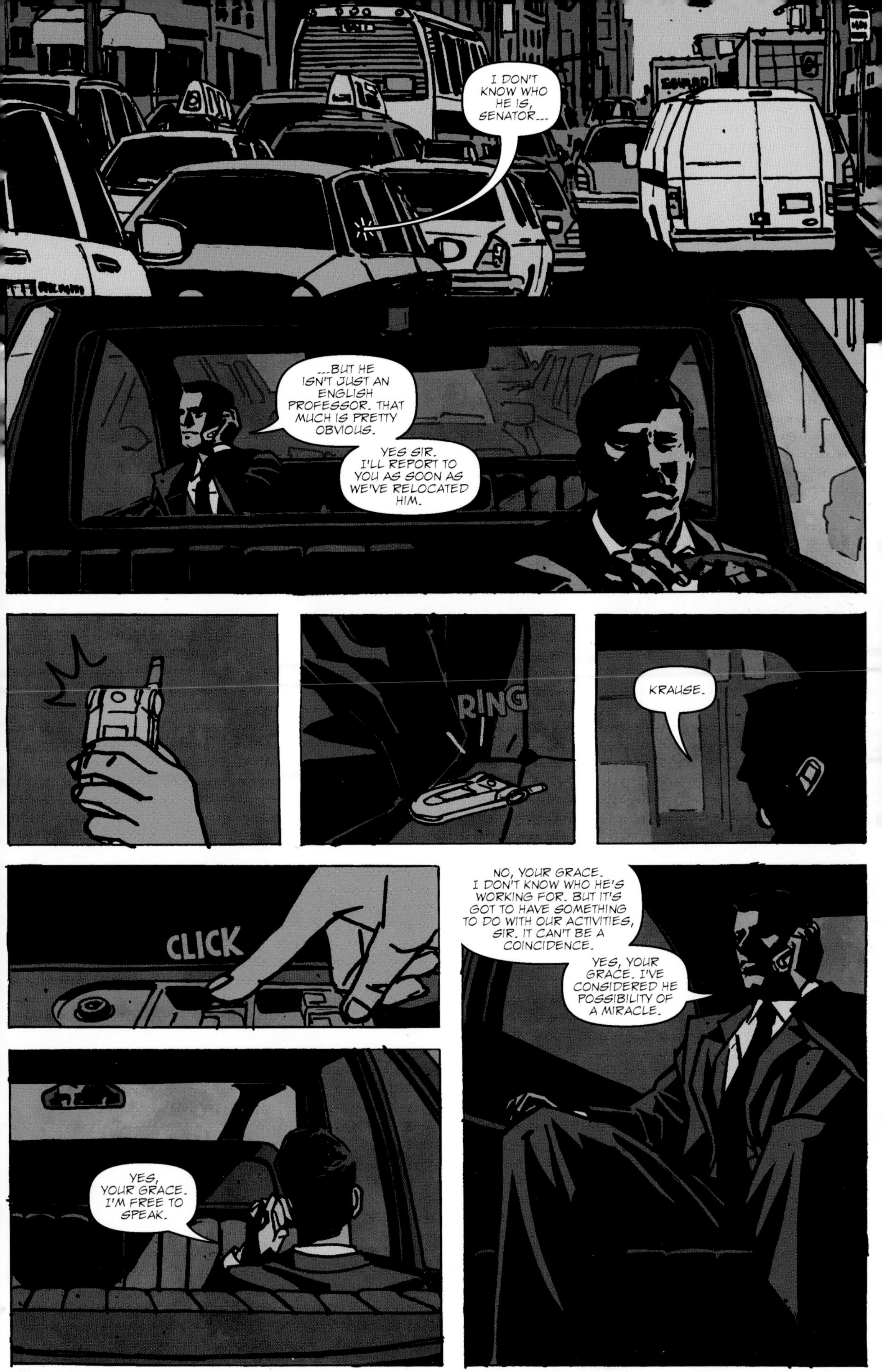
I DON'T KNOW WHO HE IS, SENATOR...
...BUT HE ISN'T JUST AN ENGLISH PROFESSOR. THAT MUCH IS PRETTY OBVIOUS.
YES SIR. I'LL REPORT TO YOU AS SOON AS WE'VE RELOCATED HIM.
RING
KRAUSE.
CLICK
YES, YOUR GRACE. I'M FREE TO SPEAK.
NO, YOUR GRACE. I DON'T KNOW WHO HE'S WORKING FOR. BUT IT'S GOT TO HAVE SOMETHING TO DO WITH OUR ACTIVITIES, SIR. IT CAN'T BE A COINCIDENCE.
YES, YOUR GRACE. I'VE CONSIDERED HE POSSIBILITY OF A MIRACLE.

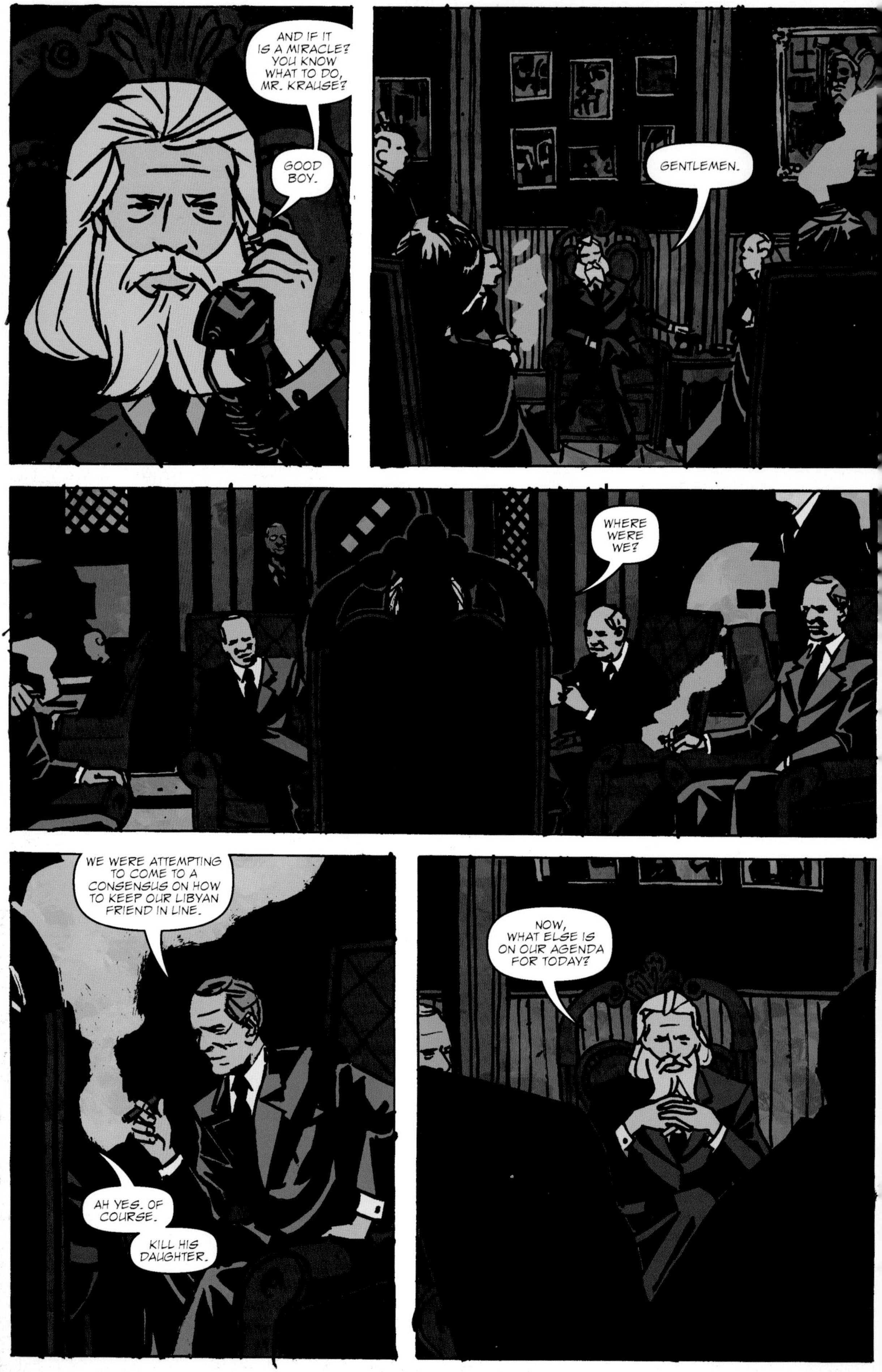
AND IF IT IS A MIRACLE? YOU KNOW WHAT TO DO, MR. KRAUSE?
GOOD BOY.
GENTLEMEN.
WHERE WERE WE?
WE WERE ATTEMPTING TO COME TO A CONSENSUS ON HOW TO KEEP OUR LIBYAN FRIEND IN LINE.
AH YES. OF COURSE.
KILL HIS DAUGHTER.
NOW, WHAT ELSE IS ON OUR AGENDA FOR TODAY?

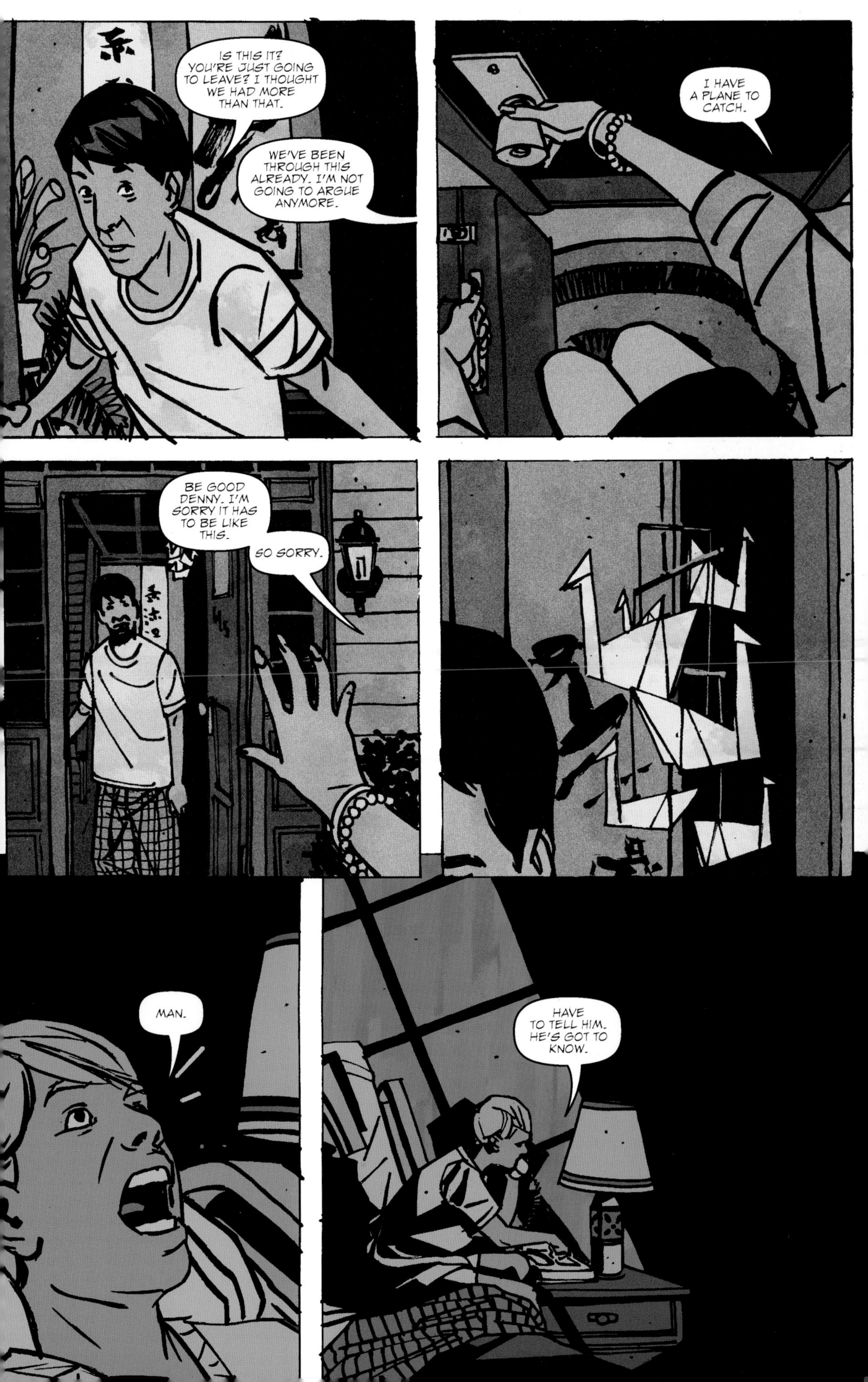
IS THIS IT? YOU'RE JUST GOING TO LEAVE? I THOUGHT WE HAD MORE THAN THAT.
WE'VE BEEN THROUGH THIS ALREADY. I'M NOT GOING TO ARGUE ANYMORE.
I HAVE A PLANE TO CATCH.
BE GOOD DENNY. I'M SORRY IT HAS TO BE LIKE THIS.
SO SORRY.
MAN.
HAVE TO TELL HIM. HE'S GOT TO KNOW.

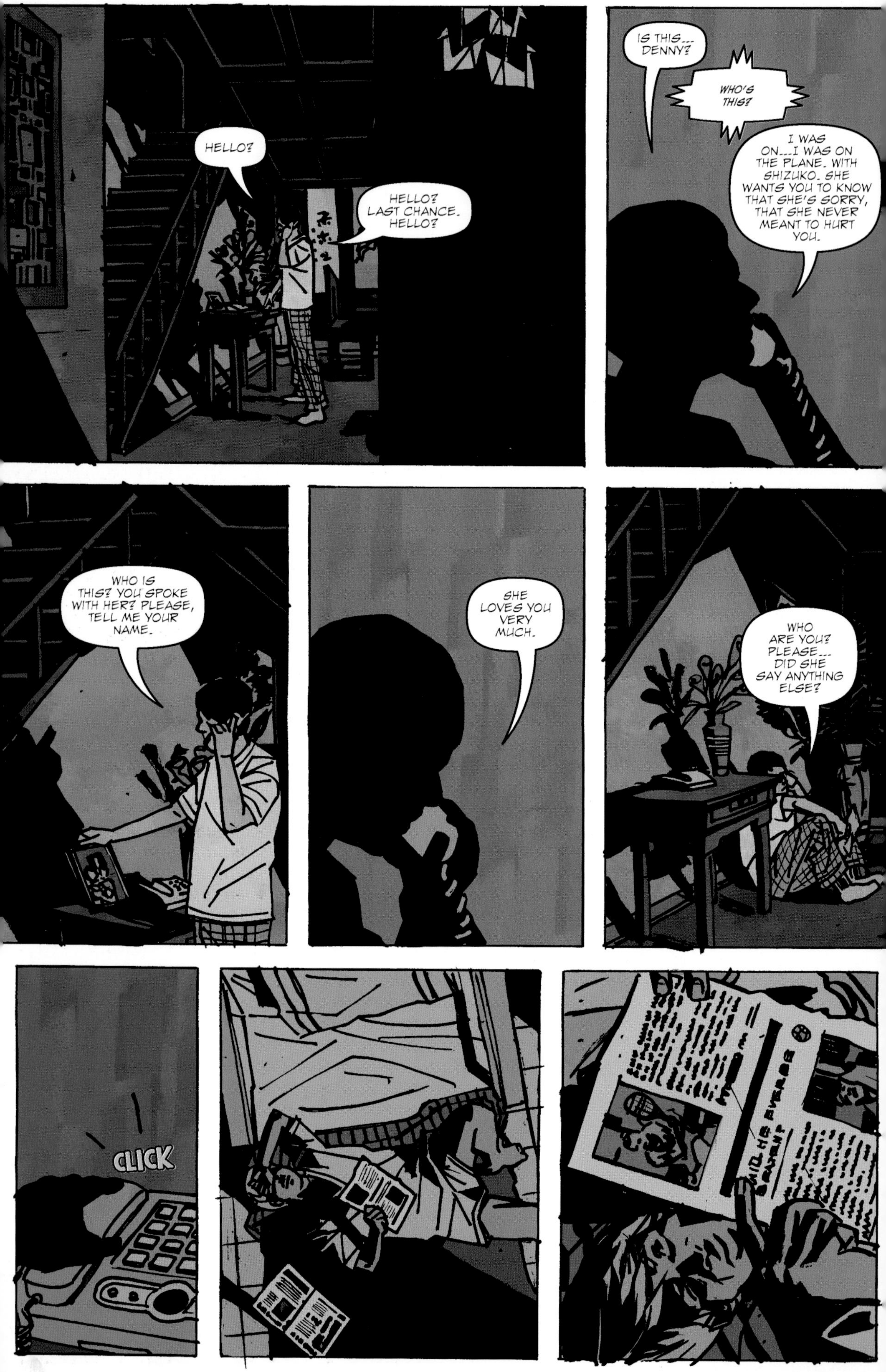
HELLO?
HELLO? LAST CHANCE. HELLO?
IS THIS... DENNY?
WHO'S THIS?
I WAS ON...I WAS ON THE PLANE. WITH SHIZUKO. SHE WANTS YOU TO KNOW THAT SHE'S SORRY, THAT SHE NEVER MEANT TO HURT YOU.
WHO IS THIS? YOU SPOKE WITH HER? PLEASE, TELL ME YOUR NAME.
SHE LOVES YOU VERY MUCH.
WHO ARE YOU? PLEASE... DID SHE SAY ANYTHING ELSE?
CLICK

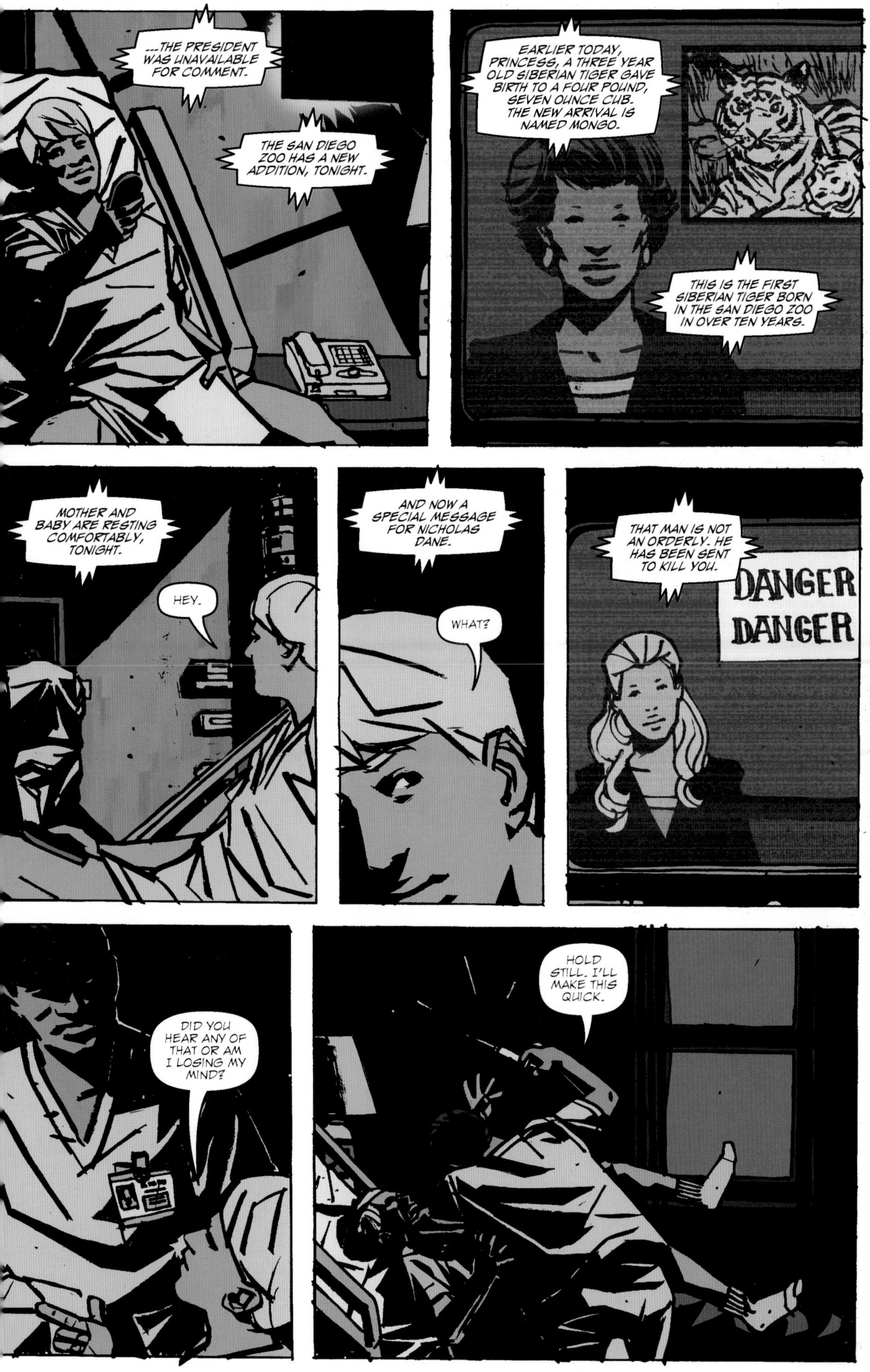

...THE PRESIDENT WAS UNAVAILABLE FOR COMMENT.
THE SAN DIEGO ZOO HAS A NEW ADDITION, TONIGHT.
EARLIER TODAY, PRINCESS, A THREE YEAR OLD SIBERIAN TIGER GAVE BIRTH TO A FOUR POUND, SEVEN OUNCE CUB. THE NEW ARRIVAL IS NAMED MONGO.
THIS IS THE FIRST SIBERIAN TIGER BORN IN THE SAN DIEGO ZOO IN OVER TEN YEARS.
MOTHER AND BABY ARE RESTING COMFORTABLY, TONIGHT.
HEY.
AND NOW A SPECIAL MESSAGE FOR NICHOLAS DANE.
WHAT?
THAT MAN IS NOT AN ORDERLY. HE HAS BEEN SENT TO KILL YOU.
DANGER
DANGER
DID YOU HEAR ANY OF THAT OR AM I LOSING MY MIND?
HOLD STILL. I'LL MAKE THIS QUICK.

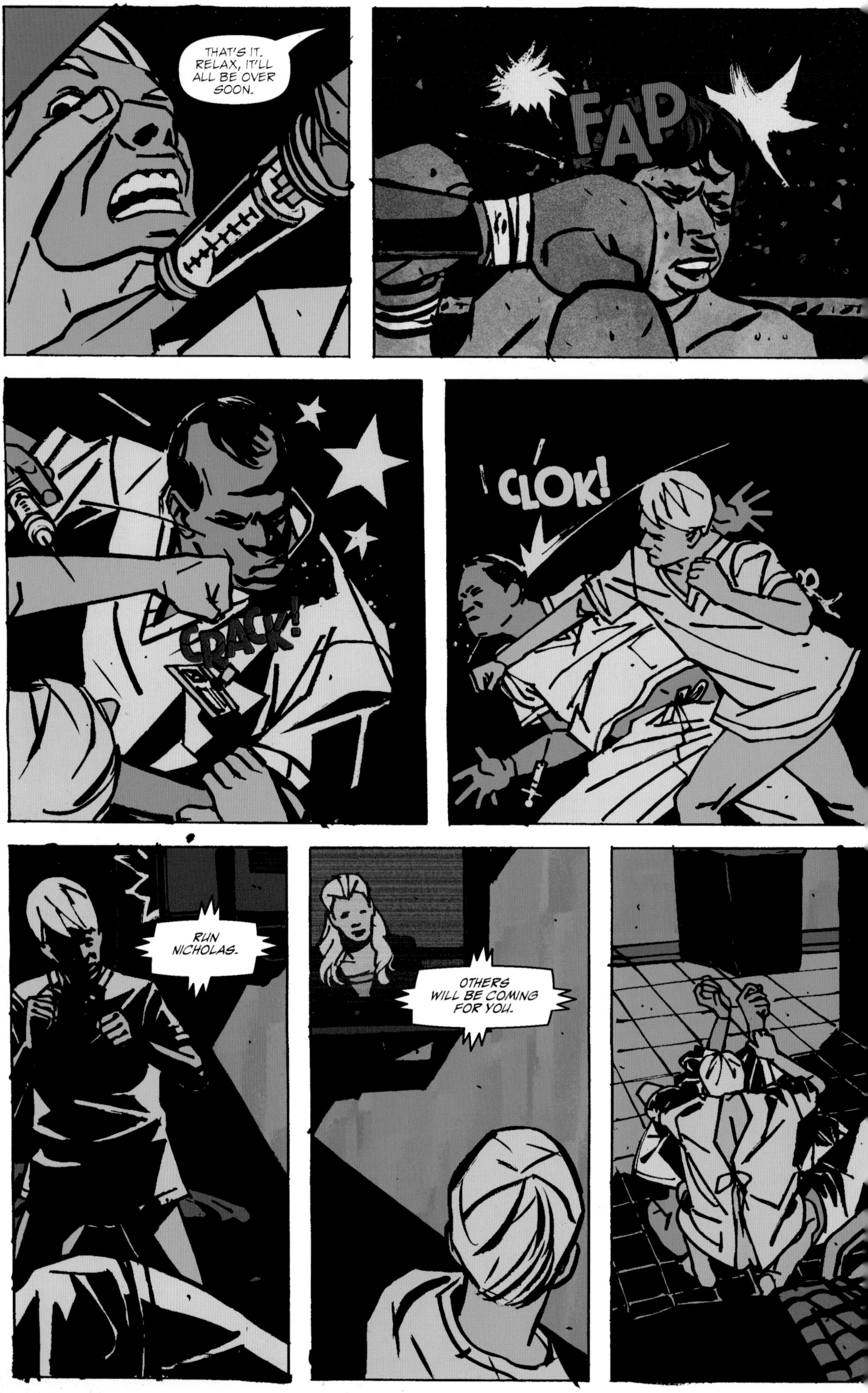
THAT'S IT. RELAX, IT'LL ALL BE OVER SOON.
FAP
CRACK!
CLOK!
RUN NICHOLAS.
OTHERS WILL BE COMING FOR YOU.

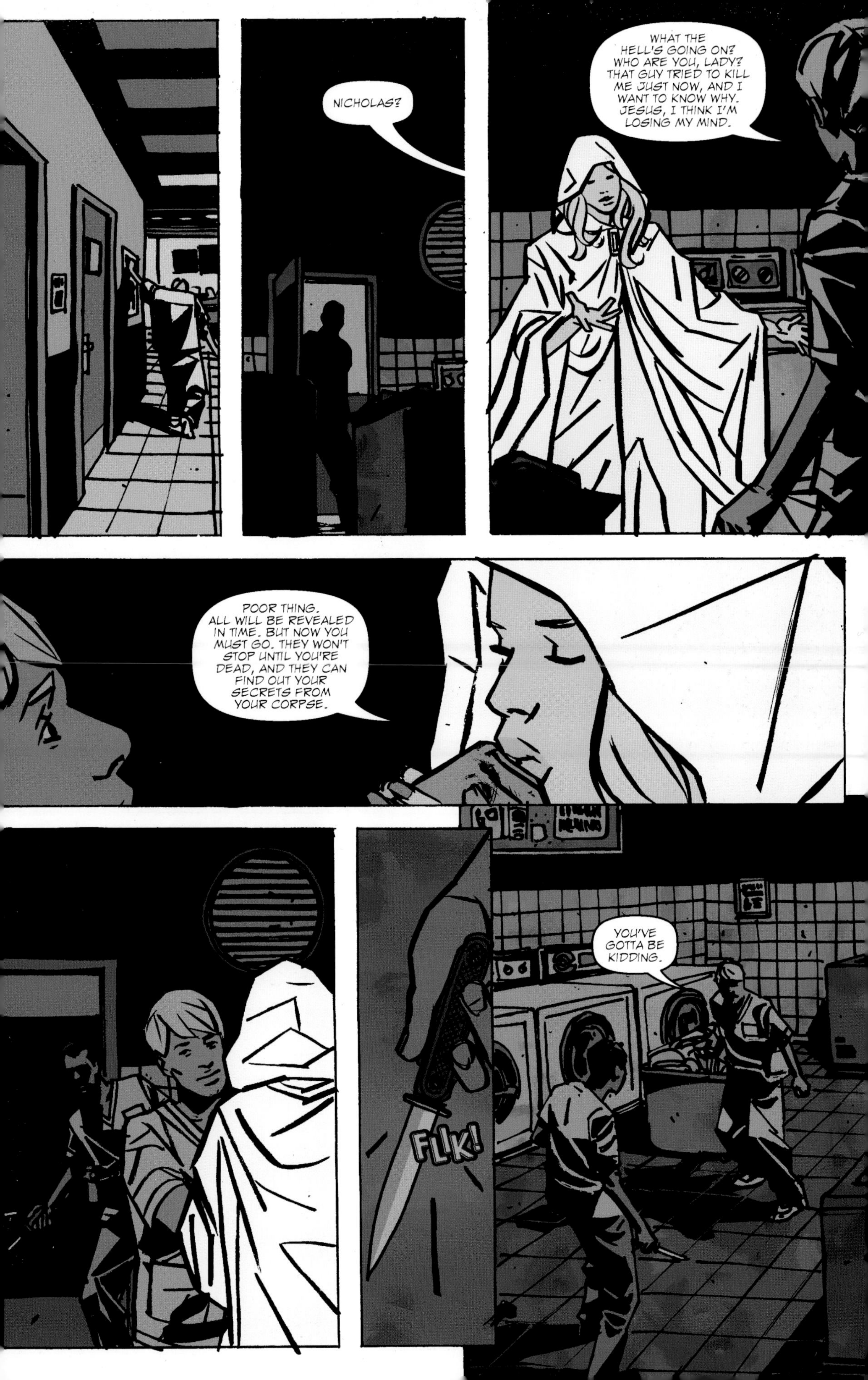
NICHOLAS?
WHAT THE HELL'S GOING ON? WHO ARE YOU, LADY? THAT GUY TRIED TO KILL ME JUST NOW, AND I WANT TO KNOW WHY. JESUS, I THINK I'M LOSING MY MIND.
POOR THING. ALL WILL BE REVEALED IN TIME. BUT NOW YOU MUST GO. THEY WON'T STOP UNTIL YOU'RE DEAD, AND THEY CAN FIND OUT YOUR SECRETS FROM YOUR CORPSE.
FLIK!
YOU'VE GOTTA BE KIDDING.

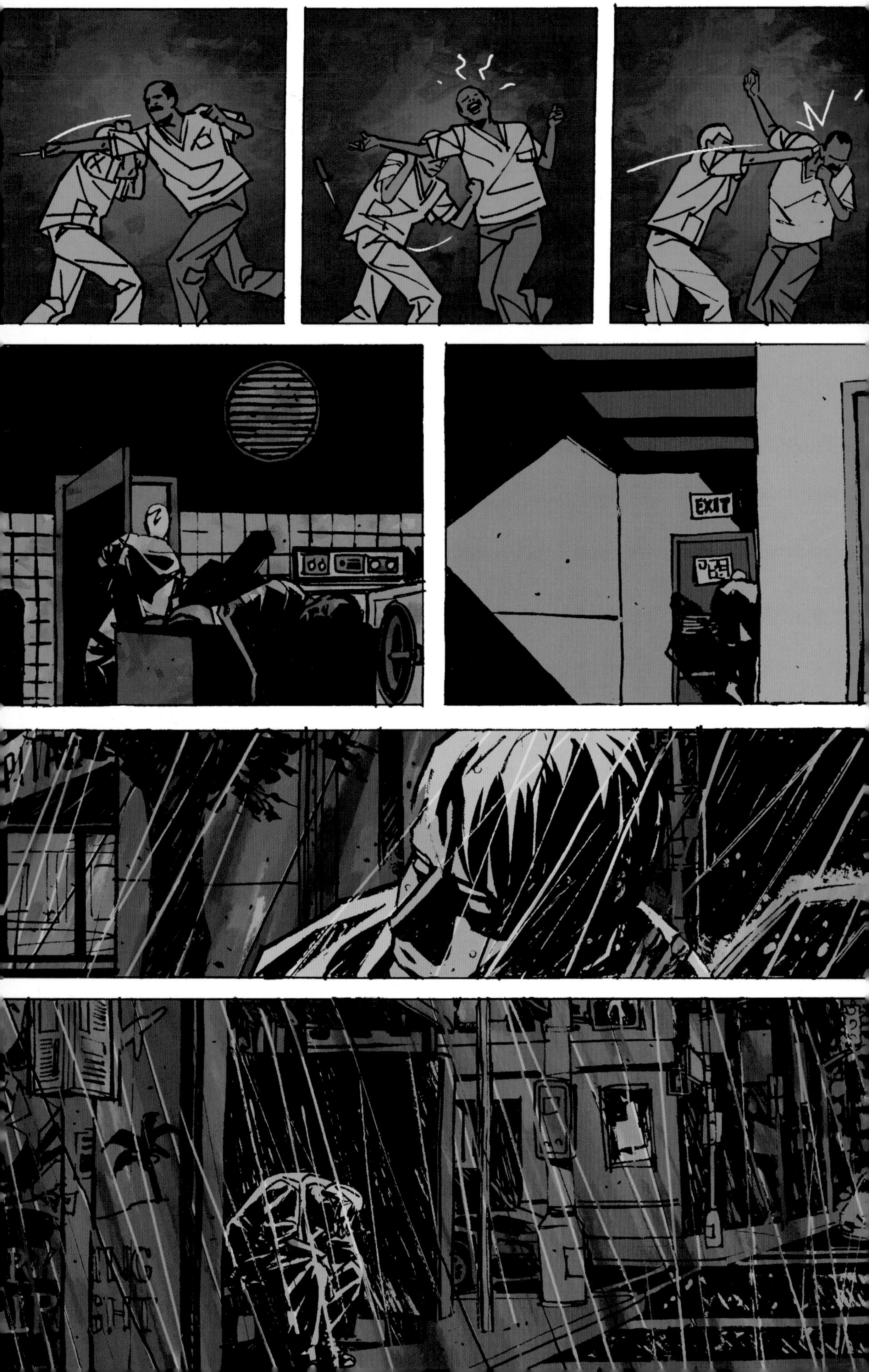
EXIT

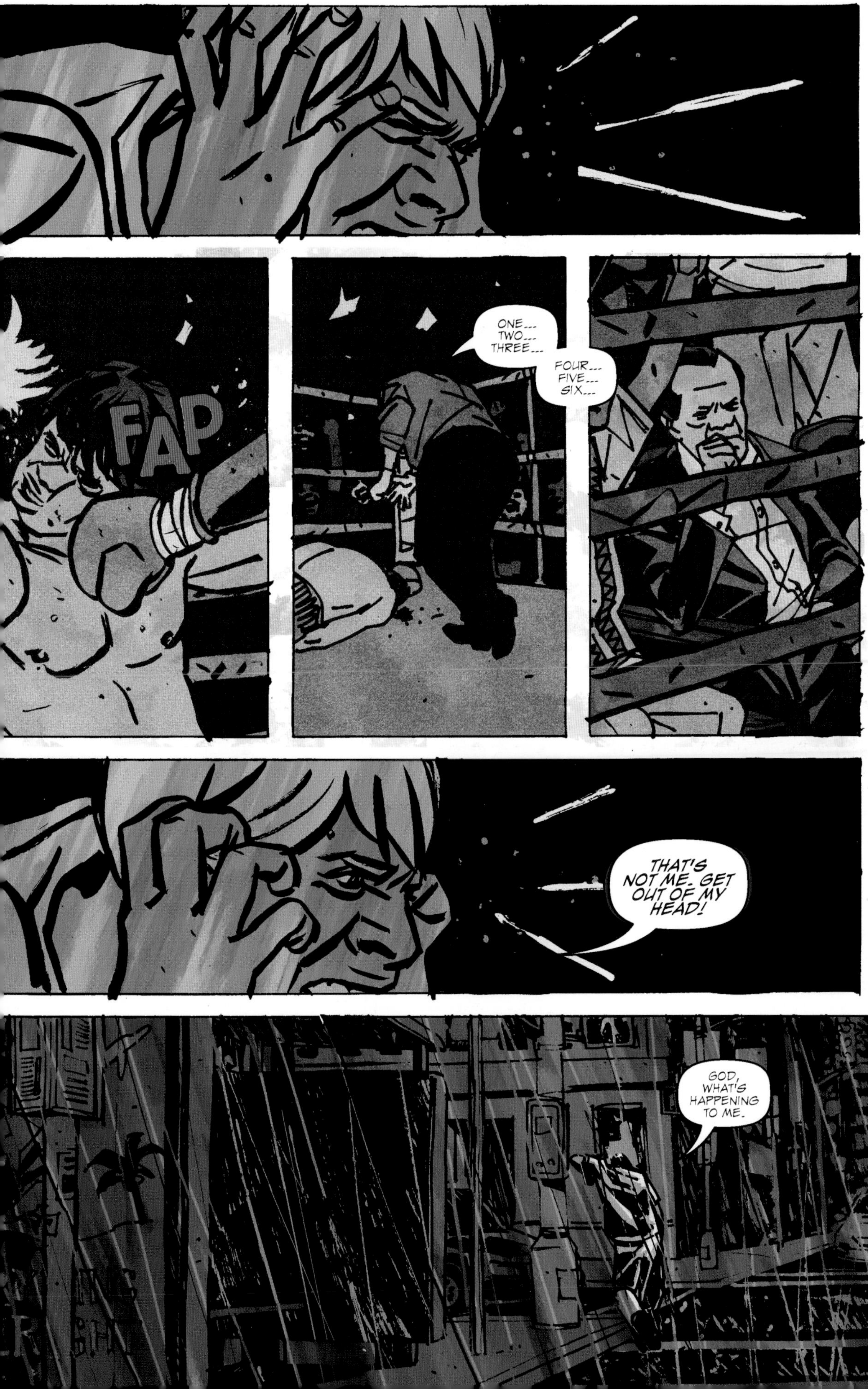
FAP
ONE... TWO... THREE...
FOUR... FIVE... SIX...
THAT'S NOT ME. GET OUT OF MY HEAD!
GOD, WHAT'S HAPPENING TO ME.

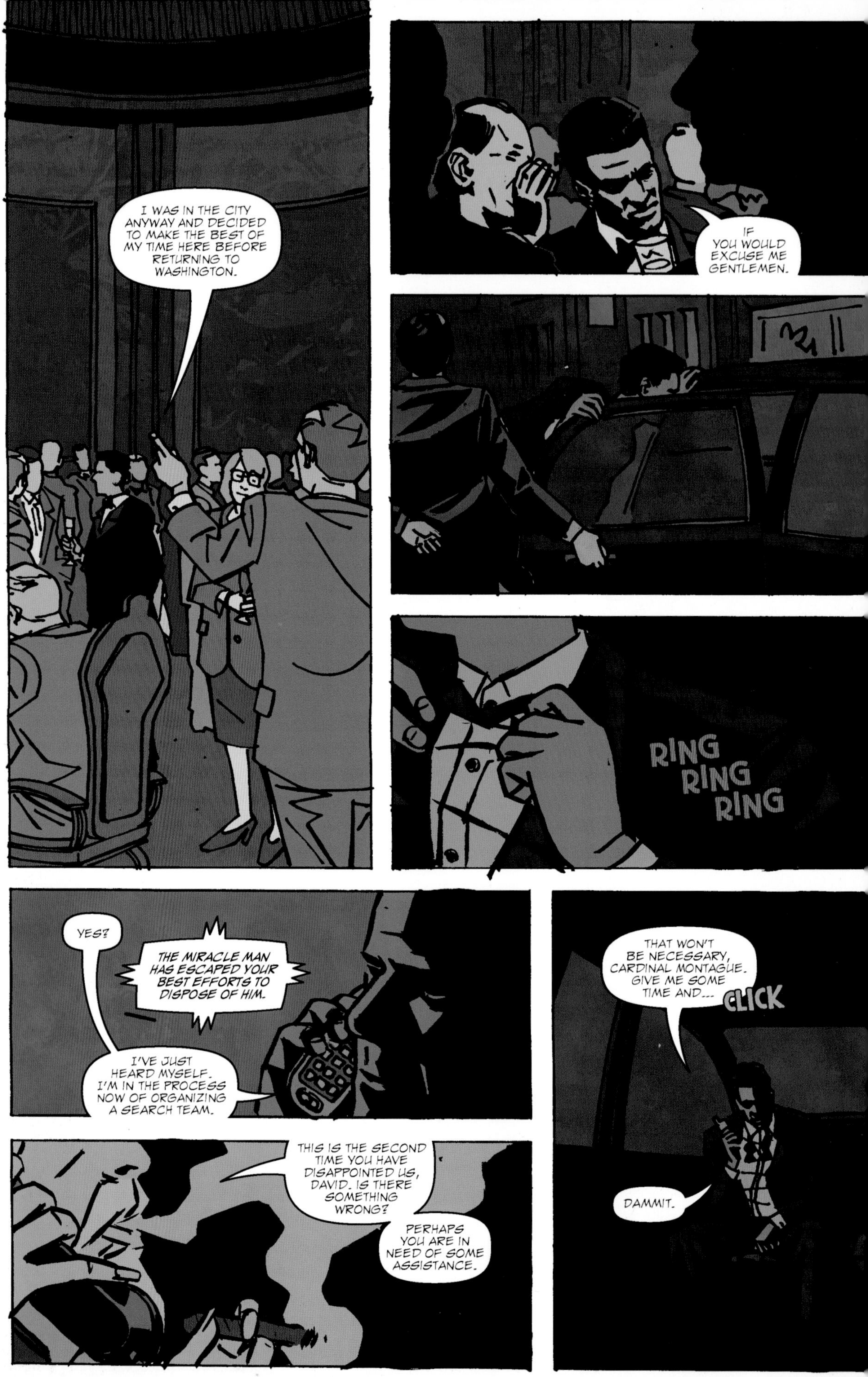
I WAS IN THE CITY ANYWAY AND DECIDED TO MAKE THE BEST OF MY TIME HERE BEFORE RETURNING TO WASHINGTON.
IF YOU WOULD EXCUSE ME GENTLEMEN.
RING RING RING
YES?
THE MIRACLE MAN HAS ESCAPED YOUR BEST EFFORTS TO DISPOSE OF HIM.
I'VE JUST HEARD MYSELF. I'M IN THE PROCESS NOW OF ORGANIZING A SEARCH TEAM.
THIS IS THE SECOND TIME YOU HAVE DISAPPOINTED US, DAVID. IS THERE SOMETHING WRONG?
PERHAPS YOU ARE IN NEED OF SOME ASSISTANCE.
THAT WON'T BE NECESSARY, CARDINAL MONTAGUE. GIVE ME SOME TIME AND...
CLICK
DAMMIT.

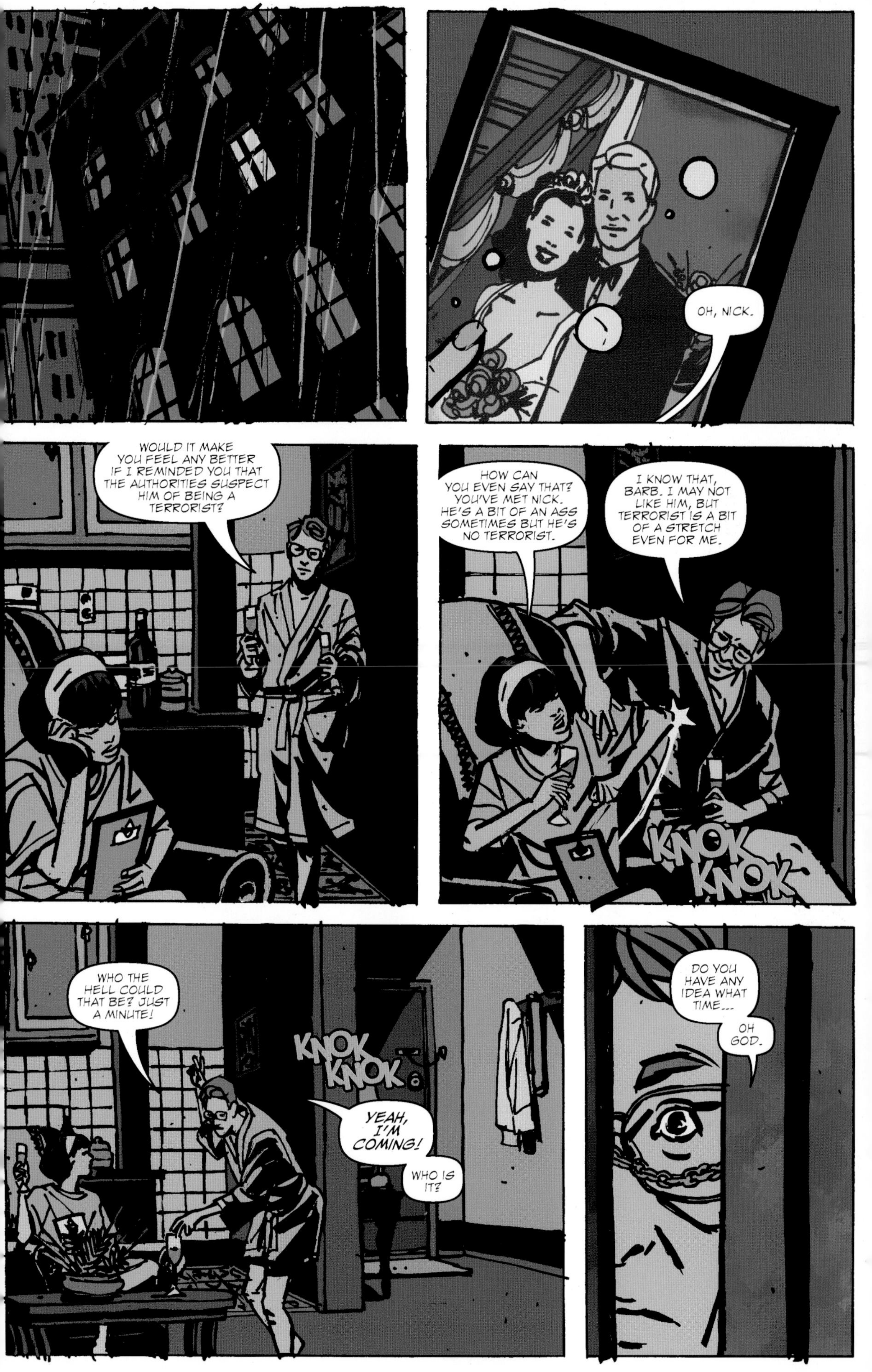
OH, NICK.
WOULD IT MAKE YOU FEEL ANY BETTER IF I REMINDED YOU THAT THE AUTHORITIES SUSPECT HIM OF BEING A TERRORIST?
HOW CAN YOU EVEN SAY THAT? YOU'VE MET NICK. HE'S A BIT OF AN ASS SOMETIMES BUT HE'S NO TERRORIST.
I KNOW THAT, BARB. I MAY NOT LIKE HIM, BUT TERRORIST IS A BIT OF A STRETCH EVEN FOR ME.
KNOK KNOK
WHO THE HELL COULD THAT BE? JUST A MINUTE!
KNOK KNOK
YEAH, I'M COMING!
WHO IS IT?
DO YOU HAVE ANY IDEA WHAT TIME...
OH GOD.

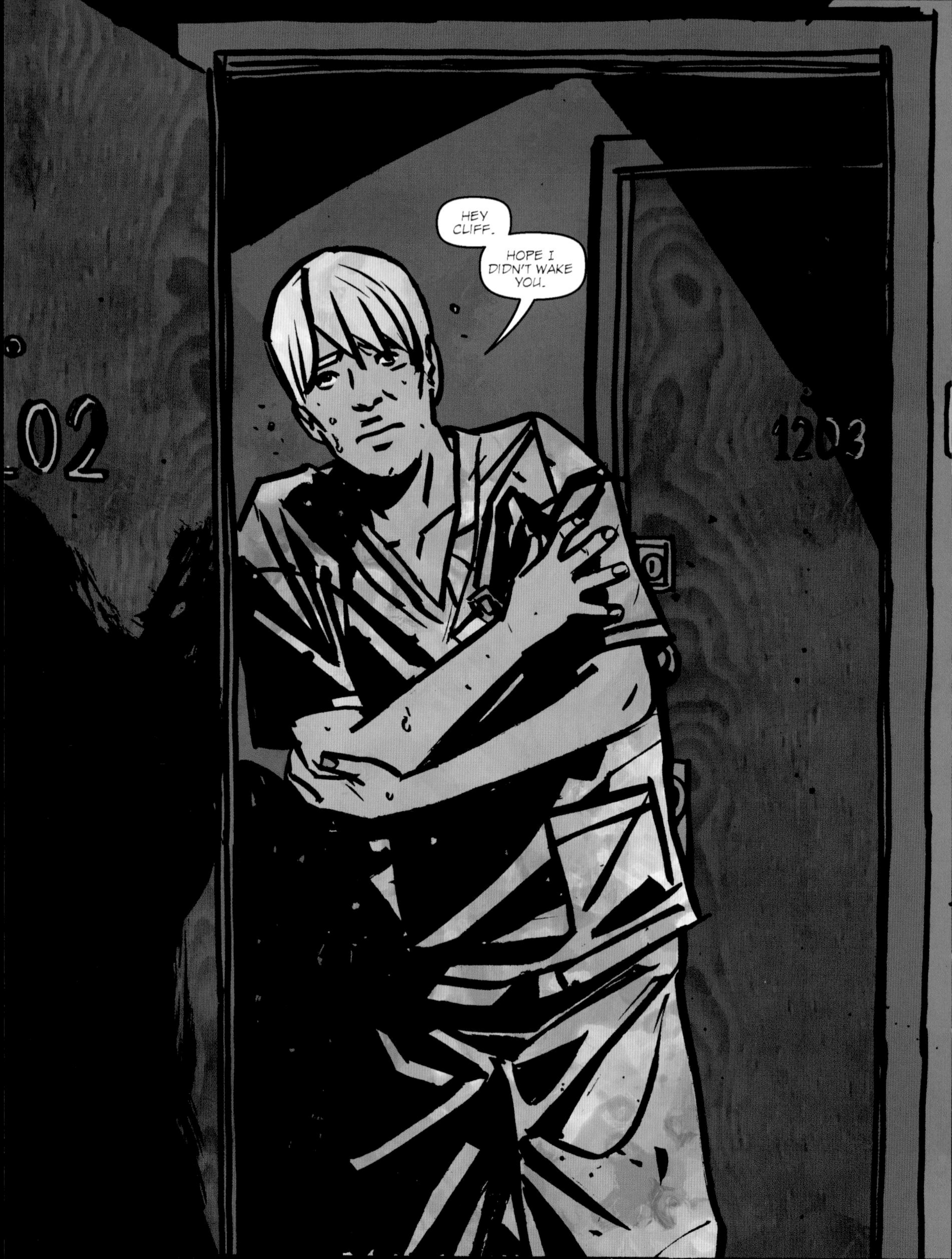

HEY CLIFF.
HOPE I DIDN'T WAKE YOU.
1203

**PAUL AZACETA**
**original series cover**

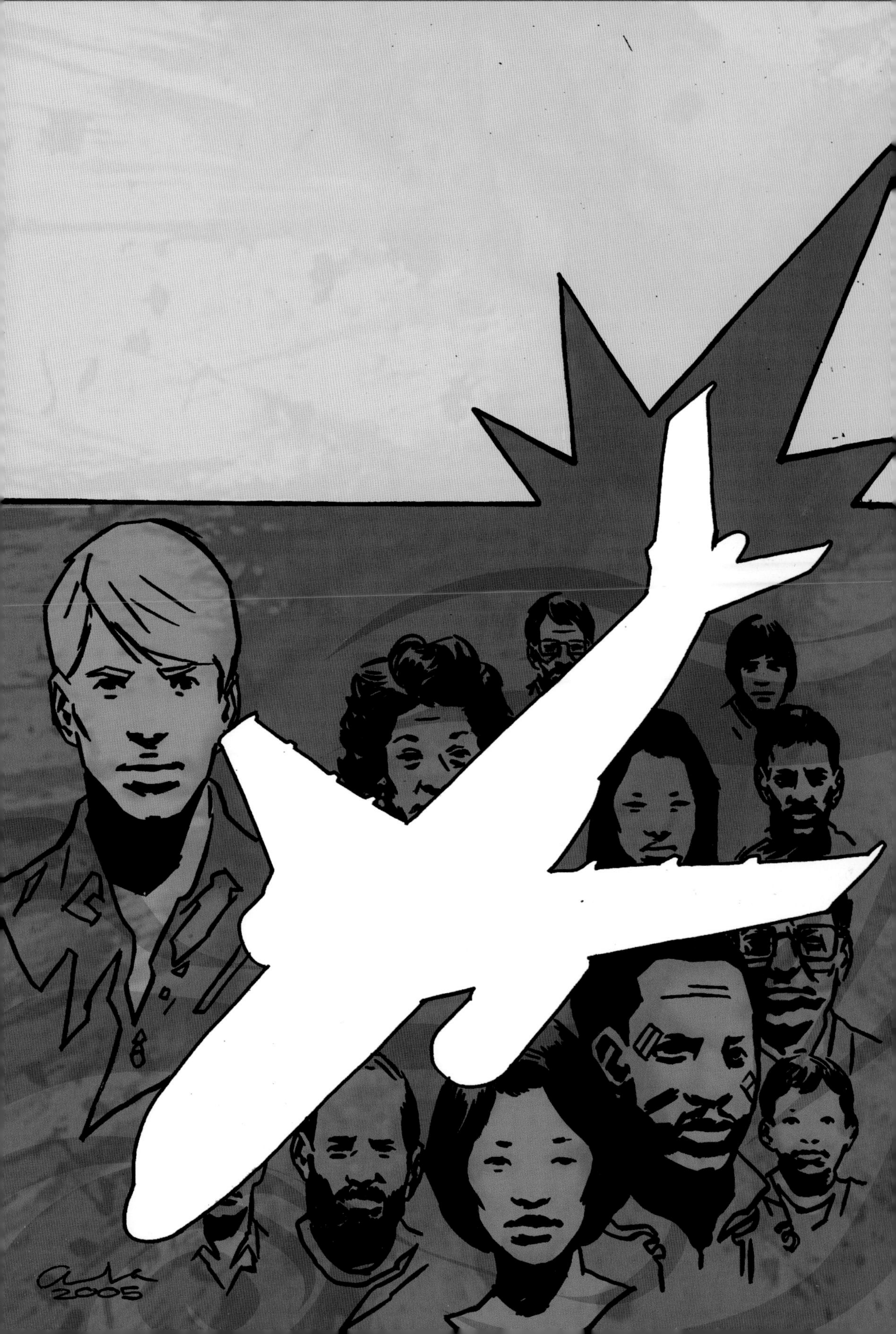
2005

# CHAPTER TWO 2

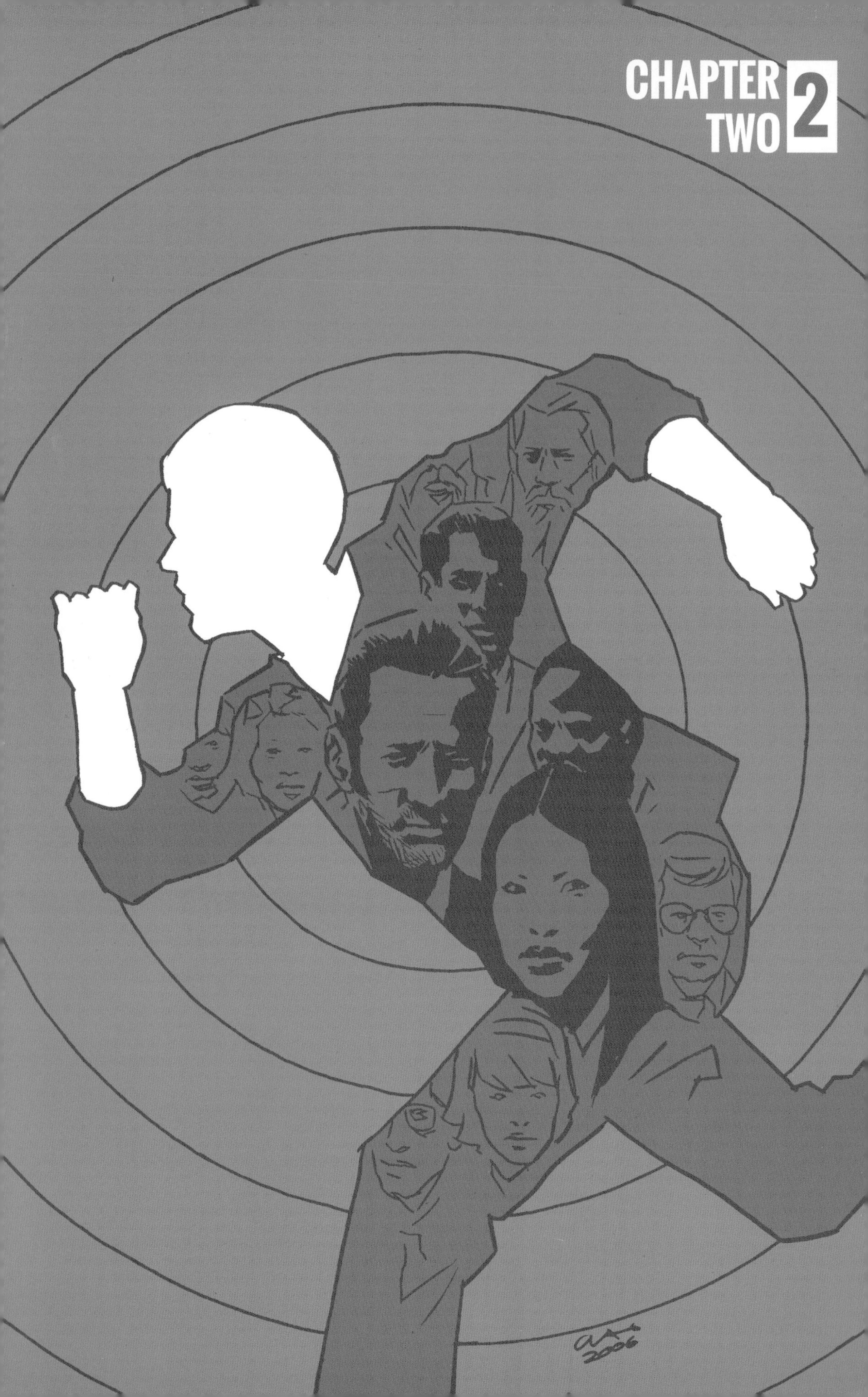

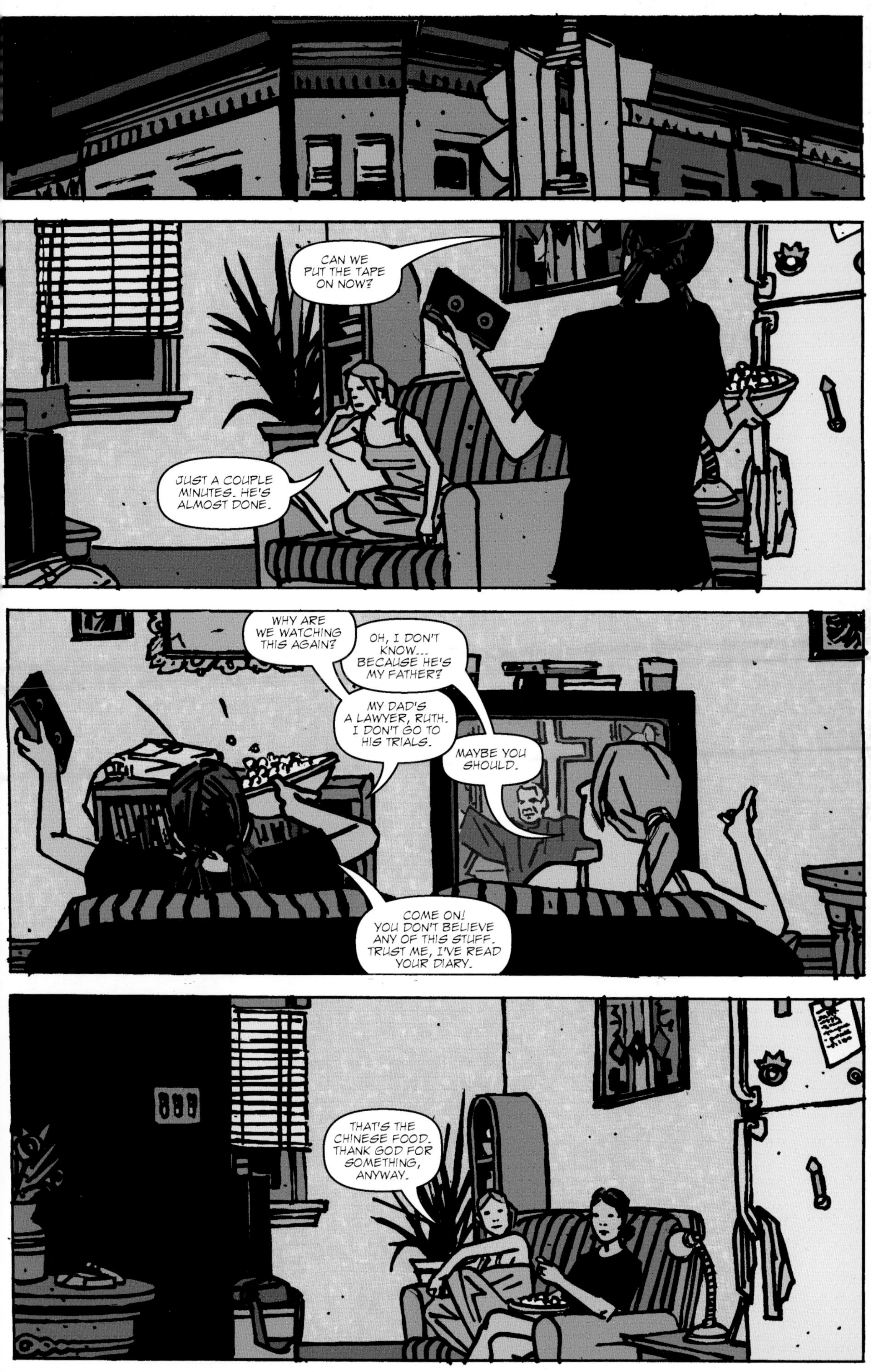

CAN WE PUT THE TAPE ON NOW?
JUST A COUPLE MINUTES. HE'S ALMOST DONE.
WHY ARE WE WATCHING THIS AGAIN?
OH, I DON'T KNOW... BECAUSE HE'S MY FATHER?
MY DAD'S A LAWYER, RUTH. I DON'T GO TO HIS TRIALS.
MAYBE YOU SHOULD.
COME ON! YOU DON'T BELIEVE ANY OF THIS STUFF. TRUST ME, I'VE READ YOUR DIARY.
THAT'S THE CHINESE FOOD. THANK GOD FOR SOMETHING, ANYWAY.

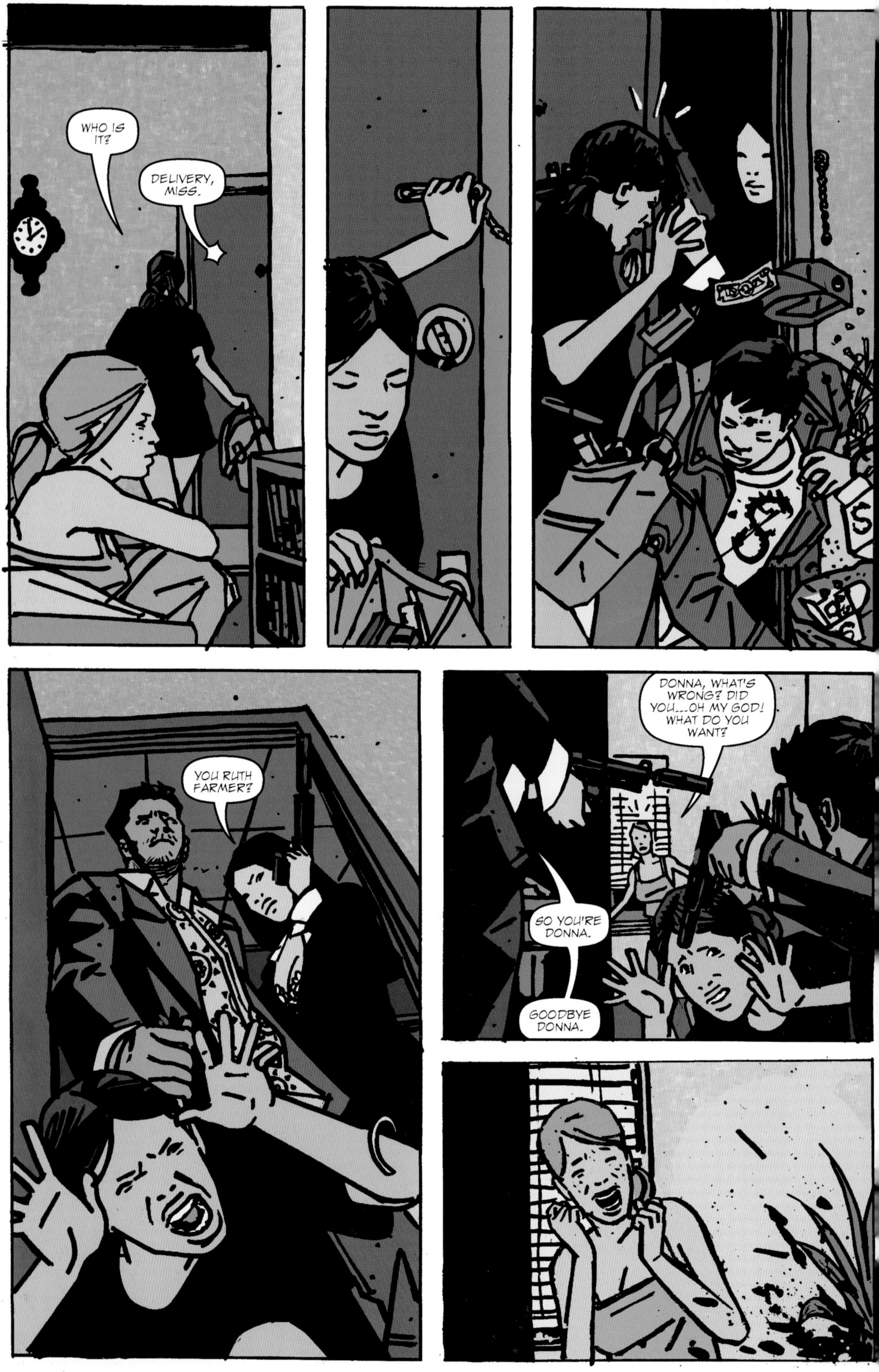
WHO IS IT?
DELIVERY, MISS.
YOU RUTH FARMER?
DONNA, WHAT'S WRONG? DID YOU...OH MY GOD! WHAT DO YOU WANT?
SO YOU'RE DONNA.
GOODBYE DONNA.

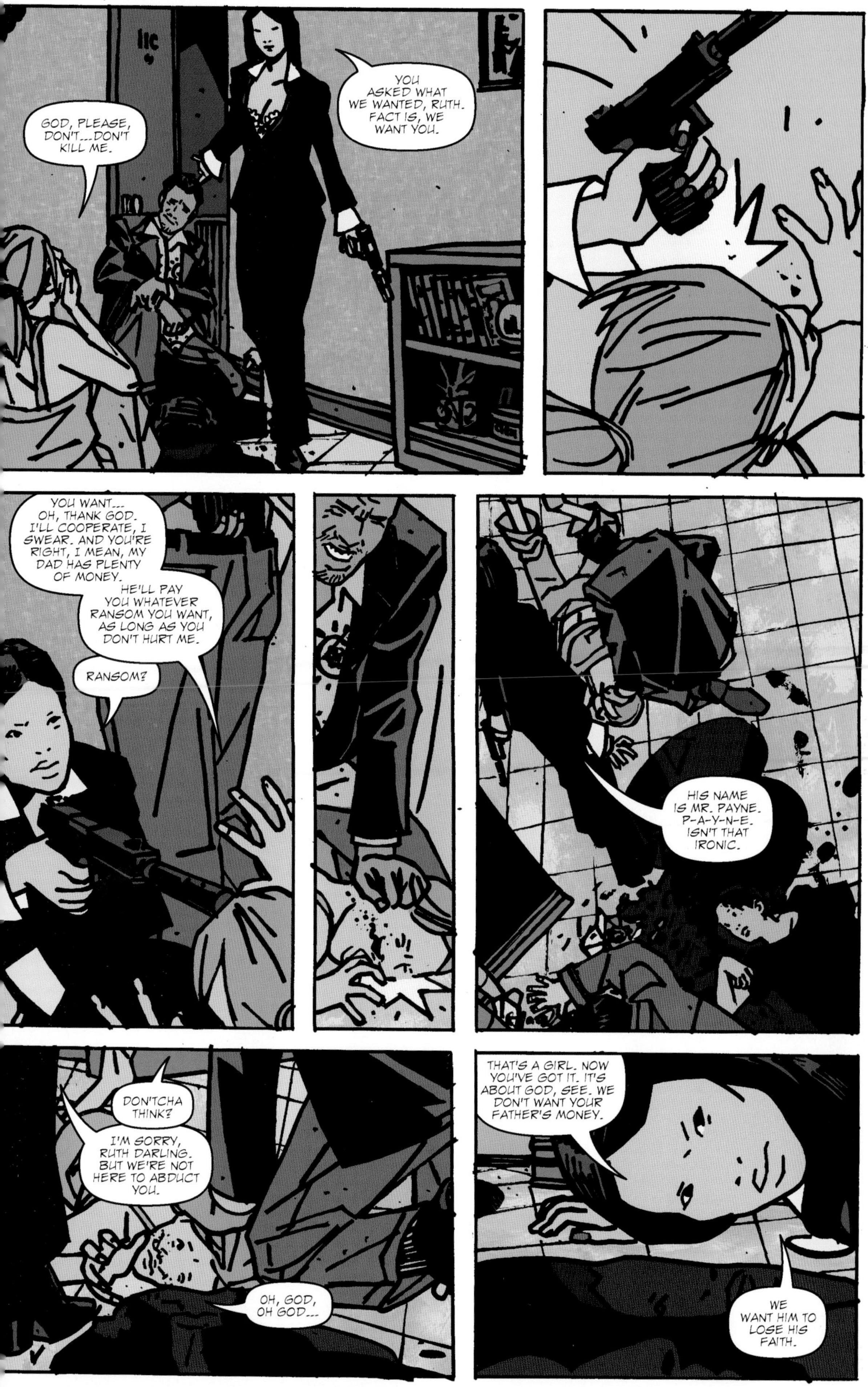
GOD, PLEASE, DON'T...DON'T KILL ME.
YOU ASKED WHAT WE WANTED, RUTH. FACT IS, WE WANT YOU.
YOU WANT... OH, THANK GOD. I'LL COOPERATE, I SWEAR. AND YOU'RE RIGHT, I MEAN, MY DAD HAS PLENTY OF MONEY.
HE'LL PAY YOU WHATEVER RANSOM YOU WANT, AS LONG AS YOU DON'T HURT ME.
RANSOM?
HIS NAME IS MR. PAYNE. P-A-Y-N-E. ISN'T THAT IRONIC.
DON'TCHA THINK?
I'M SORRY, RUTH DARLING. BUT WE'RE NOT HERE TO ABDUCT YOU.
OH, GOD, OH GOD...
THAT'S A GIRL. NOW YOU'VE GOT IT. IT'S ABOUT GOD, SEE. WE DON'T WANT YOUR FATHER'S MONEY.
WE WANT HIM TO LOSE HIS FAITH.

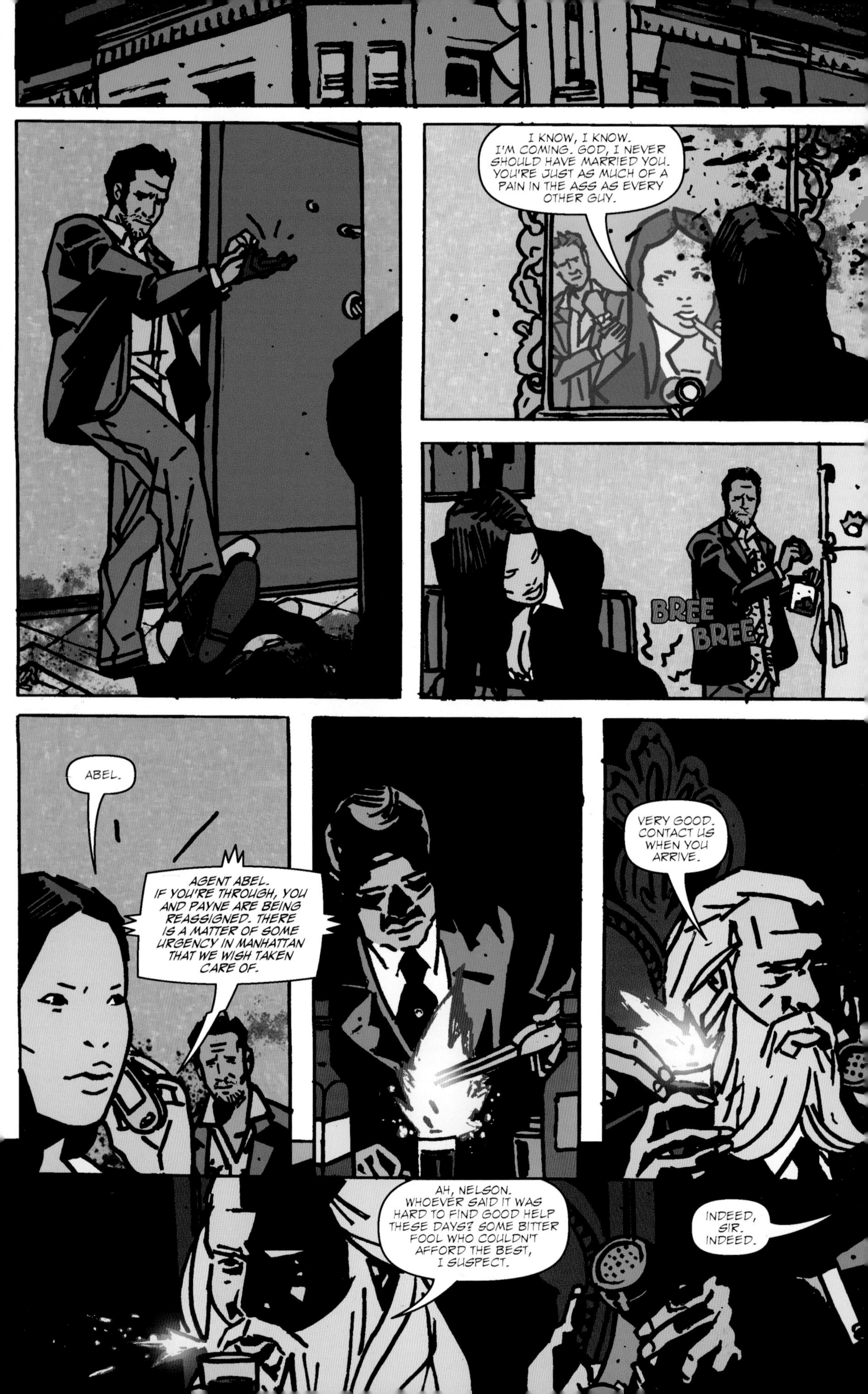
I KNOW, I KNOW. I'M COMING. GOD, I NEVER SHOULD HAVE MARRIED YOU. YOU'RE JUST AS MUCH OF A PAIN IN THE ASS AS EVERY OTHER GUY.
BREE
BREE
ABEL.
AGENT ABEL. IF YOU'RE THROUGH, YOU AND PAYNE ARE BEING REASSIGNED. THERE IS A MATTER OF SOME URGENCY IN MANHATTAN THAT WE WISH TAKEN CARE OF.
VERY GOOD. CONTACT US WHEN YOU ARRIVE.
AH, NELSON. WHOEVER SAID IT WAS HARD TO FIND GOOD HELP THESE DAYS? SOME BITTER FOOL WHO COULDN'T AFFORD THE BEST, I SUSPECT.
INDEED, SIR. INDEED.

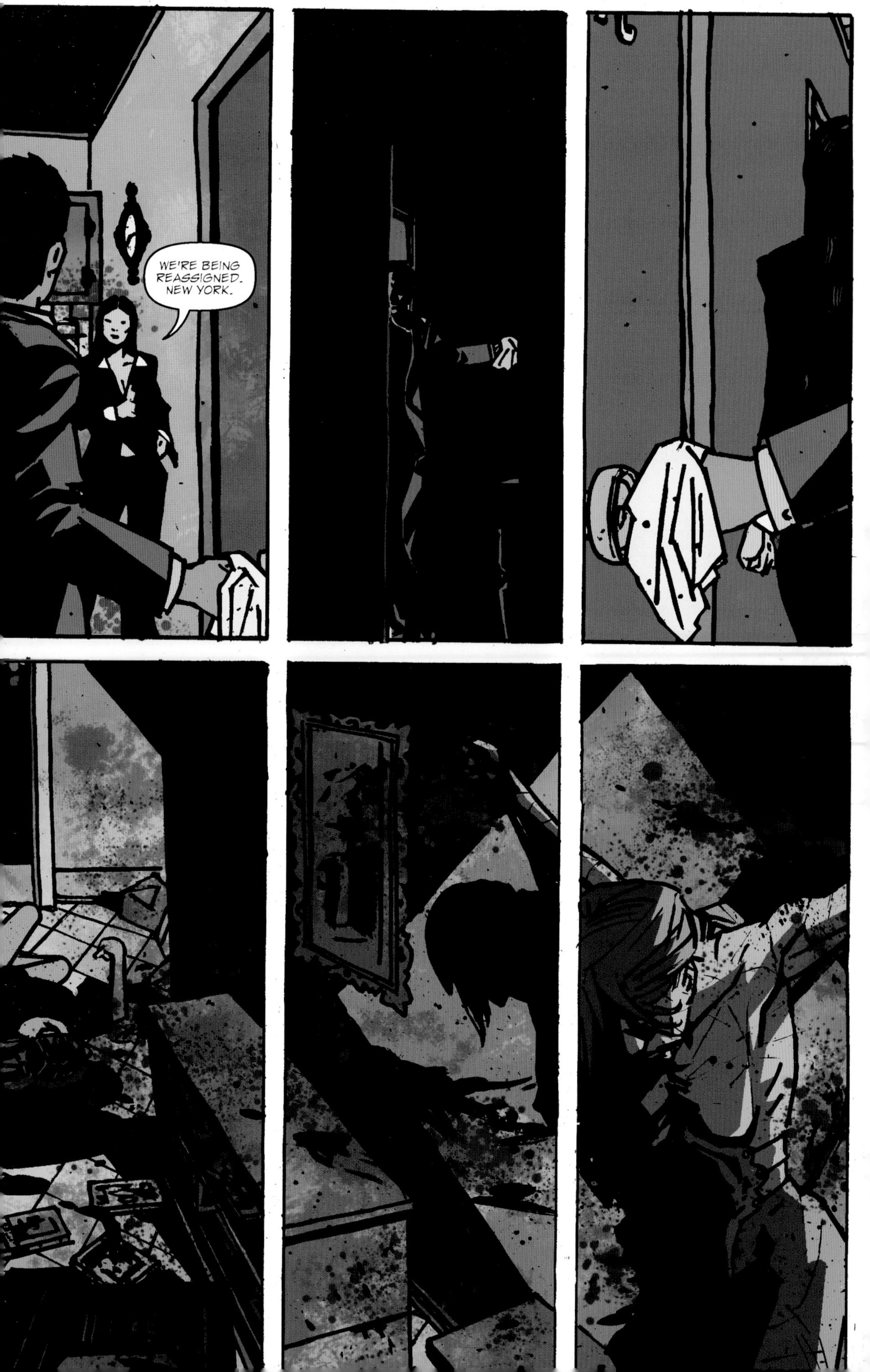
WE'RE BEING REASSIGNED. NEW YORK.

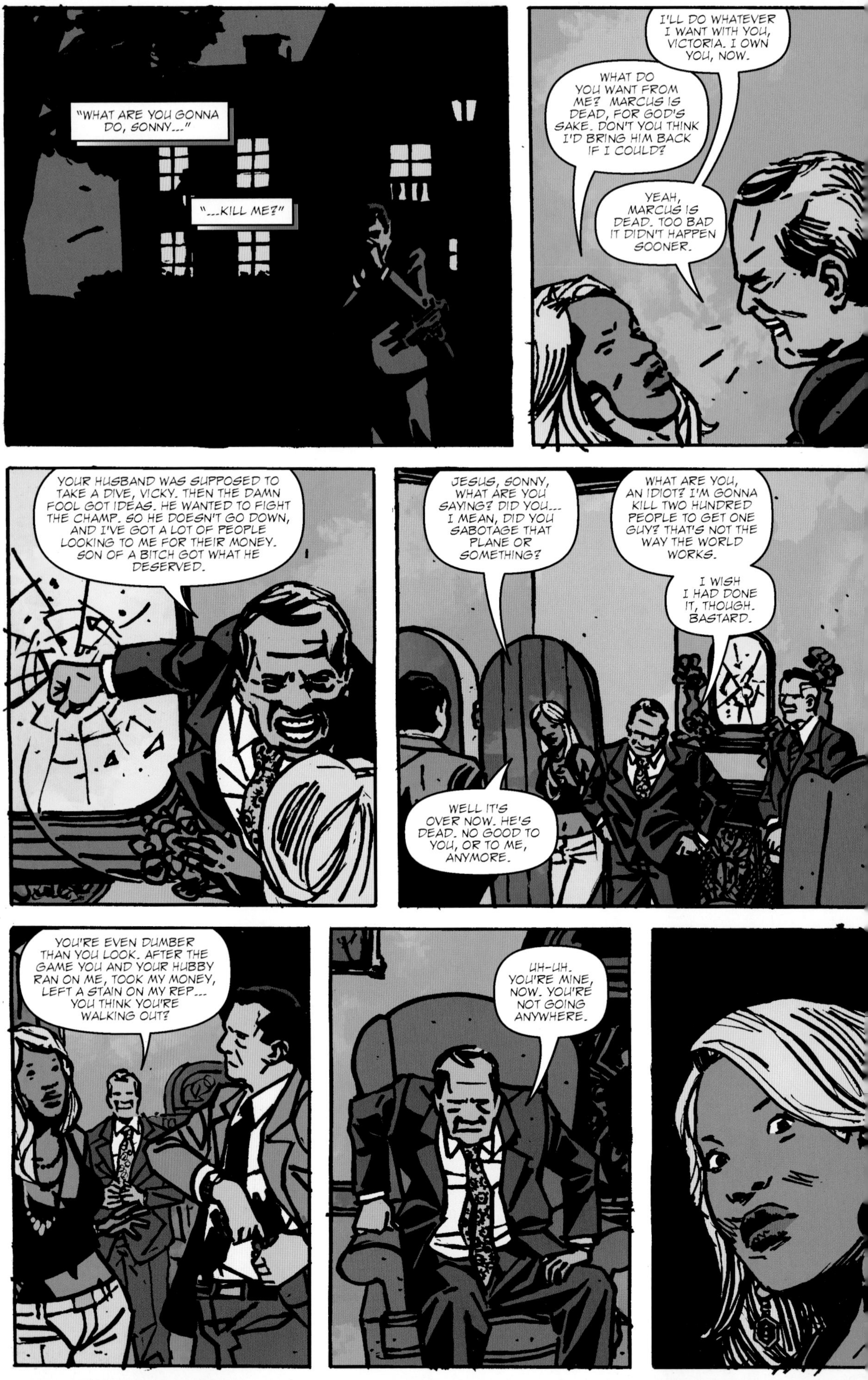
"WHAT ARE YOU GONNA DO, SONNY..."
"...KILL ME?"
WHAT DO YOU WANT FROM ME? MARCUS IS DEAD, FOR GOD'S SAKE. DON'T YOU THINK I'D BRING HIM BACK IF I COULD?
I'LL DO WHATEVER I WANT WITH YOU, VICTORIA. I OWN YOU, NOW.
YEAH, MARCUS IS DEAD. TOO BAD IT DIDN'T HAPPEN SOONER.
YOUR HUSBAND WAS SUPPOSED TO TAKE A DIVE, VICKY. THEN THE DAMN FOOL GOT IDEAS. HE WANTED TO FIGHT THE CHAMP. SO HE DOESN'T GO DOWN, AND I'VE GOT A LOT OF PEOPLE LOOKING TO ME FOR THEIR MONEY. SON OF A BITCH GOT WHAT HE DESERVED.
JESUS, SONNY, WHAT ARE YOU SAYING? DID YOU... I MEAN, DID YOU SABOTAGE THAT PLANE OR SOMETHING?
WHAT ARE YOU, AN IDIOT? I'M GONNA KILL TWO HUNDRED PEOPLE TO GET ONE GUY? THAT'S NOT THE WAY THE WORLD WORKS.
I WISH I HAD DONE IT, THOUGH. BASTARD.
WELL IT'S OVER NOW. HE'S DEAD. NO GOOD TO YOU, OR TO ME, ANYMORE.
YOU'RE EVEN DUMBER THAN YOU LOOK. AFTER THE GAME YOU AND YOUR HUBBY RAN ON ME, TOOK MY MONEY, LEFT A STAIN ON MY REP... YOU THINK YOU'RE WALKING OUT?
UH-UH. YOU'RE MINE, NOW. YOU'RE NOT GOING ANYWHERE.

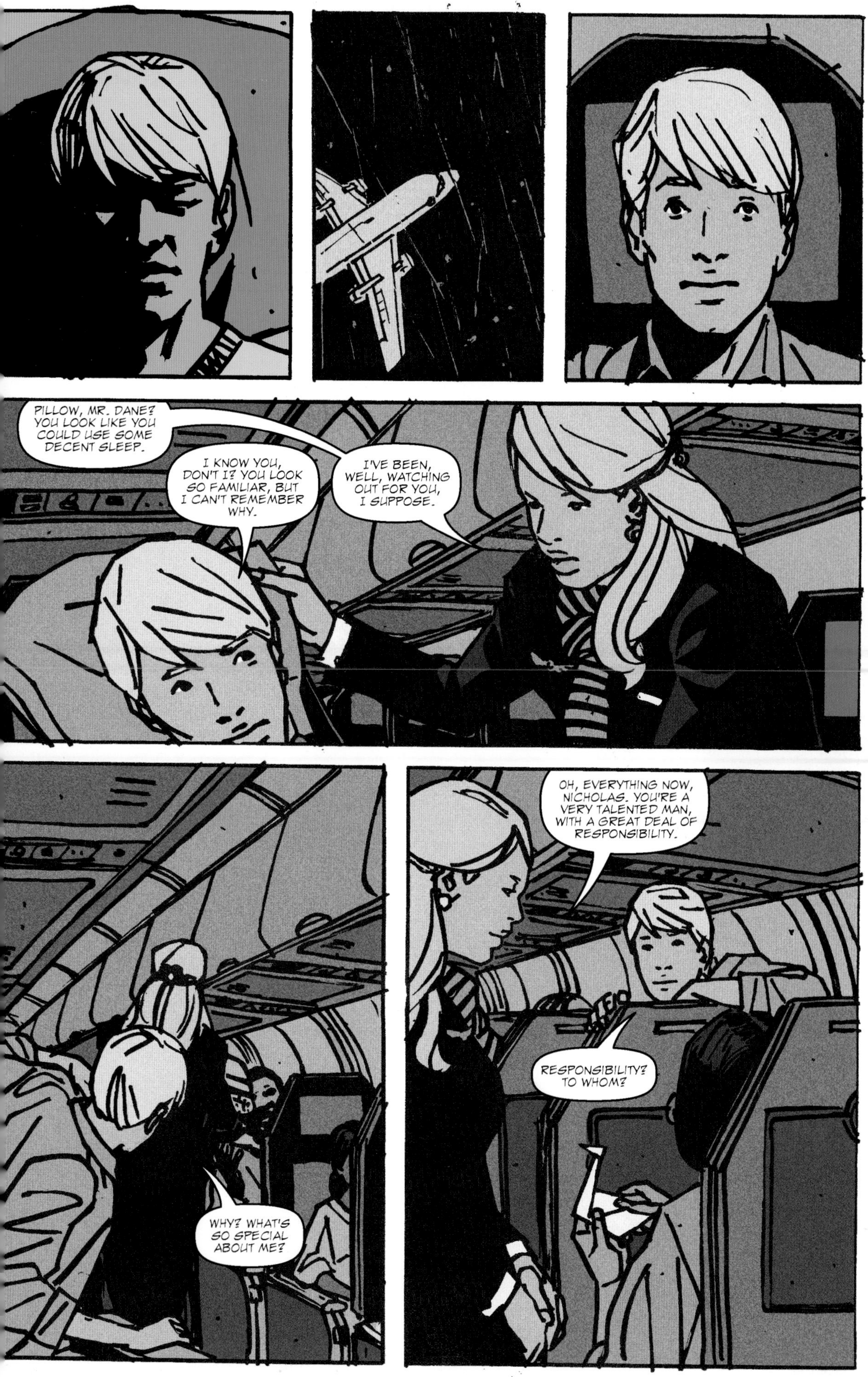
PILLOW, MR. DANE? YOU LOOK LIKE YOU COULD USE SOME DECENT SLEEP.
I KNOW YOU, DON'T I? YOU LOOK SO FAMILIAR, BUT I CAN'T REMEMBER WHY.
I'VE BEEN, WELL, WATCHING OUT FOR YOU, I SUPPOSE.
WHY? WHAT'S SO SPECIAL ABOUT ME?
OH, EVERYTHING NOW, NICHOLAS. YOU'RE A VERY TALENTED MAN, WITH A GREAT DEAL OF RESPONSIBILITY.
RESPONSIBILITY? TO WHOM?

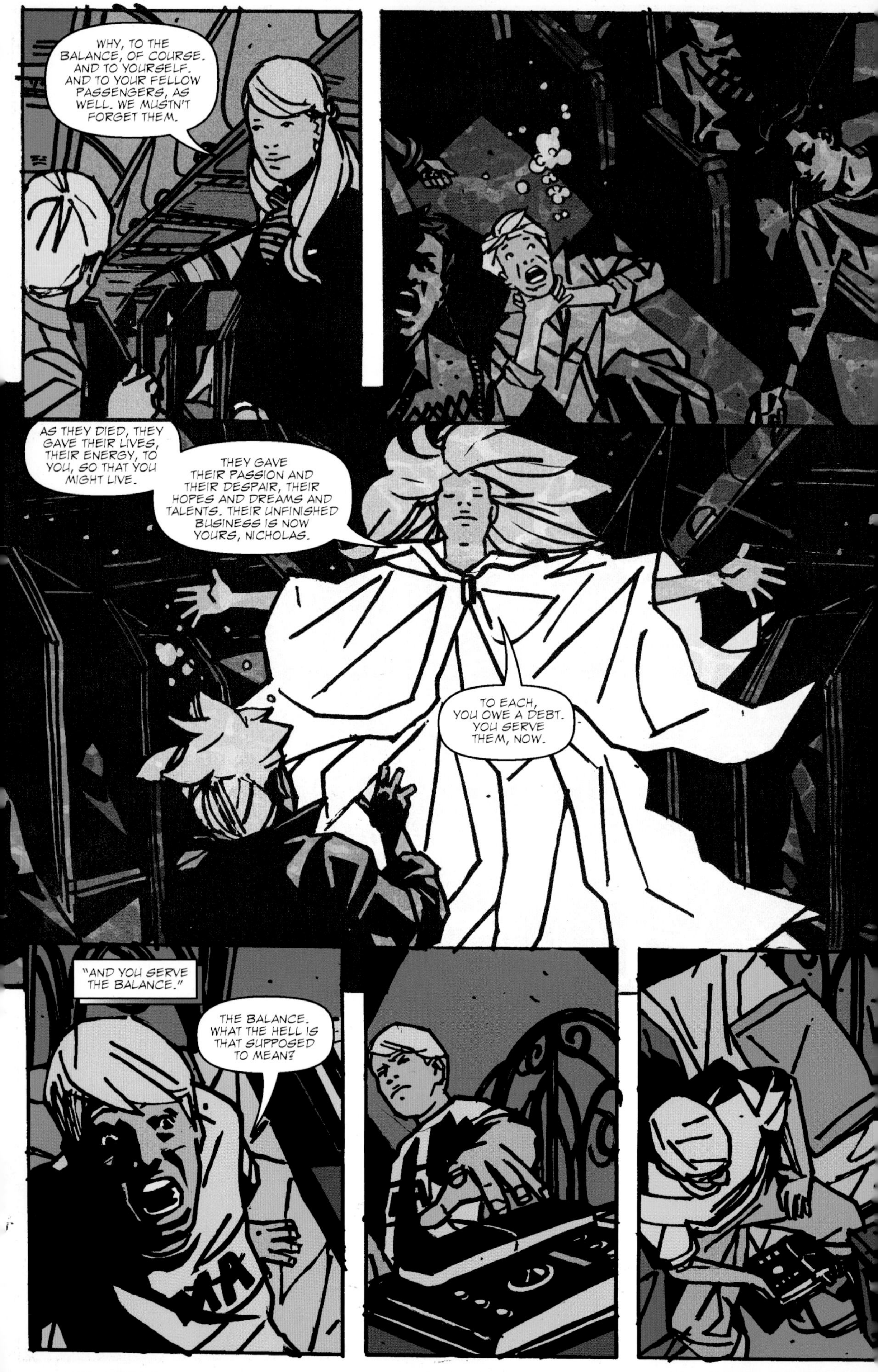
WHY, TO THE BALANCE, OF COURSE. AND TO YOURSELF. AND TO YOUR FELLOW PASSENGERS, AS WELL. WE MUSTN'T FORGET THEM.
AS THEY DIED, THEY GAVE THEIR LIVES, THEIR ENERGY, TO YOU, SO THAT YOU MIGHT LIVE.
THEY GAVE THEIR PASSION AND THEIR DESPAIR, THEIR HOPES AND DREAMS AND TALENTS. THEIR UNFINISHED BUSINESS IS NOW YOURS, NICHOLAS.
TO EACH, YOU OWE A DEBT. YOU SERVE THEM, NOW.
"AND YOU SERVE THE BALANCE."
THE BALANCE. WHAT THE HELL IS THAT SUPPOSED TO MEAN?

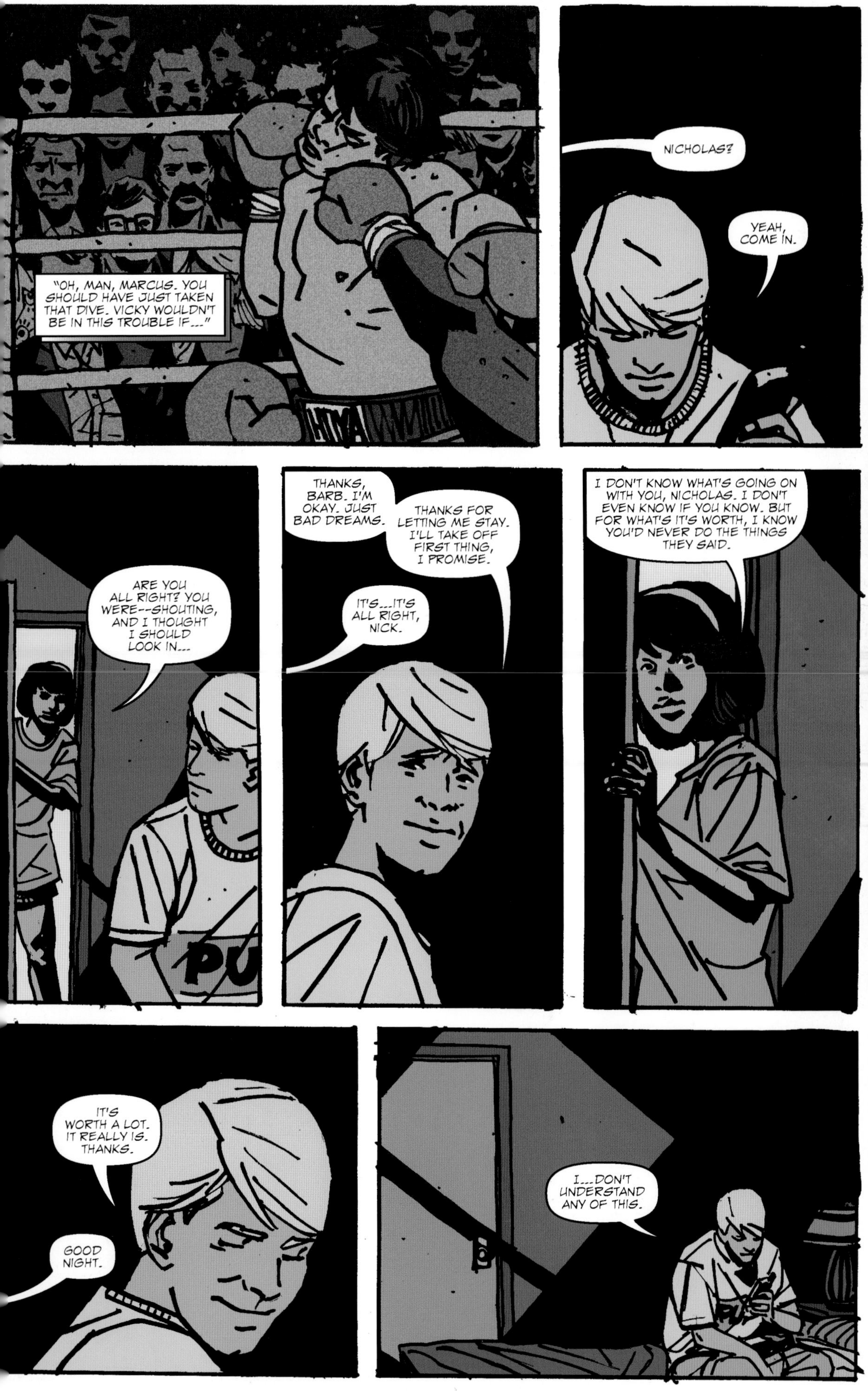
"OH, MAN, MARCUS. YOU SHOULD HAVE JUST TAKEN THAT DIVE. VICKY WOULDN'T BE IN THIS TROUBLE IF..."
NICHOLAS?
YEAH, COME IN.
ARE YOU ALL RIGHT? YOU WERE--SHOUTING, AND I THOUGHT I SHOULD LOOK IN...
THANKS, BARB. I'M OKAY. JUST BAD DREAMS.
THANKS FOR LETTING ME STAY. I'LL TAKE OFF FIRST THING, I PROMISE.
IT'S...IT'S ALL RIGHT, NICK.
I DON'T KNOW WHAT'S GOING ON WITH YOU, NICHOLAS. I DON'T EVEN KNOW IF YOU KNOW. BUT FOR WHAT'S IT'S WORTH, I KNOW YOU'D NEVER DO THE THINGS THEY SAID.
IT'S WORTH A LOT. IT REALLY IS. THANKS.
GOOD NIGHT.
I...DON'T UNDERSTAND ANY OF THIS.

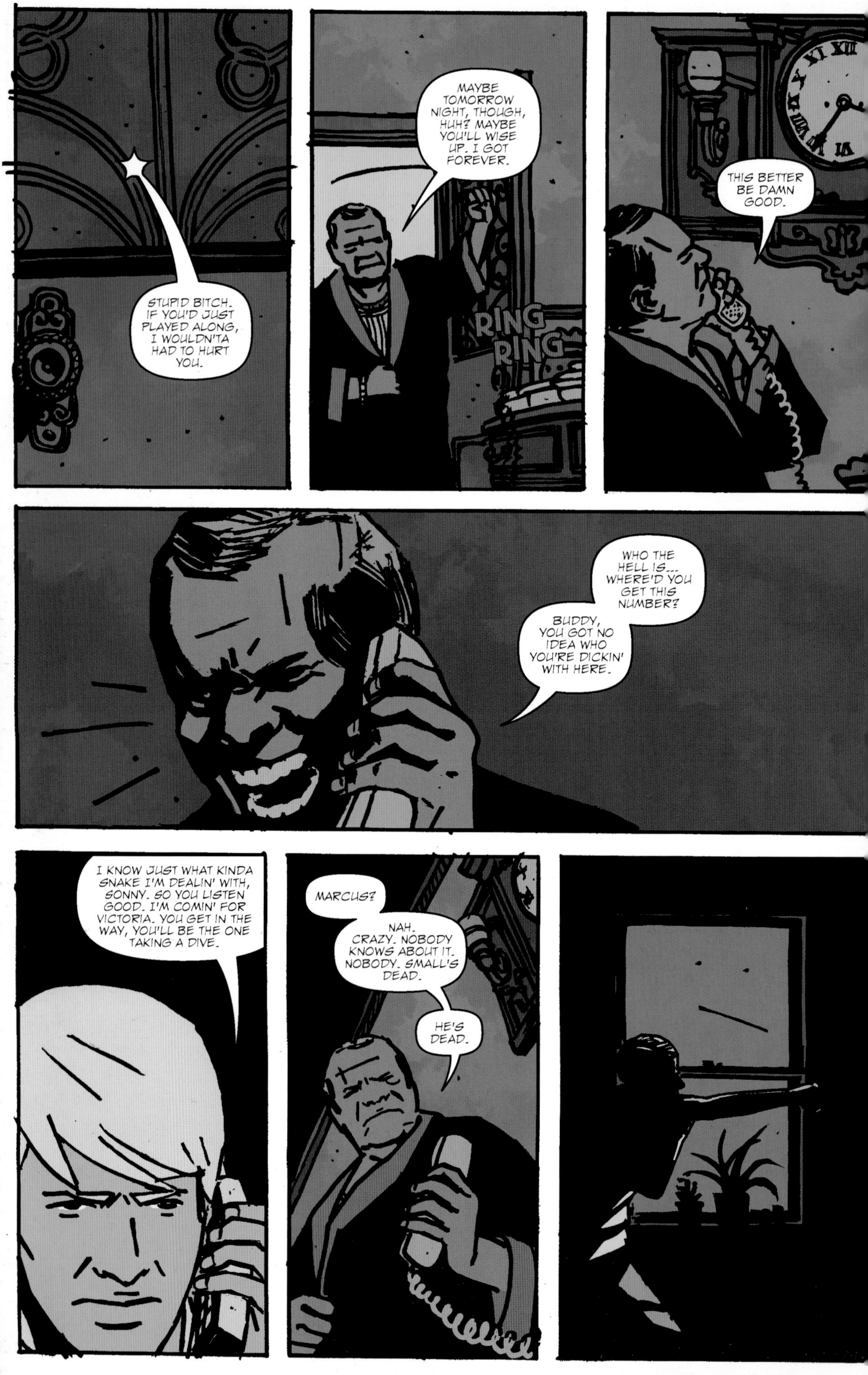
STUPID BITCH. IF YOU'D JUST PLAYED ALONG, I WOULDN'TA HAD TO HURT YOU.
MAYBE TOMORROW NIGHT, THOUGH, HUH? MAYBE YOU'LL WISE UP. I GOT FOREVER.
RING RING
THIS BETTER BE DAMN GOOD.
WHO THE HELL IS... WHERE'D YOU GET THIS NUMBER?
BUDDY, YOU GOT NO IDEA WHO YOU'RE DICKIN' WITH HERE.
I KNOW JUST WHAT KINDA SNAKE I'M DEALIN' WITH, SONNY. SO YOU LISTEN GOOD. I'M COMIN' FOR VICTORIA. YOU GET IN THE WAY, YOU'LL BE THE ONE TAKING A DIVE.
MARCUS?
NAH. CRAZY. NOBODY KNOWS ABOUT IT. NOBODY. SMALL'S DEAD.
HE'S DEAD.

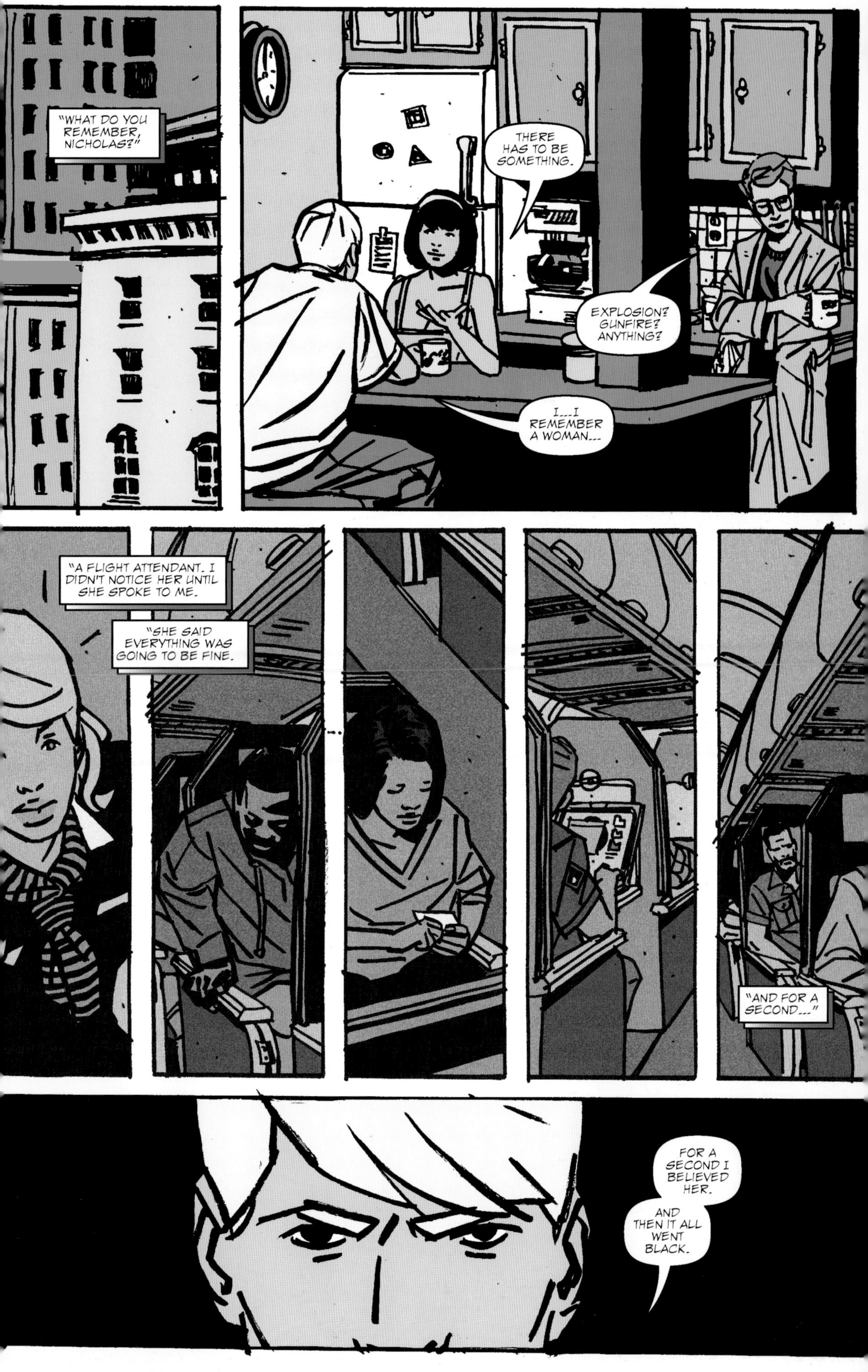
"WHAT DO YOU REMEMBER, NICHOLAS?"
THERE HAS TO BE SOMETHING.
EXPLOSION? GUNFIRE? ANYTHING?
I...I REMEMBER A WOMAN...
"A FLIGHT ATTENDANT. I DIDN'T NOTICE HER UNTIL SHE SPOKE TO ME.
"SHE SAID EVERYTHING WAS GOING TO BE FINE.
"AND FOR A SECOND..."
FOR A SECOND I BELIEVED HER.
AND THEN IT ALL WENT BLACK.

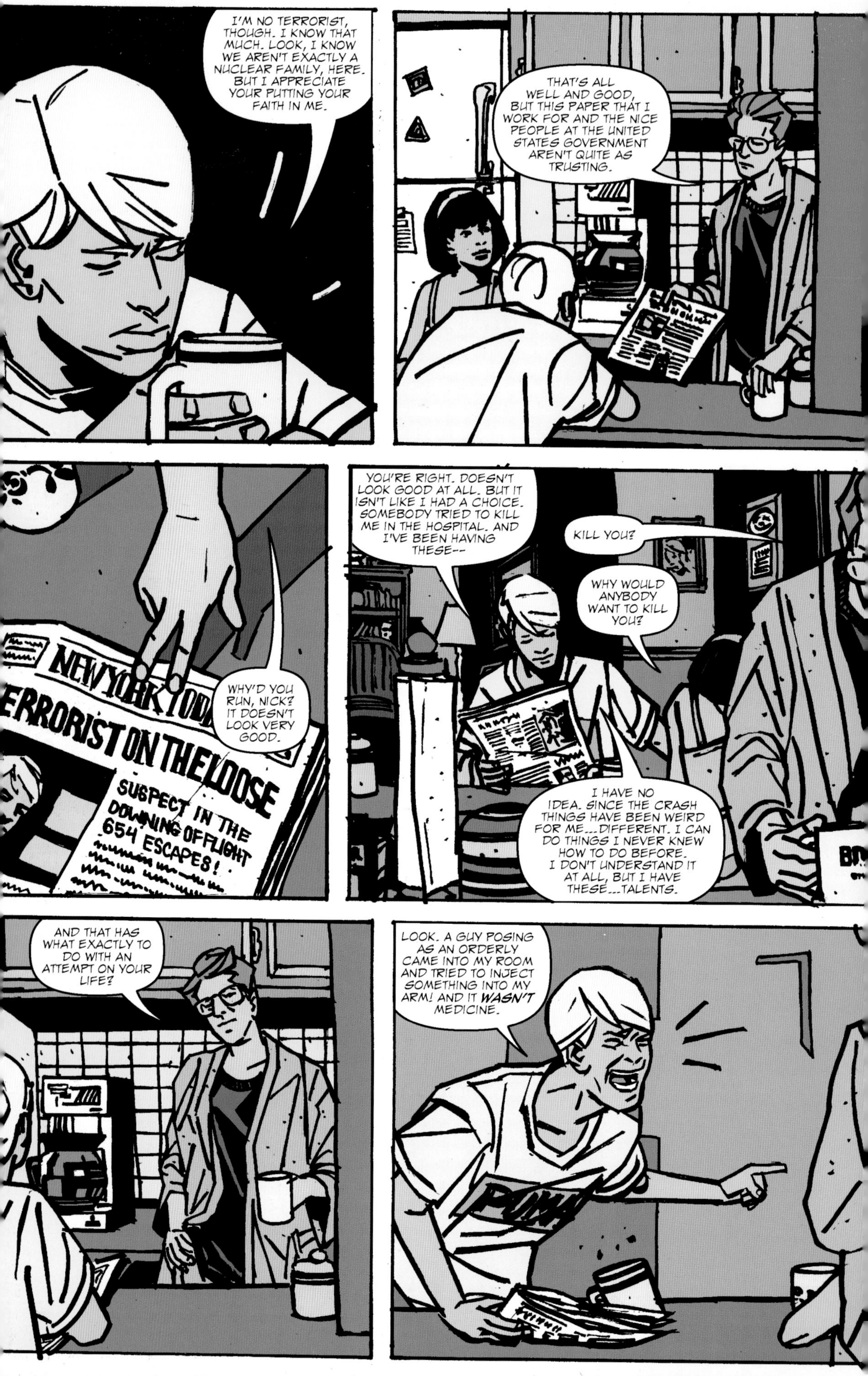
I'M NO TERRORIST, THOUGH. I KNOW THAT MUCH. LOOK, I KNOW WE AREN'T EXACTLY A NUCLEAR FAMILY, HERE. BUT I APPRECIATE YOUR PUTTING YOUR FAITH IN ME.
THAT'S ALL WELL AND GOOD, BUT THIS PAPER THAT I WORK FOR AND THE NICE PEOPLE AT THE UNITED STATES GOVERNMENT AREN'T QUITE AS TRUSTING.
NEW YORK TODA
TERRORIST ON THE LOOSE
SUSPECT IN THE DOWNING OF FLIGHT 654 ESCAPES!
WHY'D YOU RUN, NICK? IT DOESN'T LOOK VERY GOOD.
YOU'RE RIGHT. DOESN'T LOOK GOOD AT ALL. BUT IT ISN'T LIKE I HAD A CHOICE. SOMEBODY TRIED TO KILL ME IN THE HOSPITAL. AND I'VE BEEN HAVING THESE--
KILL YOU?
WHY WOULD ANYBODY WANT TO KILL YOU?
I HAVE NO IDEA. SINCE THE CRASH THINGS HAVE BEEN WEIRD FOR ME...DIFFERENT. I CAN DO THINGS I NEVER KNEW HOW TO DO BEFORE. I DON'T UNDERSTAND IT AT ALL, BUT I HAVE THESE...TALENTS.
AND THAT HAS WHAT EXACTLY TO DO WITH AN ATTEMPT ON YOUR LIFE?
LOOK. A GUY POSING AS AN ORDERLY CAME INTO MY ROOM AND TRIED TO INJECT SOMETHING INTO MY ARM! AND IT *WASN'T* MEDICINE.
PUMA

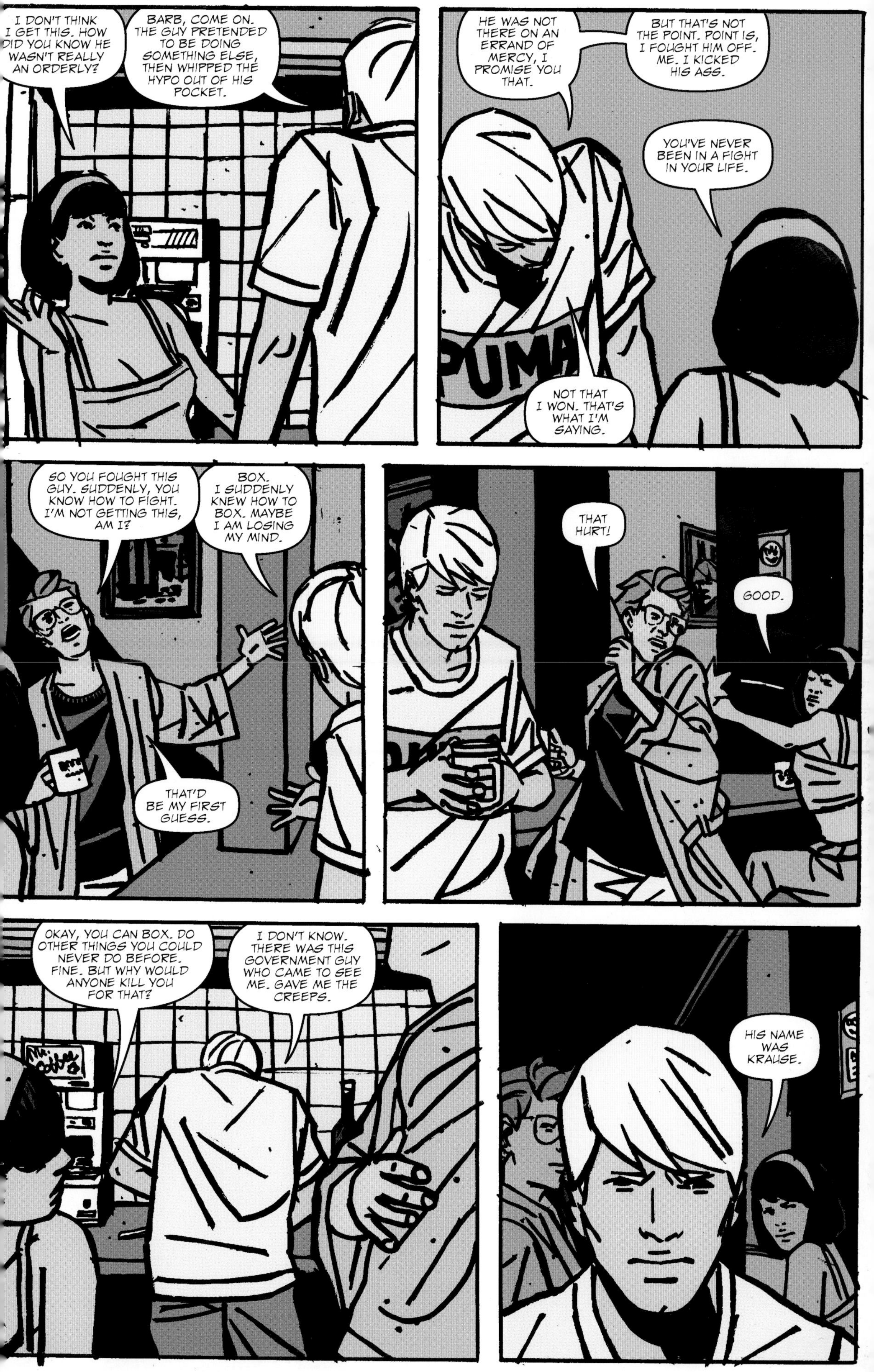
I DON'T THINK I GET THIS. HOW DID YOU KNOW HE WASN'T REALLY AN ORDERLY?
BARB, COME ON. THE GUY PRETENDED TO BE DOING SOMETHING ELSE, THEN WHIPPED THE HYPO OUT OF HIS POCKET.
HE WAS NOT THERE ON AN ERRAND OF MERCY, I PROMISE YOU THAT.
BUT THAT'S NOT THE POINT. POINT IS, I FOUGHT HIM OFF. ME. I KICKED HIS ASS.
YOU'VE NEVER BEEN IN A FIGHT IN YOUR LIFE.
PUMA
NOT THAT I WON. THAT'S WHAT I'M SAYING.
SO YOU FOUGHT THIS GUY. SUDDENLY, YOU KNOW HOW TO FIGHT. I'M NOT GETTING THIS, AM I?
BOX. I SUDDENLY KNEW HOW TO BOX. MAYBE I AM LOSING MY MIND.
THAT'D BE MY FIRST GUESS.
THAT HURT!
GOOD.
OKAY, YOU CAN BOX. DO OTHER THINGS YOU COULD NEVER DO BEFORE. FINE. BUT WHY WOULD ANYONE KILL YOU FOR THAT?
I DON'T KNOW. THERE WAS THIS GOVERNMENT GUY WHO CAME TO SEE ME. GAVE ME THE CREEPS.
HIS NAME WAS KRAUSE.

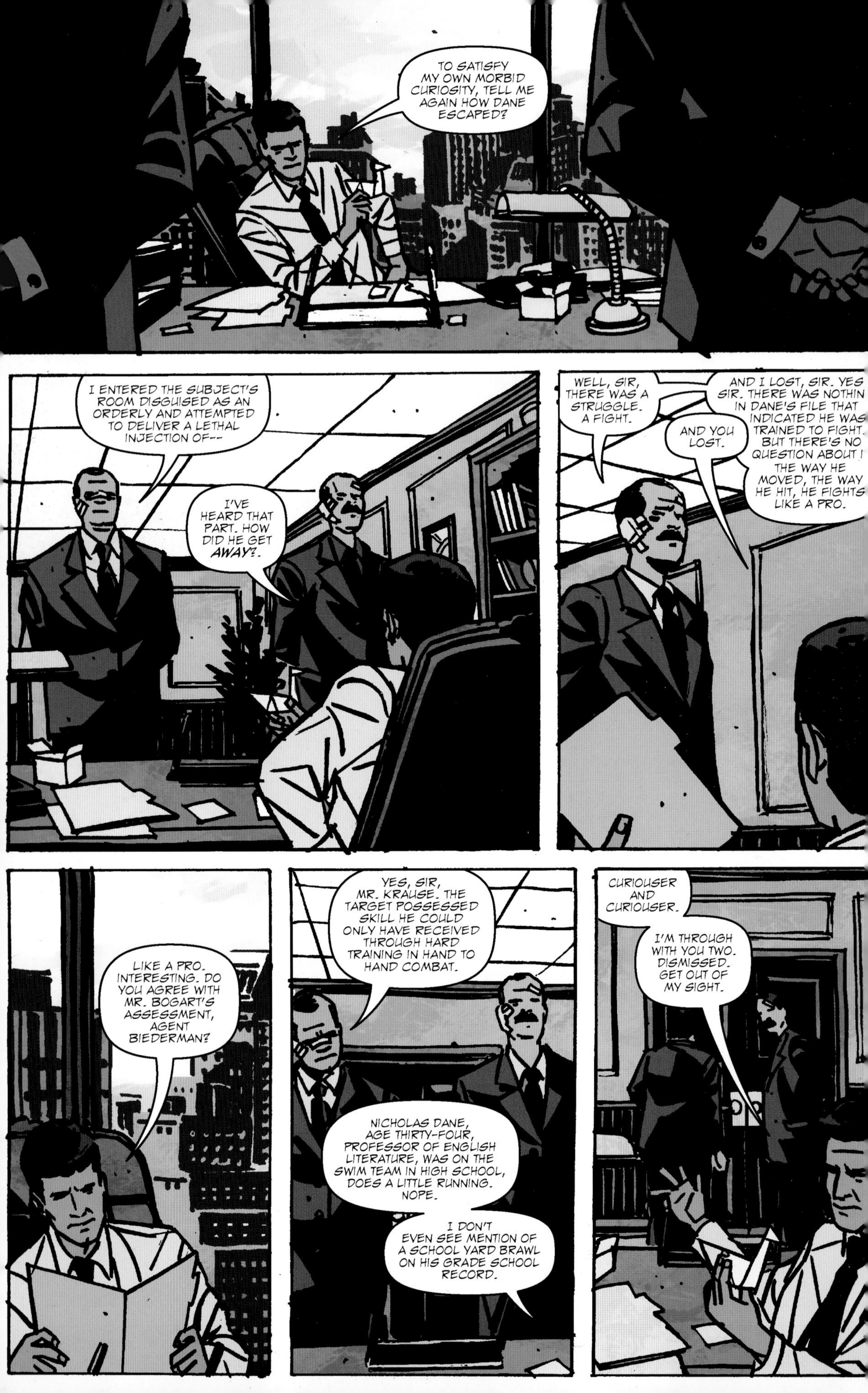
TO SATISFY MY OWN MORBID CURIOSITY, TELL ME AGAIN HOW DANE ESCAPED?
I ENTERED THE SUBJECT'S ROOM DISGUISED AS AN ORDERLY AND ATTEMPTED TO DELIVER A LETHAL INJECTION OF--
I'VE HEARD THAT PART. HOW DID HE GET *AWAY*?.
WELL, SIR, THERE WAS A STRUGGLE. A FIGHT.
AND YOU LOST.
AND I LOST, SIR. YES SIR. THERE WAS NOTHIN IN DANE'S FILE THAT INDICATED HE WAS TRAINED TO FIGHT. BUT THERE'S NO QUESTION ABOUT I THE WAY HE MOVED, THE WAY HE HIT, HE FIGHTS LIKE A PRO.
LIKE A PRO. INTERESTING. DO YOU AGREE WITH MR. BOGART'S ASSESSMENT, AGENT BIEDERMAN?
YES, SIR, MR. KRAUSE. THE TARGET POSSESSED SKILL HE COULD ONLY HAVE RECEIVED THROUGH HARD TRAINING IN HAND TO HAND COMBAT.
NICHOLAS DANE, AGE THIRTY-FOUR, PROFESSOR OF ENGLISH LITERATURE, WAS ON THE SWIM TEAM IN HIGH SCHOOL, DOES A LITTLE RUNNING. NOPE.
I DON'T EVEN SEE MENTION OF A SCHOOL YARD BRAWL ON HIS GRADE SCHOOL RECORD.
CURIOUSER AND CURIOUSER.
I'M THROUGH WITH YOU TWO. DISMISSED. GET OUT OF MY SIGHT.

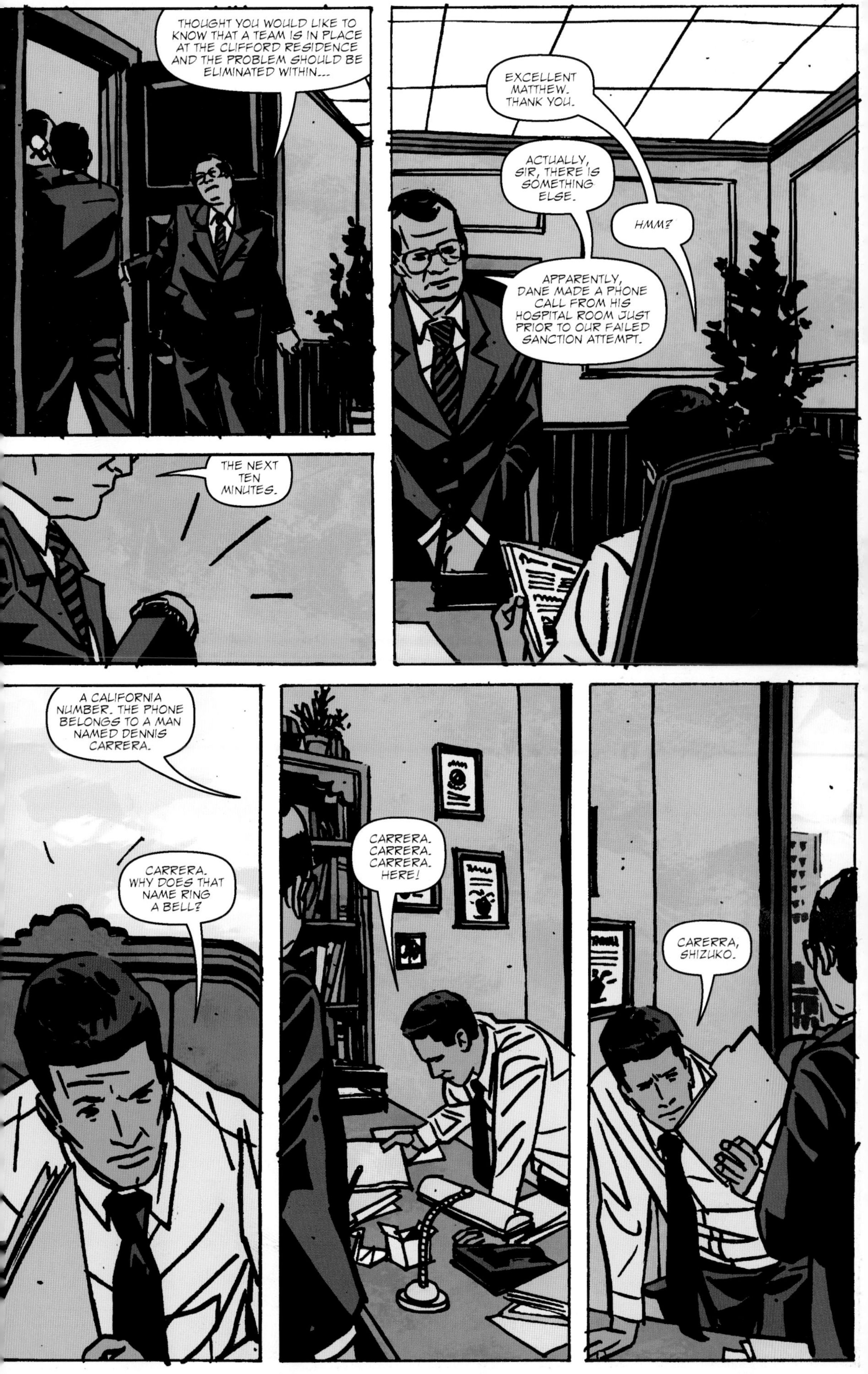
THOUGHT YOU WOULD LIKE TO KNOW THAT A TEAM IS IN PLACE AT THE CLIFFORD RESIDENCE AND THE PROBLEM SHOULD BE ELIMINATED WITHIN...
THE NEXT TEN MINUTES.
EXCELLENT MATTHEW. THANK YOU.
ACTUALLY, SIR, THERE IS SOMETHING ELSE.
HMM?
APPARENTLY, DANE MADE A PHONE CALL FROM HIS HOSPITAL ROOM JUST PRIOR TO OUR FAILED SANCTION ATTEMPT.
A CALIFORNIA NUMBER. THE PHONE BELONGS TO A MAN NAMED DENNIS CARRERA.
CARRERA. WHY DOES THAT NAME RING A BELL?
CARRERA. CARRERA. CARRERA. HERE!
CARERRA, SHIZUKO.

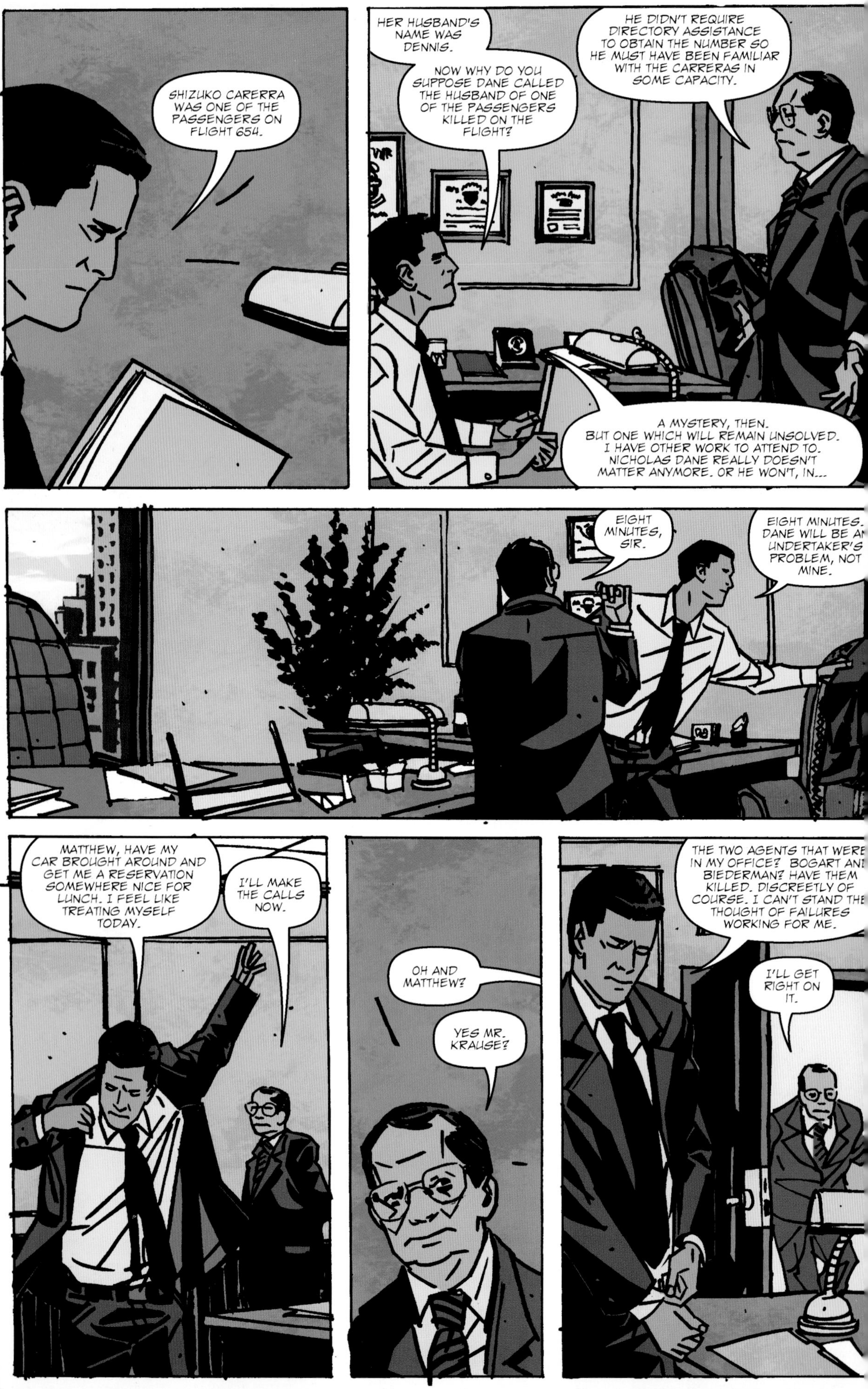
SHIZUKO CARERRA WAS ONE OF THE PASSENGERS ON FLIGHT 654.
HER HUSBAND'S NAME WAS DENNIS.
NOW WHY DO YOU SUPPOSE DANE CALLED THE HUSBAND OF ONE OF THE PASSENGERS KILLED ON THE FLIGHT?
HE DIDN'T REQUIRE DIRECTORY ASSISTANCE TO OBTAIN THE NUMBER SO HE MUST HAVE BEEN FAMILIAR WITH THE CARRERAS IN SOME CAPACITY.
A MYSTERY, THEN. BUT ONE WHICH WILL REMAIN UNSOLVED. I HAVE OTHER WORK TO ATTEND TO. NICHOLAS DANE REALLY DOESN'T MATTER ANYMORE. OR HE WON'T, IN...
EIGHT MINUTES, SIR.
EIGHT MINUTES. DANE WILL BE AN UNDERTAKER'S PROBLEM, NOT MINE.
MATTHEW, HAVE MY CAR BROUGHT AROUND AND GET ME A RESERVATION SOMEWHERE NICE FOR LUNCH. I FEEL LIKE TREATING MYSELF TODAY.
I'LL MAKE THE CALLS NOW.
OH AND MATTHEW?
YES MR. KRAUSE?
THE TWO AGENTS THAT WERE IN MY OFFICE? BOGART AND BIEDERMAN? HAVE THEM KILLED. DISCREETLY OF COURSE. I CAN'T STAND THE THOUGHT OF FAILURES WORKING FOR ME.
I'LL GET RIGHT ON IT.

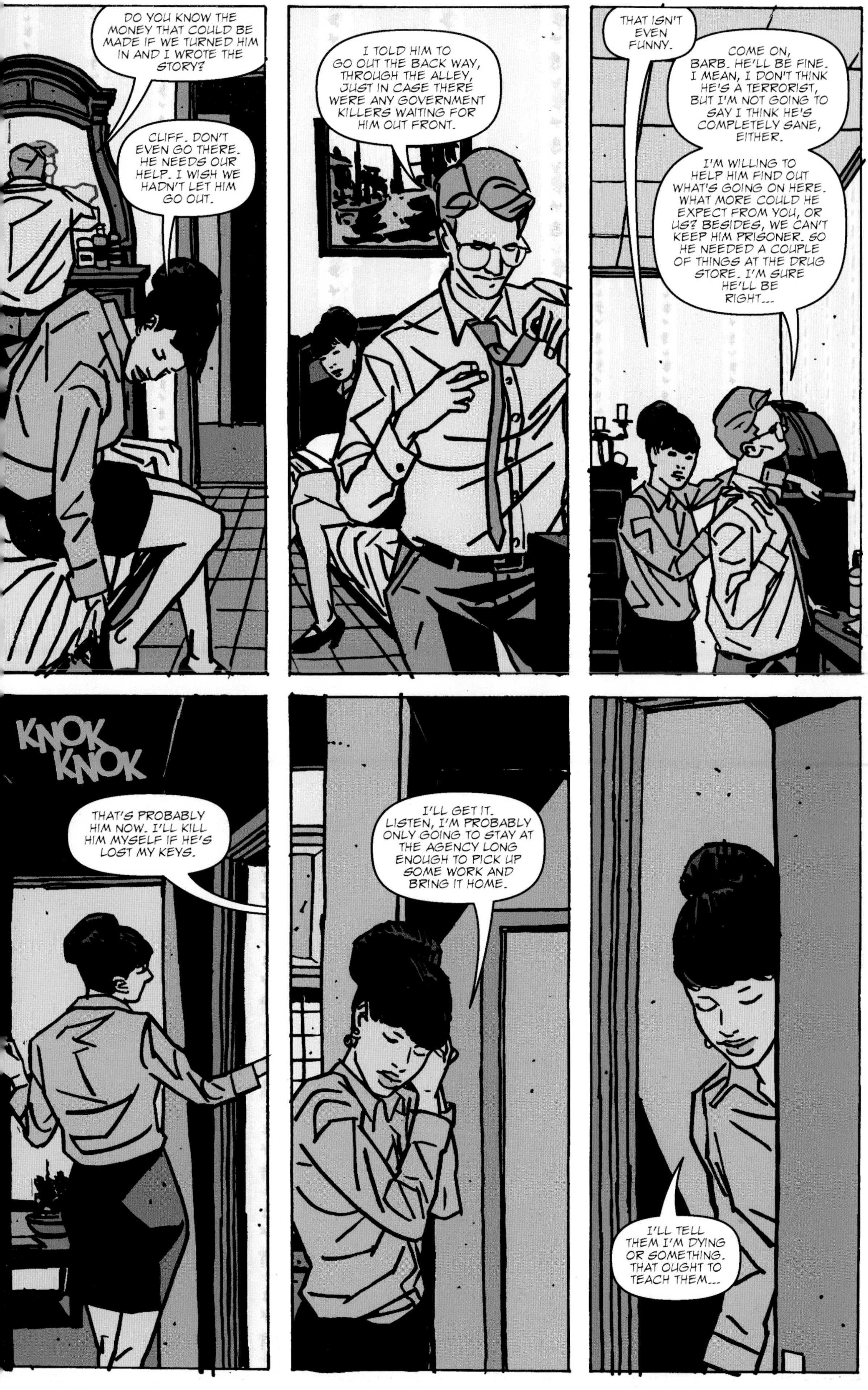
DO YOU KNOW THE MONEY THAT COULD BE MADE IF WE TURNED HIM IN AND I WROTE THE STORY?
CLIFF. DON'T EVEN GO THERE. HE NEEDS OUR HELP. I WISH WE HADN'T LET HIM GO OUT.
I TOLD HIM TO GO OUT THE BACK WAY, THROUGH THE ALLEY, JUST IN CASE THERE WERE ANY GOVERNMENT KILLERS WAITING FOR HIM OUT FRONT.
THAT ISN'T EVEN FUNNY.
COME ON, BARB. HE'LL BE FINE. I MEAN, I DON'T THINK HE'S A TERRORIST, BUT I'M NOT GOING TO SAY I THINK HE'S COMPLETELY SANE, EITHER.
I'M WILLING TO HELP HIM FIND OUT WHAT'S GOING ON HERE. WHAT MORE COULD HE EXPECT FROM YOU, OR US? BESIDES, WE CAN'T KEEP HIM PRISONER. SO HE NEEDED A COUPLE OF THINGS AT THE DRUG STORE. I'M SURE HE'LL BE RIGHT...
KNOK KNOK
THAT'S PROBABLY HIM NOW. I'LL KILL HIM MYSELF IF HE'S LOST MY KEYS.
I'LL GET IT. LISTEN, I'M PROBABLY ONLY GOING TO STAY AT THE AGENCY LONG ENOUGH TO PICK UP SOME WORK AND BRING IT HOME.
I'LL TELL THEM I'M DYING OR SOMETHING. THAT OUGHT TO TEACH THEM...

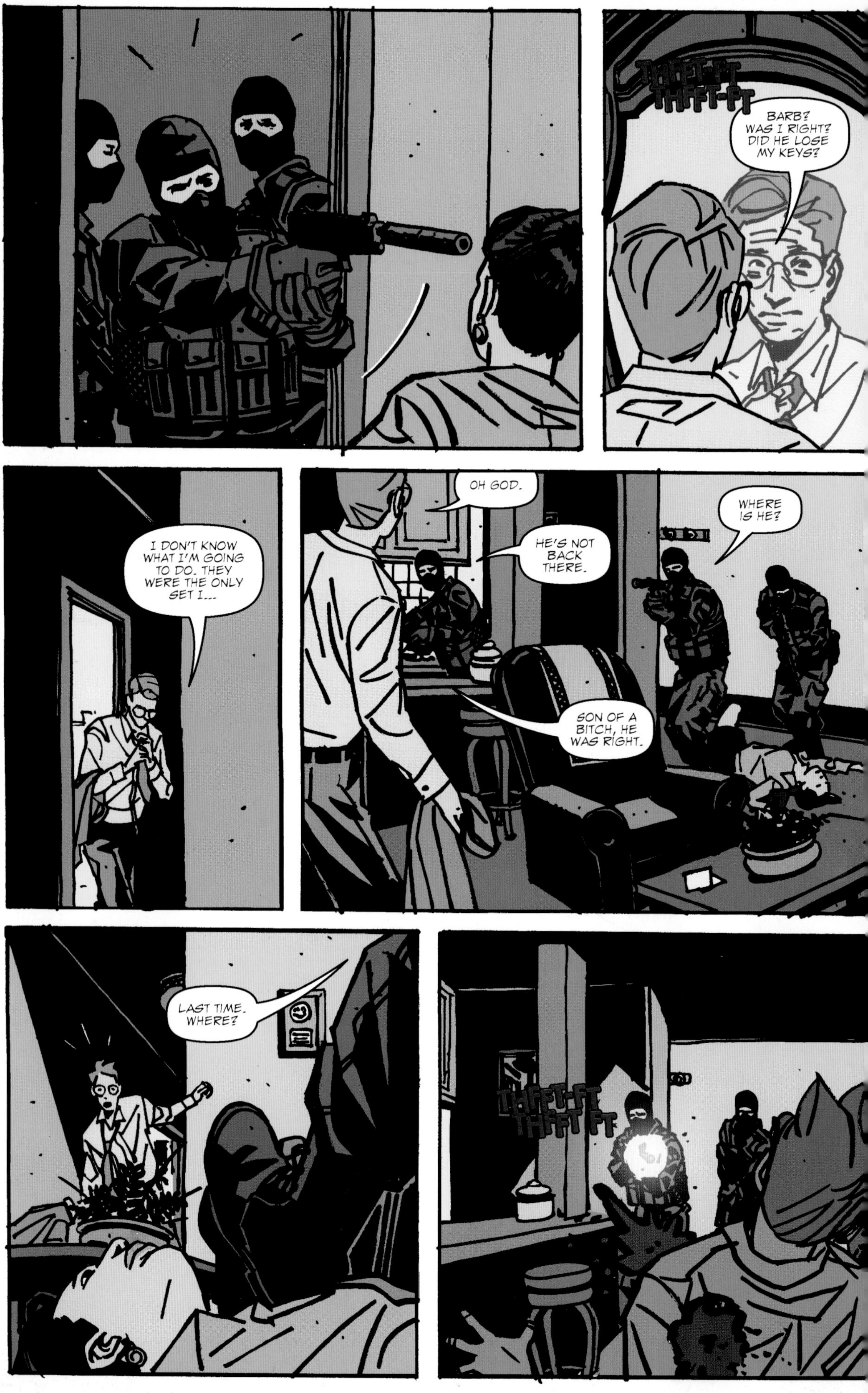
THFFT-FT
THFFT-FT
BARB? WAS I RIGHT? DID HE LOSE MY KEYS?
I DON'T KNOW WHAT I'M GOING TO DO. THEY WERE THE ONLY SET I...
OH GOD.
HE'S NOT BACK THERE.
WHERE IS HE?
SON OF A BITCH, HE WAS RIGHT.
LAST TIME. WHERE?
THFFT-FT
THFFT-FT

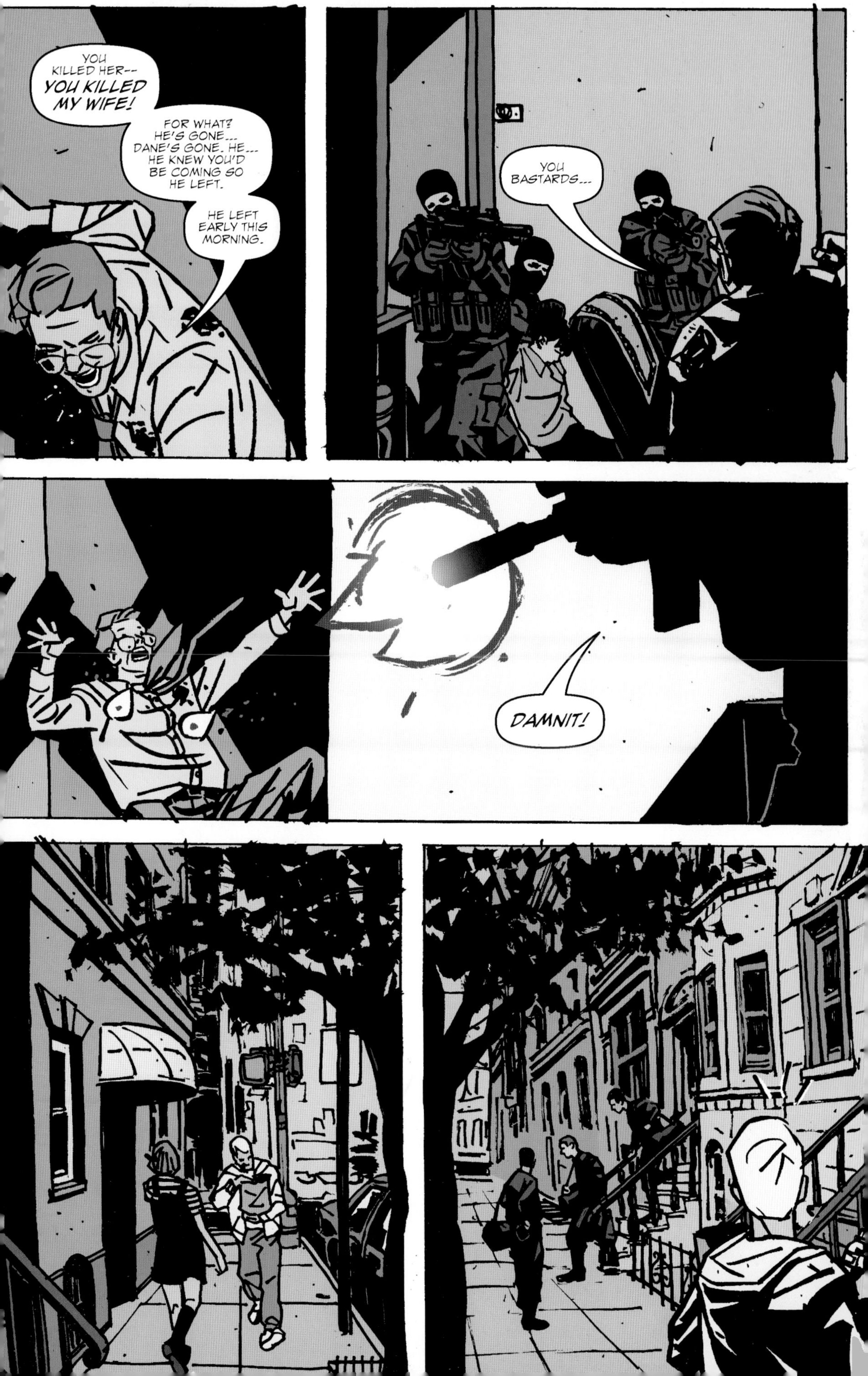
YOU KILLED HER-- YOU KILLED MY WIFE!
FOR WHAT? HE'S GONE... DANE'S GONE. HE... HE KNEW YOU'D BE COMING SO HE LEFT.
HE LEFT EARLY THIS MORNING.
YOU BASTARDS...
DAMNIT!

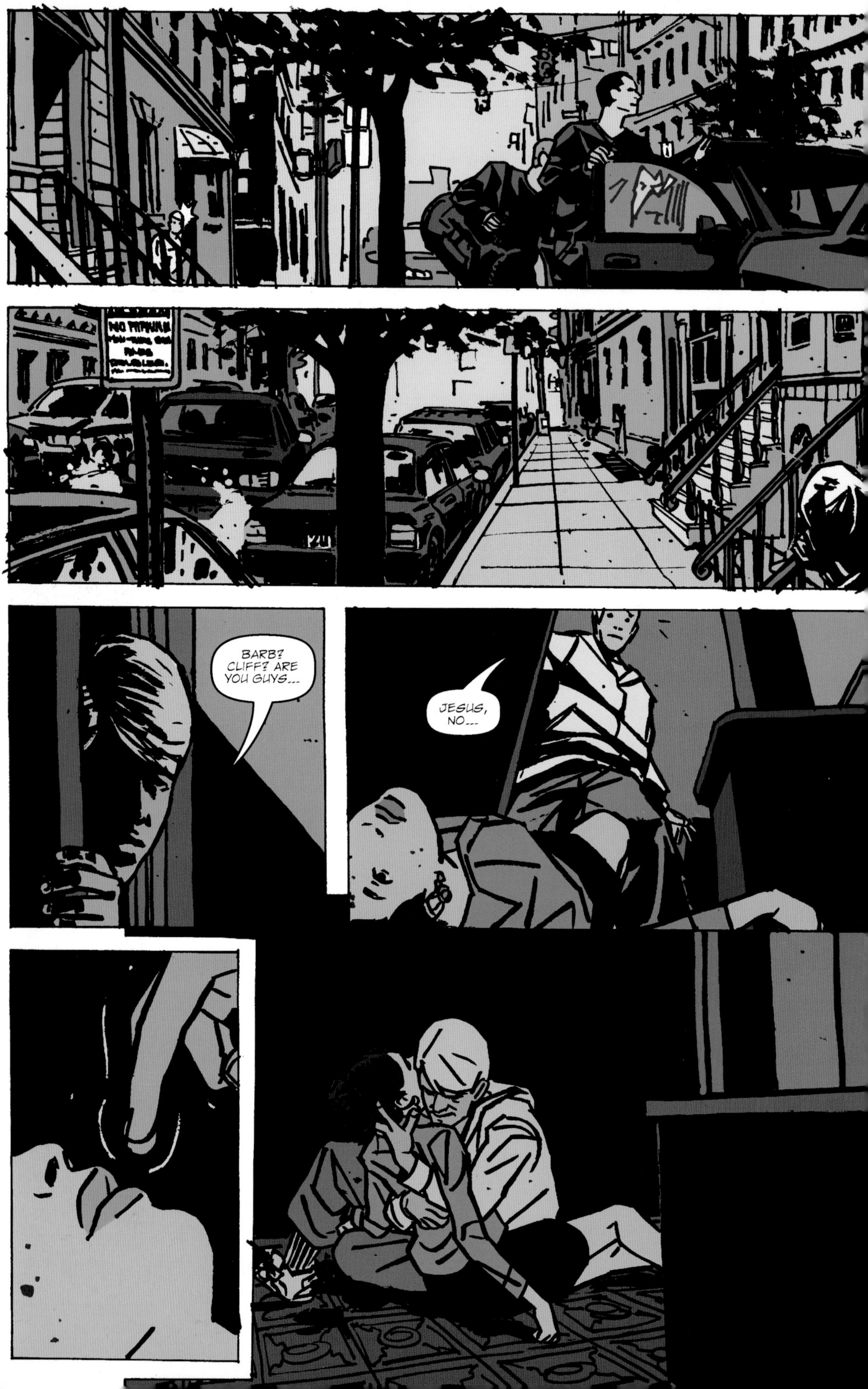
BARB? CLIFF? ARE YOU GUYS...
JESUS, NO...

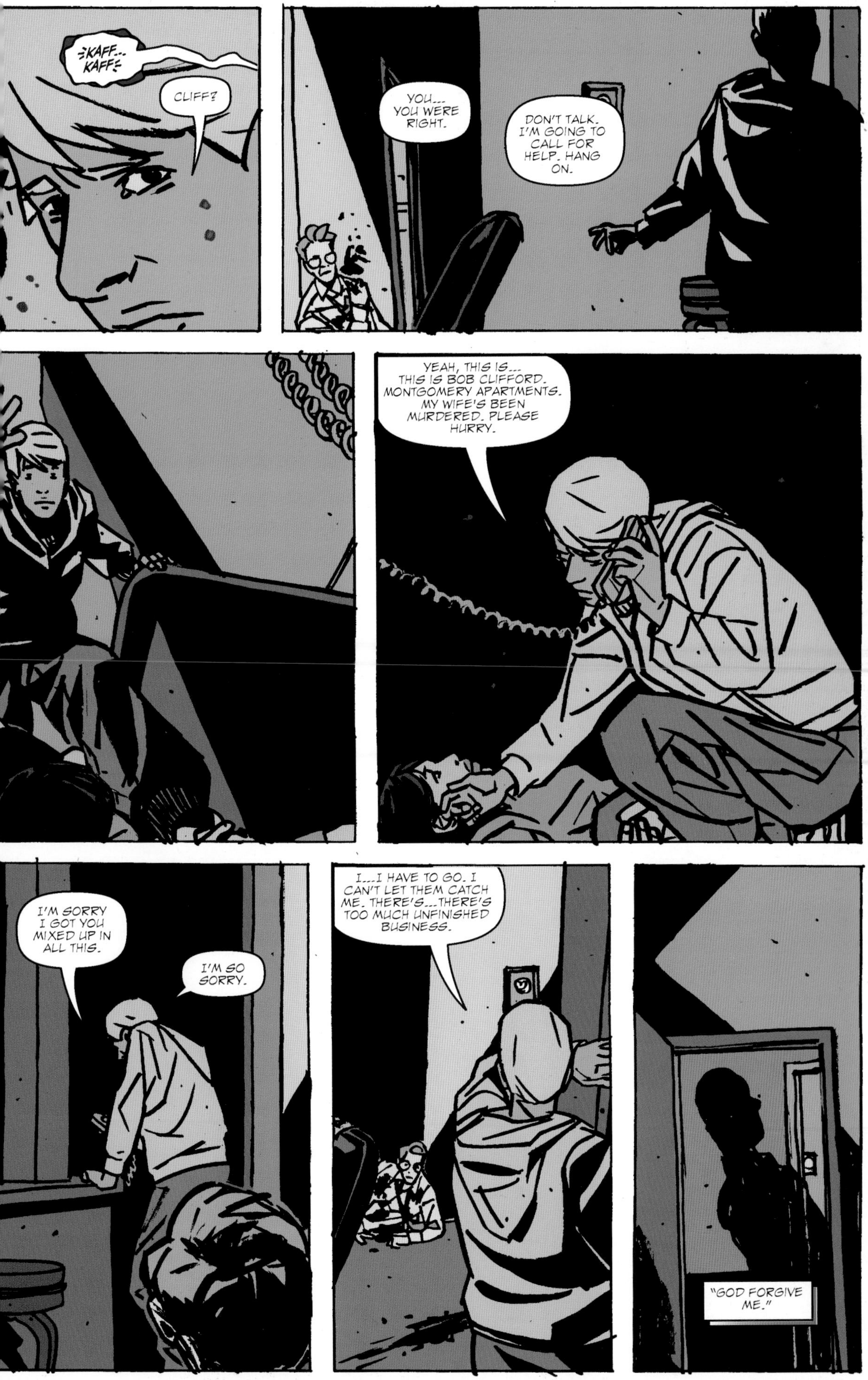

KAFF... KAFF
CLIFF?
YOU... YOU WERE RIGHT.
DON'T TALK. I'M GOING TO CALL FOR HELP. HANG ON.
YEAH, THIS IS... THIS IS BOB CLIFFORD. MONTGOMERY APARTMENTS. MY WIFE'S BEEN MURDERED. PLEASE HURRY.
I'M SORRY I GOT YOU MIXED UP IN ALL THIS.
I'M SO SORRY.
I...I HAVE TO GO. I CAN'T LET THEM CATCH ME. THERE'S...THERE'S TOO MUCH UNFINISHED BUSINESS.
"GOD FORGIVE ME."

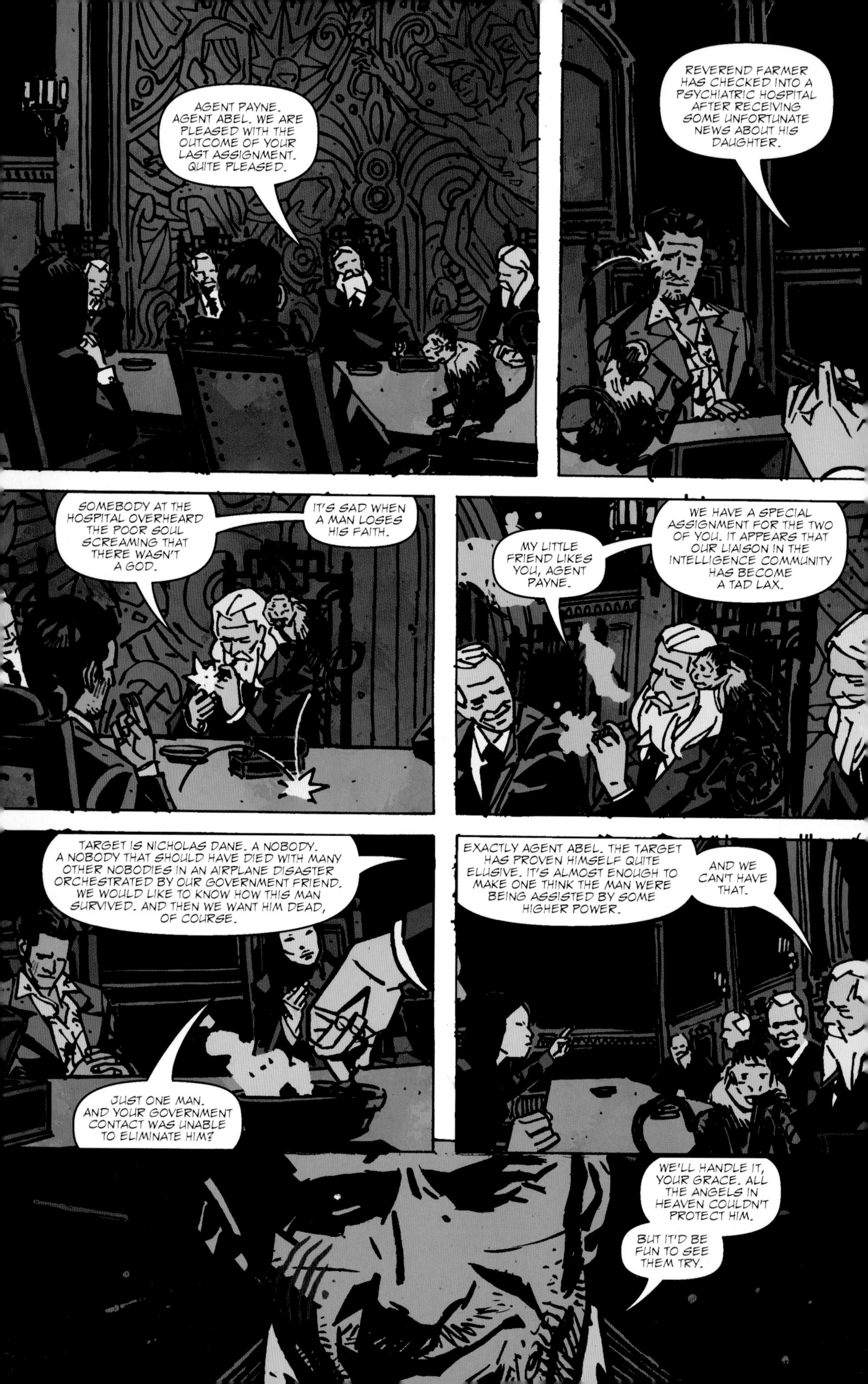
AGENT PAYNE. AGENT ABEL. WE ARE PLEASED WITH THE OUTCOME OF YOUR LAST ASSIGNMENT. QUITE PLEASED.
REVEREND FARMER HAS CHECKED INTO A PSYCHIATRIC HOSPITAL AFTER RECEIVING SOME UNFORTUNATE NEWS ABOUT HIS DAUGHTER.
SOMEBODY AT THE HOSPITAL OVERHEARD THE POOR SOUL SCREAMING THAT THERE WASN'T A GOD.
IT'S SAD WHEN A MAN LOSES HIS FAITH.
MY LITTLE FRIEND LIKES YOU, AGENT PAYNE.
WE HAVE A SPECIAL ASSIGNMENT FOR THE TWO OF YOU. IT APPEARS THAT OUR LIAISON IN THE INTELLIGENCE COMMUNITY HAS BECOME A TAD LAX.
TARGET IS NICHOLAS DANE. A NOBODY. A NOBODY THAT SHOULD HAVE DIED WITH MANY OTHER NOBODIES IN AN AIRPLANE DISASTER ORCHESTRATED BY OUR GOVERNMENT FRIEND. WE WOULD LIKE TO KNOW HOW THIS MAN SURVIVED. AND THEN WE WANT HIM DEAD, OF COURSE.
JUST ONE MAN. AND YOUR GOVERNMENT CONTACT WAS UNABLE TO ELIMINATE HIM?
EXACTLY AGENT ABEL. THE TARGET HAS PROVEN HIMSELF QUITE ELUSIVE. IT'S ALMOST ENOUGH TO MAKE ONE THINK THE MAN WERE BEING ASSISTED BY SOME HIGHER POWER.
AND WE CAN'T HAVE THAT.
WE'LL HANDLE IT, YOUR GRACE. ALL THE ANGELS IN HEAVEN COULDN'T PROTECT HIM.
BUT IT'D BE FUN TO SEE THEM TRY.

**PAUL AZACETA**
original series cover

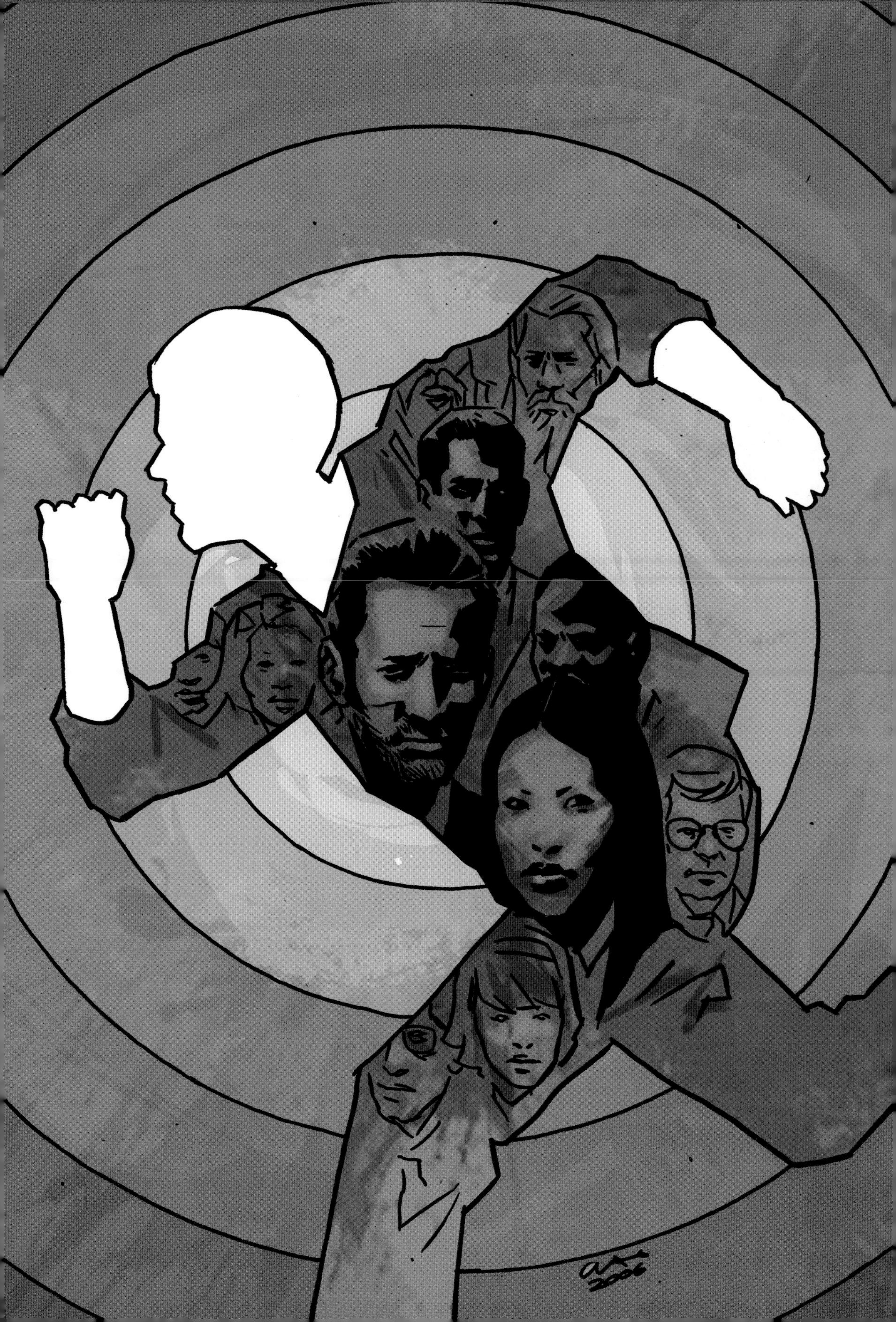

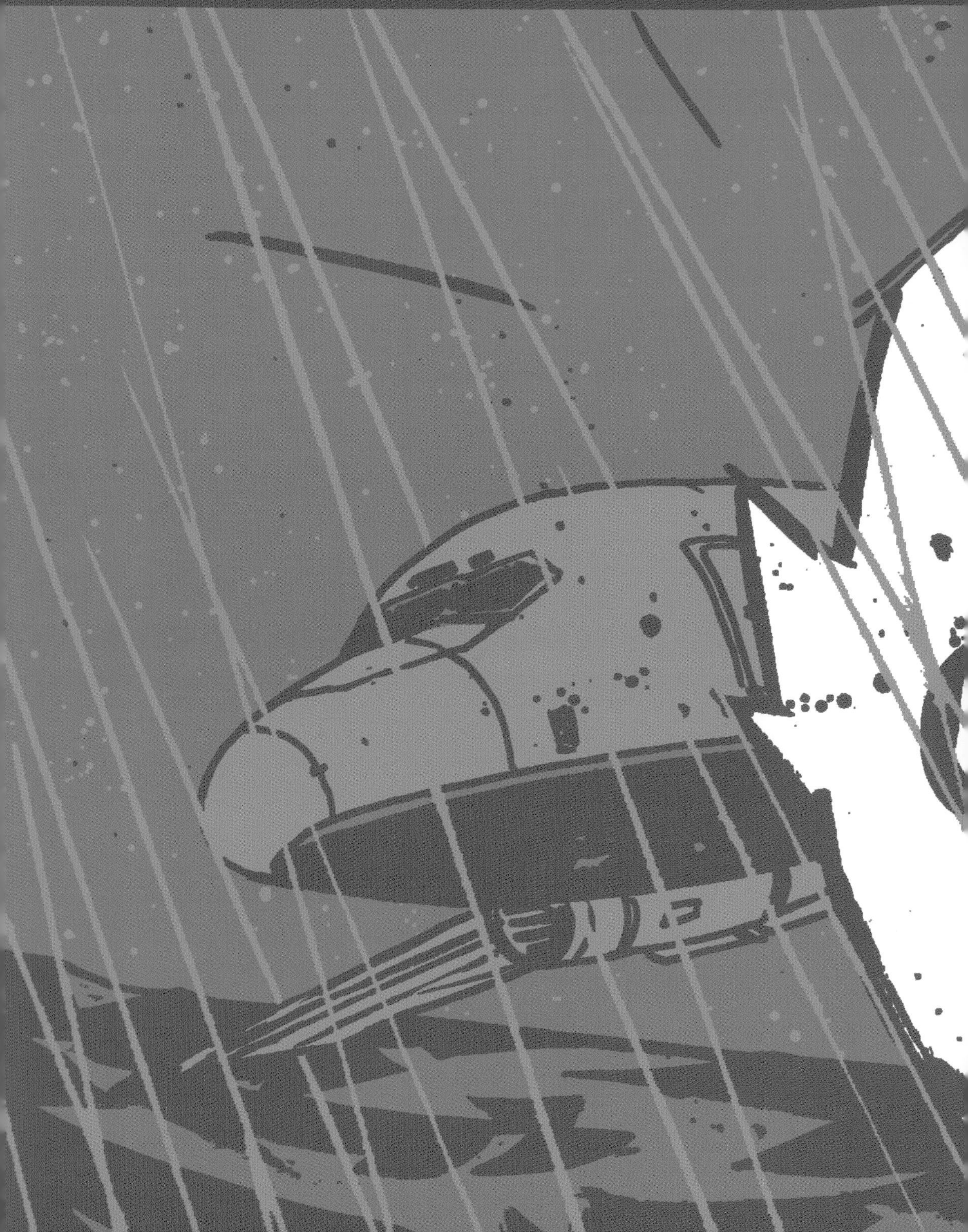

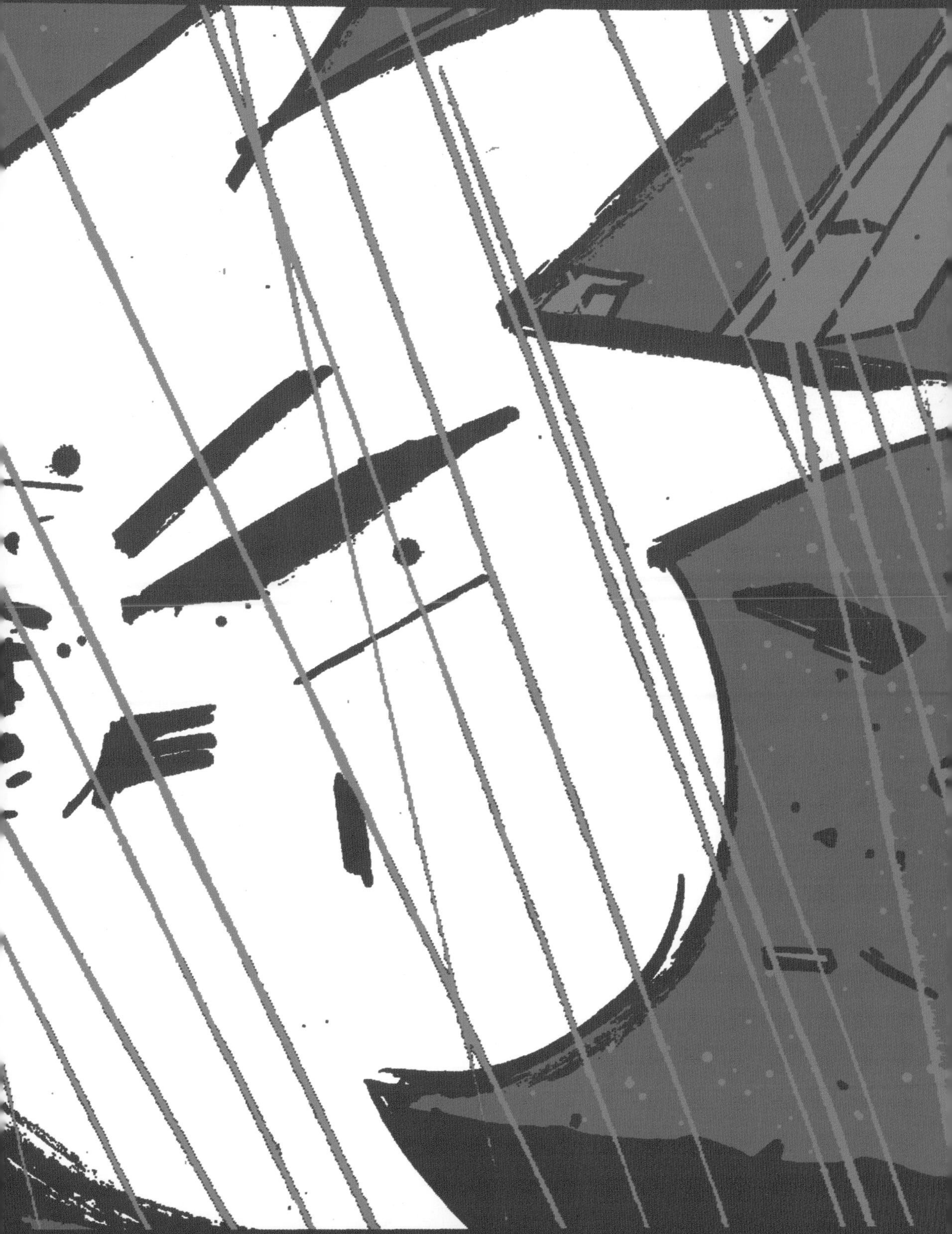

# CHAPTER THREE 3

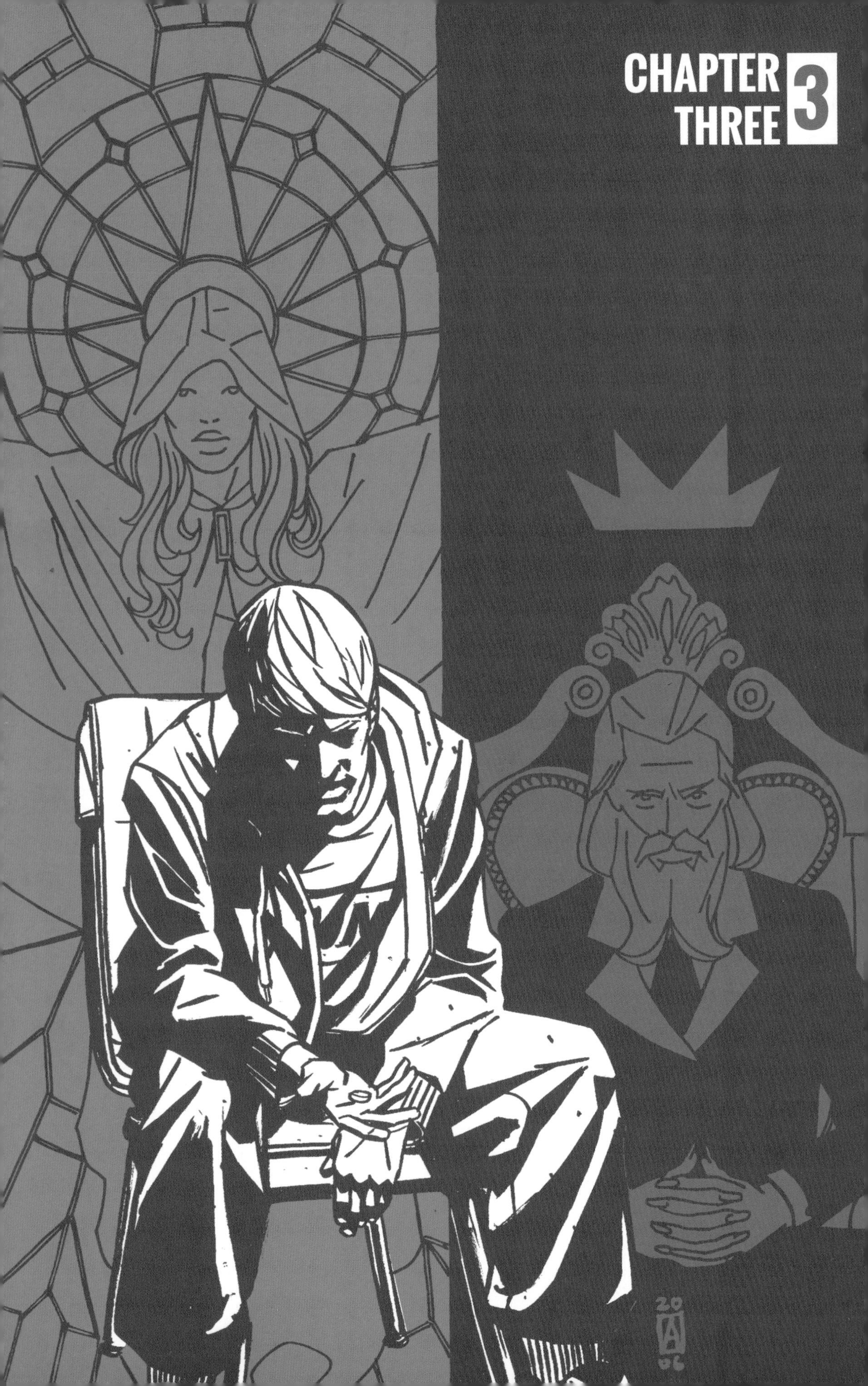

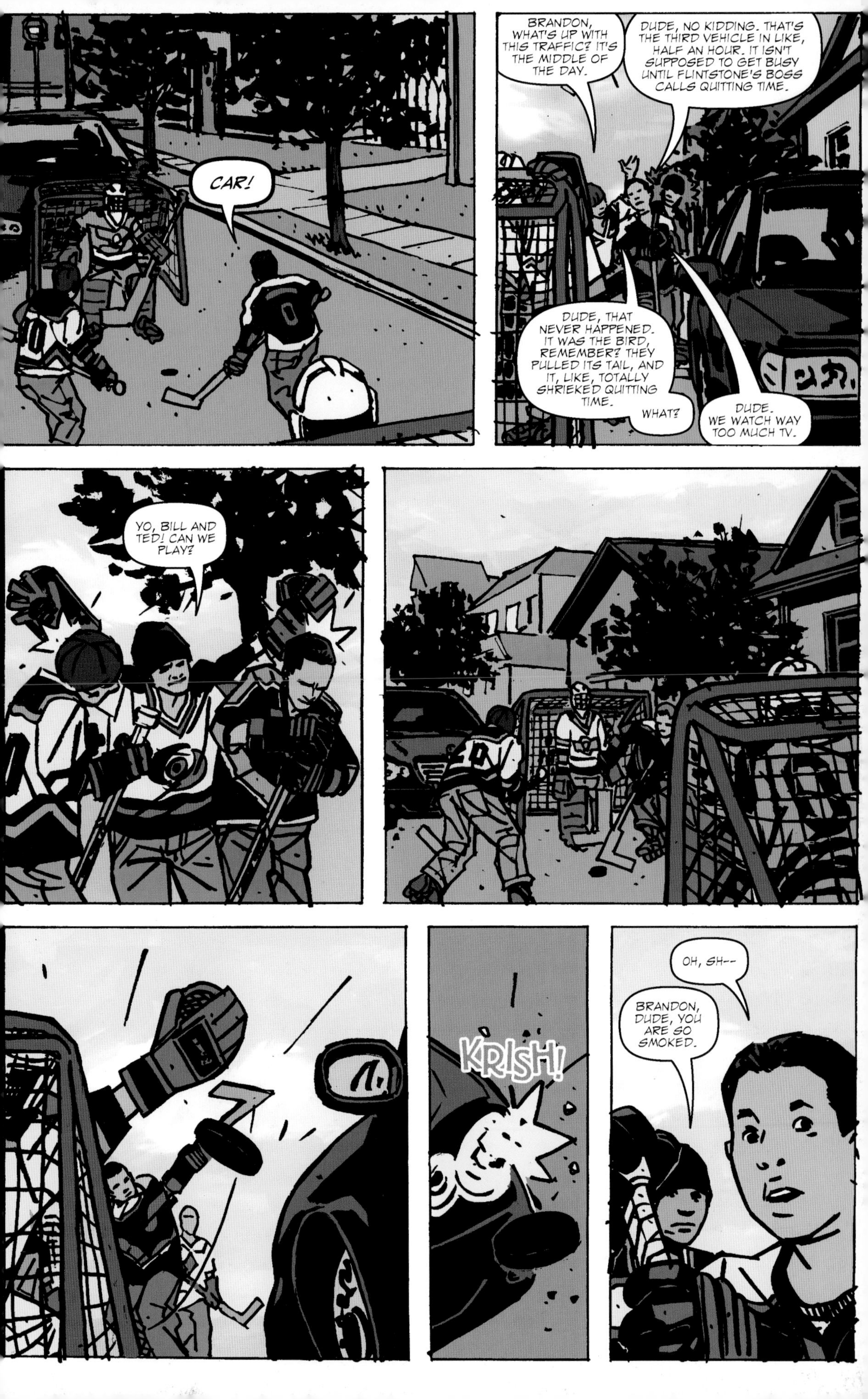
CAR!
BRANDON, WHAT'S UP WITH THIS TRAFFIC? IT'S THE MIDDLE OF THE DAY.
DUDE, NO KIDDING. THAT'S THE THIRD VEHICLE IN LIKE, HALF AN HOUR. IT ISN'T SUPPOSED TO GET BUSY UNTIL FLINTSTONE'S BOSS CALLS QUITTING TIME.
DUDE, THAT NEVER HAPPENED. IT WAS THE BIRD, REMEMBER? THEY PULLED ITS TAIL, AND IT, LIKE, TOTALLY SHRIEKED QUITTING TIME.
WHAT?
DUDE. WE WATCH WAY TOO MUCH TV.
YO, BILL AND TED! CAN WE PLAY?
KRISH!
OH, SH--
BRANDON, DUDE, YOU ARE SO SMOKED.

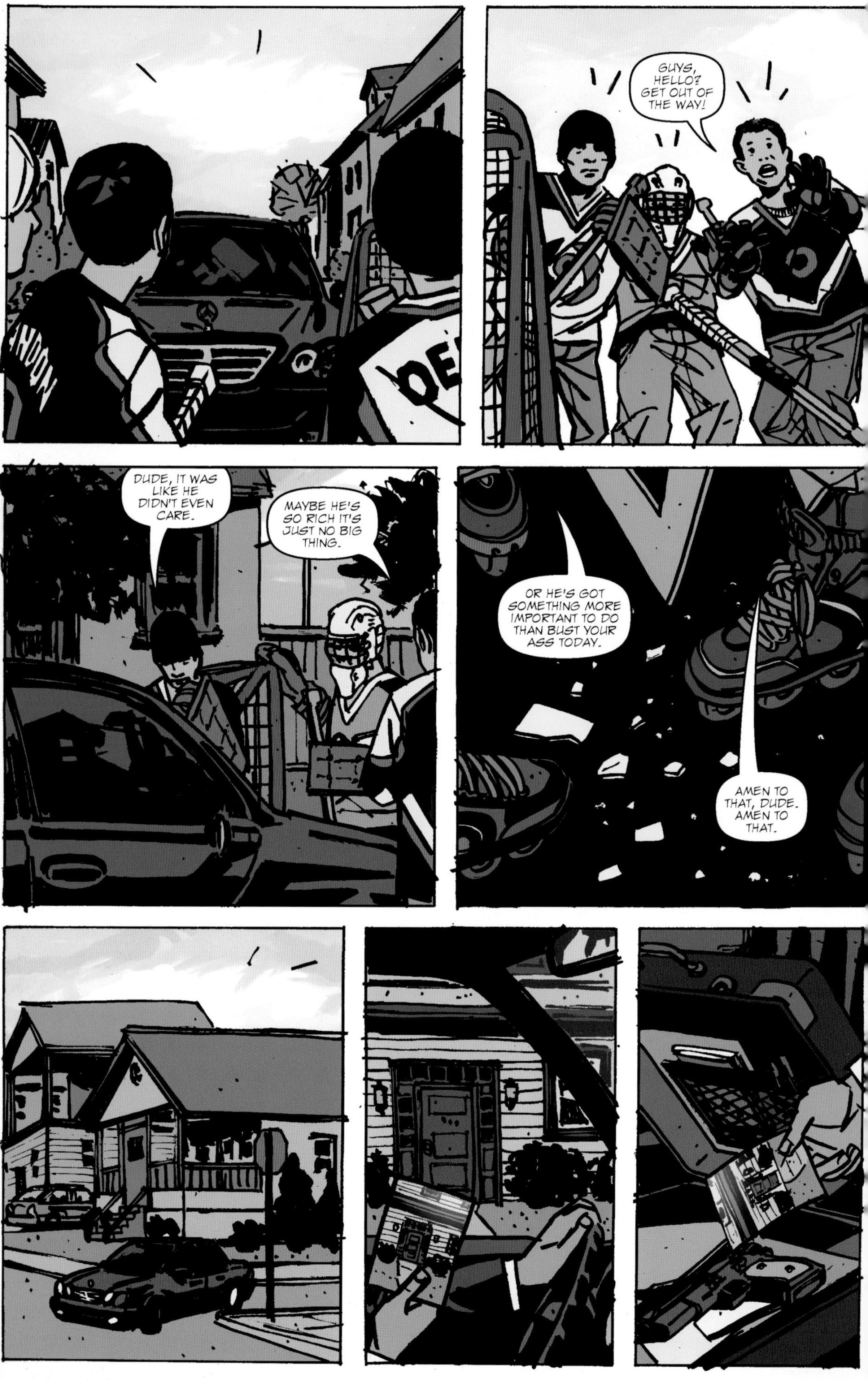
GUYS, HELLO? GET OUT OF THE WAY!
DUDE, IT WAS LIKE HE DIDN'T EVEN CARE.
MAYBE HE'S SO RICH IT'S JUST NO BIG THING.
OR HE'S GOT SOMETHING MORE IMPORTANT TO DO THAN BUST YOUR ASS TODAY.
AMEN TO THAT, DUDE. AMEN TO THAT.

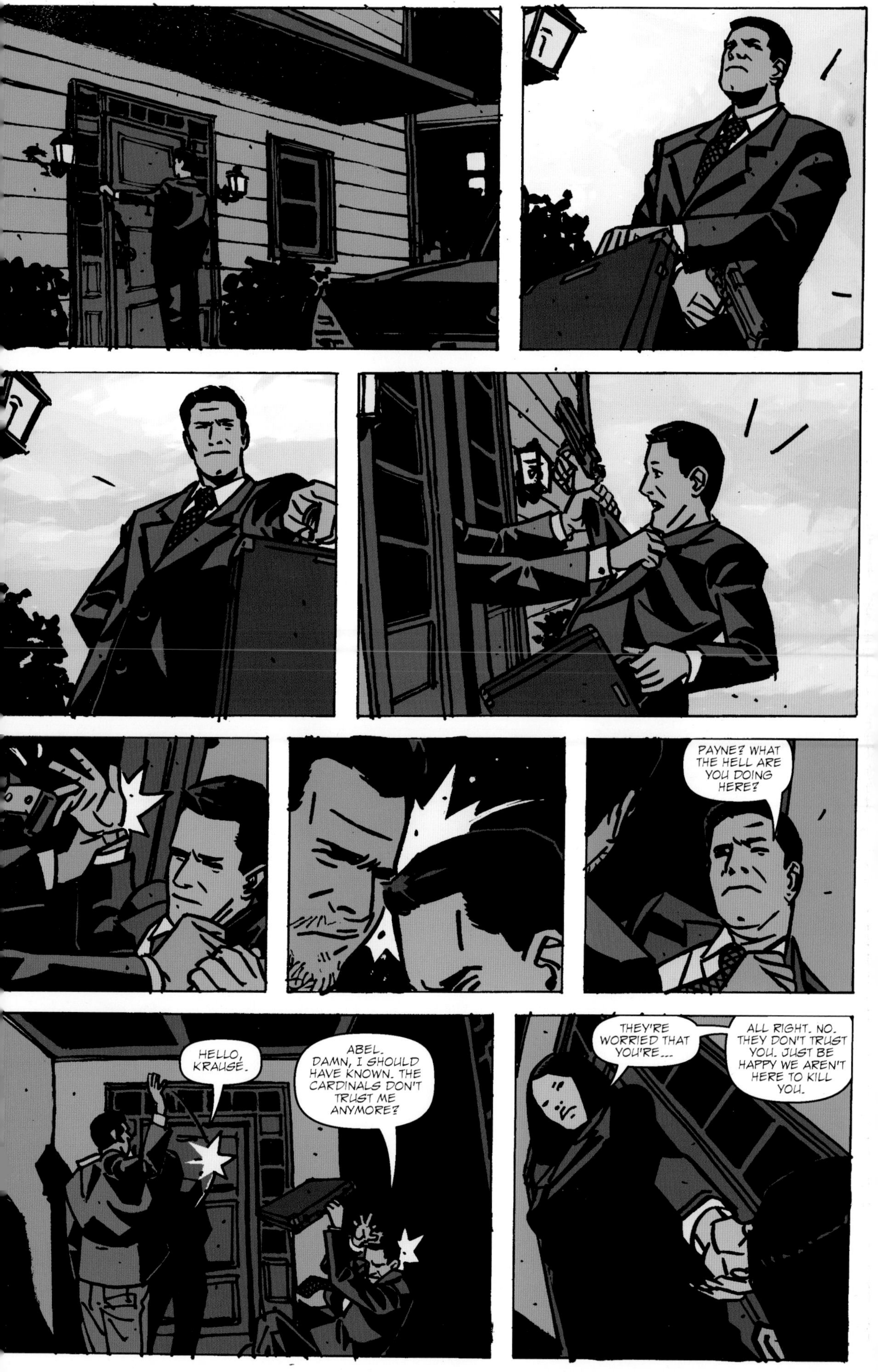
PAYNE? WHAT THE HELL ARE YOU DOING HERE?
HELLO, KRAUSE.
ABEL. DAMN, I SHOULD HAVE KNOWN. THE CARDINALS DON'T TRUST ME ANYMORE?
THEY'RE WORRIED THAT YOU'RE...
ALL RIGHT. NO. THEY DON'T TRUST YOU. JUST BE HAPPY WE AREN'T HERE TO KILL YOU.

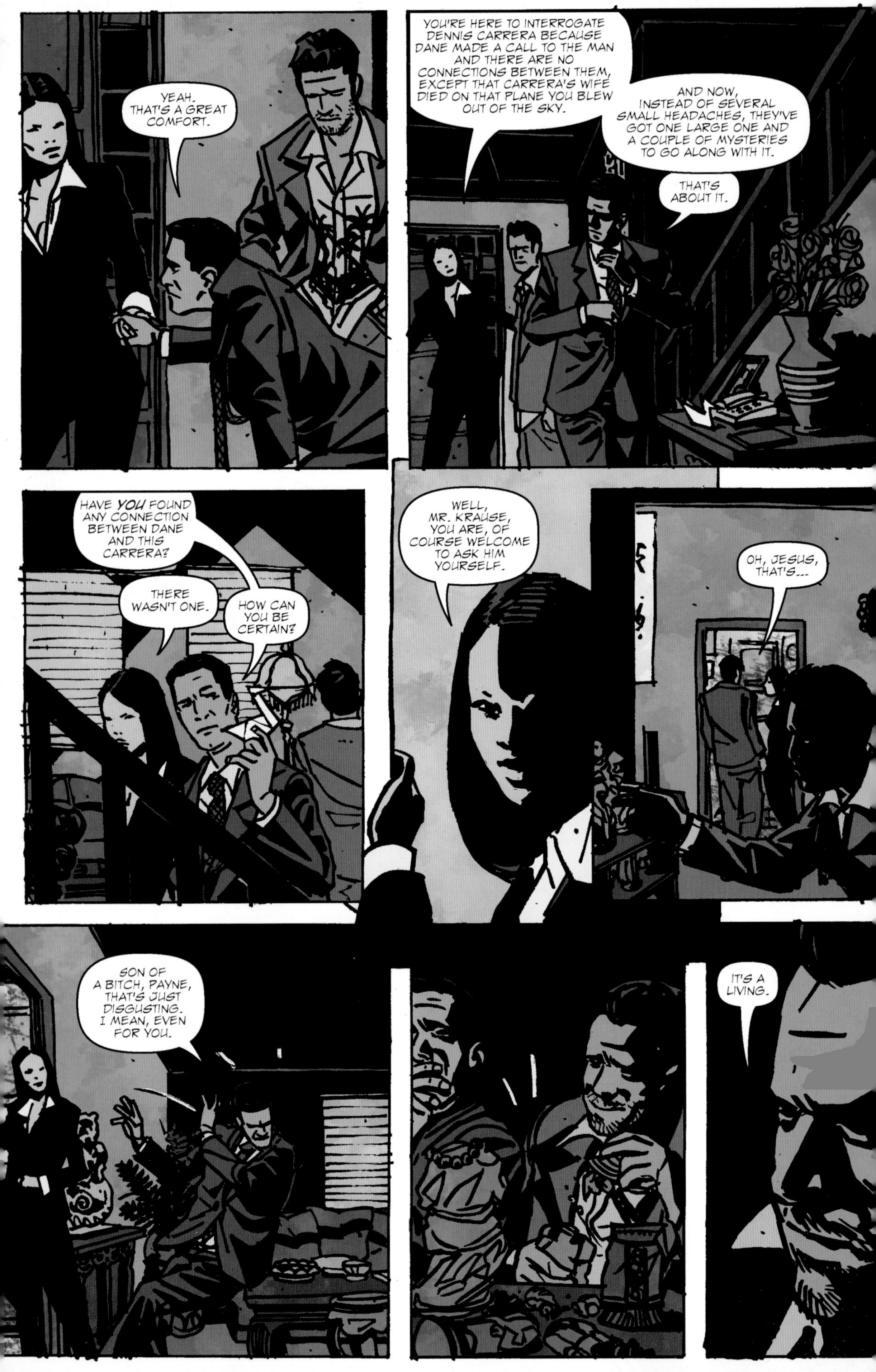
YEAH. THAT'S A GREAT COMFORT.
YOU'RE HERE TO INTERROGATE DENNIS CARRERA BECAUSE DANE MADE A CALL TO THE MAN AND THERE ARE NO CONNECTIONS BETWEEN THEM, EXCEPT THAT CARRERA'S WIFE DIED ON THAT PLANE YOU BLEW OUT OF THE SKY.
AND NOW, INSTEAD OF SEVERAL SMALL HEADACHES, THEY'VE GOT ONE LARGE ONE AND A COUPLE OF MYSTERIES TO GO ALONG WITH IT.
THAT'S ABOUT IT.
HAVE YOU FOUND ANY CONNECTION BETWEEN DANE AND THIS CARRERA?
THERE WASN'T ONE.
HOW CAN YOU BE CERTAIN?
WELL, MR. KRAUSE, YOU ARE, OF COURSE WELCOME TO ASK HIM YOURSELF.
OH, JESUS, THAT'S...
SON OF A BITCH, PAYNE, THAT'S JUST DISGUSTING. I MEAN, EVEN FOR YOU.
IT'S A LIVING.

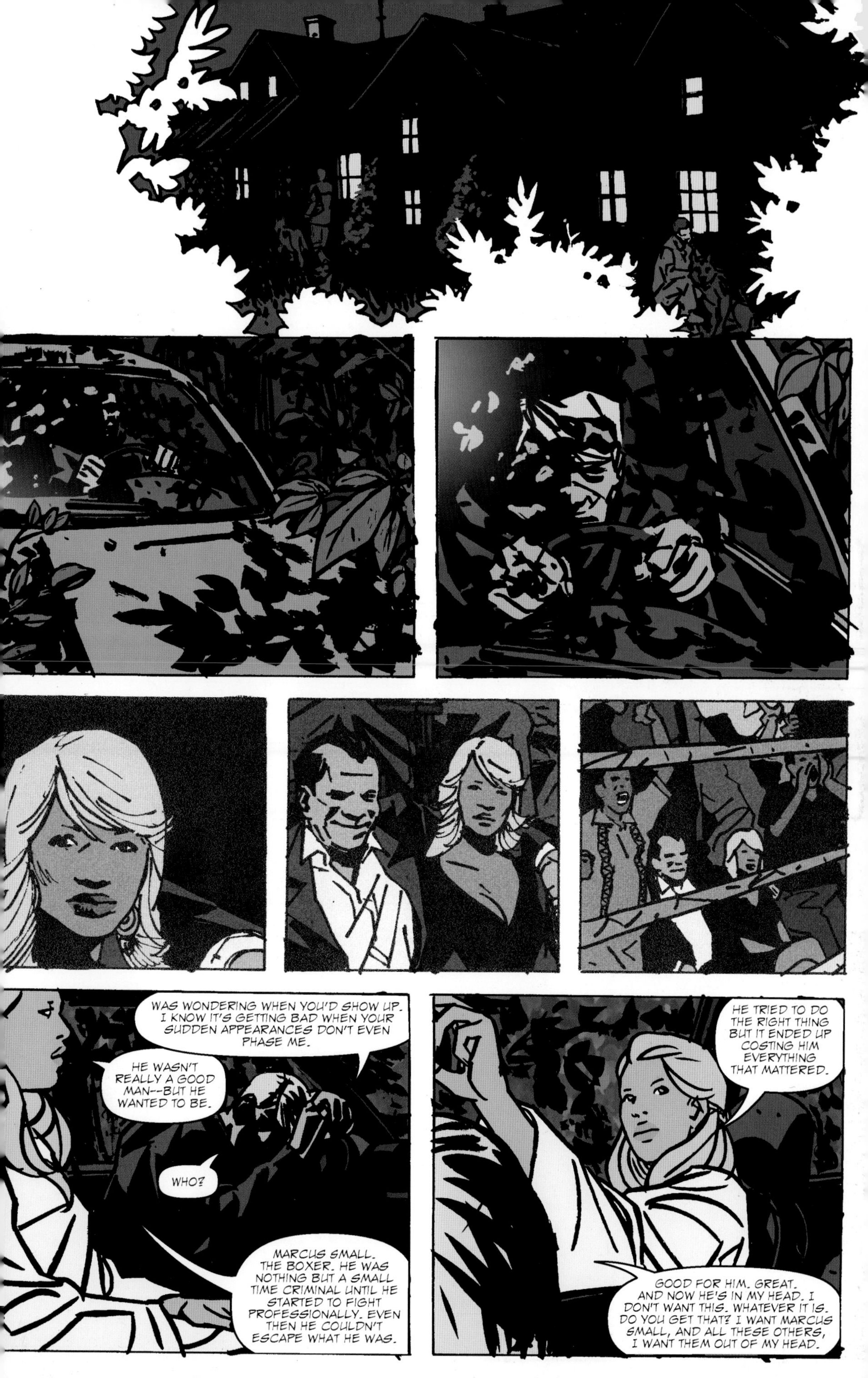
WAS WONDERING WHEN YOU'D SHOW UP. I KNOW IT'S GETTING BAD WHEN YOUR SUDDEN APPEARANCES DON'T EVEN PHASE ME.
HE WASN'T REALLY A GOOD MAN--BUT HE WANTED TO BE.
WHO?
MARCUS SMALL. THE BOXER. HE WAS NOTHING BUT A SMALL TIME CRIMINAL UNTIL HE STARTED TO FIGHT PROFESSIONALLY. EVEN THEN HE COULDN'T ESCAPE WHAT HE WAS.
HE TRIED TO DO THE RIGHT THING BUT IT ENDED UP COSTING HIM EVERYTHING THAT MATTERED.
GOOD FOR HIM. GREAT. AND NOW HE'S IN MY HEAD. I DON'T WANT THIS. WHATEVER IT IS. DO YOU GET THAT? I WANT MARCUS SMALL, AND ALL THESE OTHERS, I WANT THEM OUT OF MY HEAD.

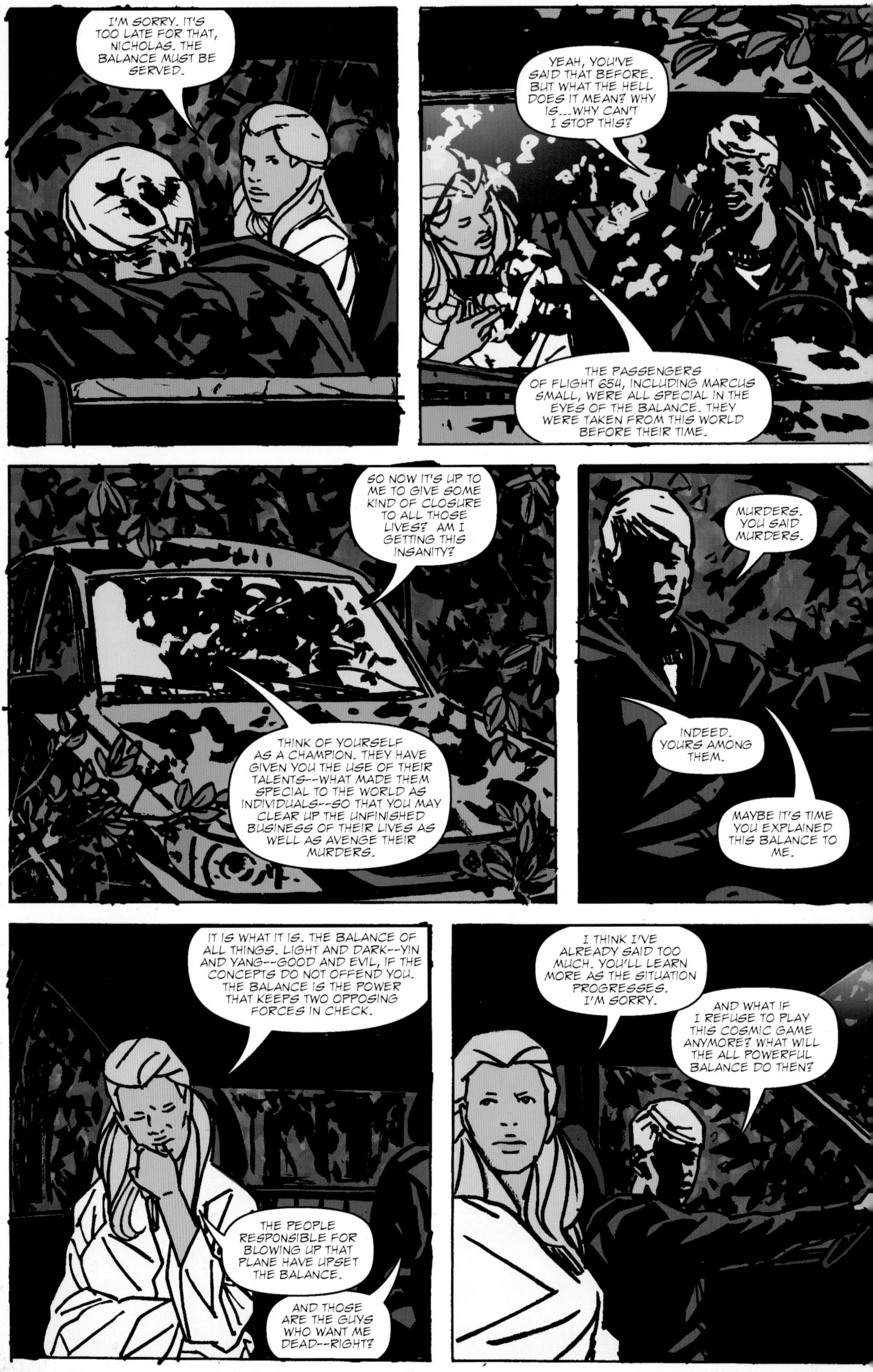
I'M SORRY. IT'S TOO LATE FOR THAT, NICHOLAS. THE BALANCE MUST BE SERVED.
YEAH, YOU'VE SAID THAT BEFORE. BUT WHAT THE HELL DOES IT MEAN? WHY IS...WHY CAN'T I STOP THIS?
THE PASSENGERS OF FLIGHT 654, INCLUDING MARCUS SMALL, WERE ALL SPECIAL IN THE EYES OF THE BALANCE. THEY WERE TAKEN FROM THIS WORLD BEFORE THEIR TIME.
SO NOW IT'S UP TO ME TO GIVE SOME KIND OF CLOSURE TO ALL THOSE LIVES? AM I GETTING THIS INSANITY?
THINK OF YOURSELF AS A CHAMPION. THEY HAVE GIVEN YOU THE USE OF THEIR TALENTS--WHAT MADE THEM SPECIAL TO THE WORLD AS INDIVIDUALS--SO THAT YOU MAY CLEAR UP THE UNFINISHED BUSINESS OF THEIR LIVES AS WELL AS AVENGE THEIR MURDERS.
MURDERS. YOU SAID MURDERS.
INDEED. YOURS AMONG THEM.
MAYBE IT'S TIME YOU EXPLAINED THIS BALANCE TO ME.
IT IS WHAT IT IS. THE BALANCE OF ALL THINGS. LIGHT AND DARK--YIN AND YANG--GOOD AND EVIL, IF THE CONCEPTS DO NOT OFFEND YOU. THE BALANCE IS THE POWER THAT KEEPS TWO OPPOSING FORCES IN CHECK.
THE PEOPLE RESPONSIBLE FOR BLOWING UP THAT PLANE HAVE UPSET THE BALANCE.
AND THOSE ARE THE GUYS WHO WANT ME DEAD--RIGHT?
I THINK I'VE ALREADY SAID TOO MUCH. YOU'LL LEARN MORE AS THE SITUATION PROGRESSES. I'M SORRY.
AND WHAT IF I REFUSE TO PLAY THIS COSMIC GAME ANYMORE? WHAT WILL THE ALL POWERFUL BALANCE DO THEN?

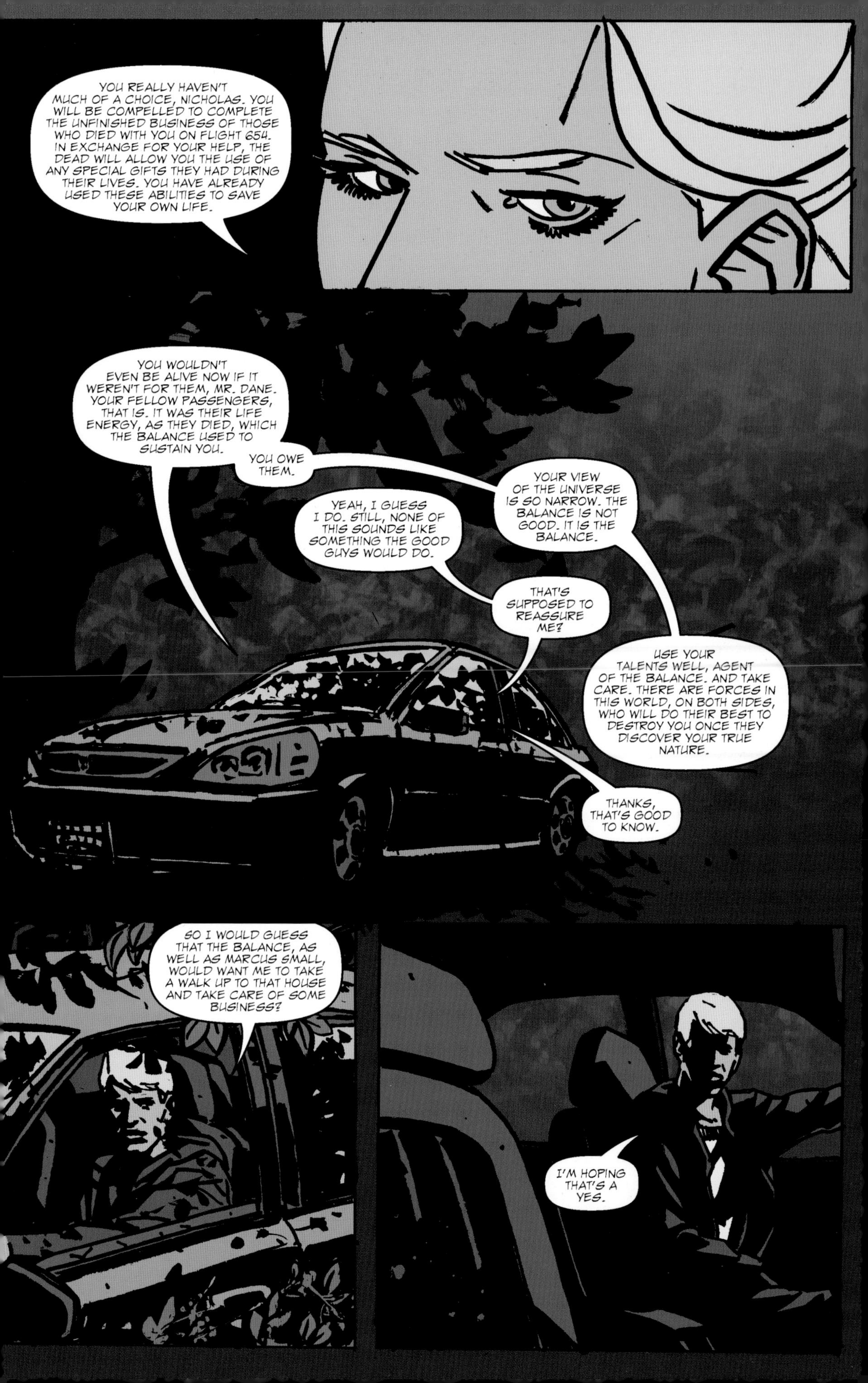
YOU REALLY HAVEN'T MUCH OF A CHOICE, NICHOLAS. YOU WILL BE COMPELLED TO COMPLETE THE UNFINISHED BUSINESS OF THOSE WHO DIED WITH YOU ON FLIGHT 654. IN EXCHANGE FOR YOUR HELP, THE DEAD WILL ALLOW YOU THE USE OF ANY SPECIAL GIFTS THEY HAD DURING THEIR LIVES. YOU HAVE ALREADY USED THESE ABILITIES TO SAVE YOUR OWN LIFE.
YOU WOULDN'T EVEN BE ALIVE NOW IF IT WEREN'T FOR THEM, MR. DANE. YOUR FELLOW PASSENGERS, THAT IS. IT WAS THEIR LIFE ENERGY, AS THEY DIED, WHICH THE BALANCE USED TO SUSTAIN YOU.
YOU OWE THEM.
YEAH, I GUESS I DO. STILL, NONE OF THIS SOUNDS LIKE SOMETHING THE GOOD GUYS WOULD DO.
YOUR VIEW OF THE UNIVERSE IS SO NARROW. THE BALANCE IS NOT GOOD. IT IS THE BALANCE.
THAT'S SUPPOSED TO REASSURE ME?
USE YOUR TALENTS WELL, AGENT OF THE BALANCE. AND TAKE CARE. THERE ARE FORCES IN THIS WORLD, ON BOTH SIDES, WHO WILL DO THEIR BEST TO DESTROY YOU ONCE THEY DISCOVER YOUR TRUE NATURE.
THANKS, THAT'S GOOD TO KNOW.
SO I WOULD GUESS THAT THE BALANCE, AS WELL AS MARCUS SMALL, WOULD WANT ME TO TAKE A WALK UP TO THAT HOUSE AND TAKE CARE OF SOME BUSINESS?
I'M HOPING THAT'S A YES.

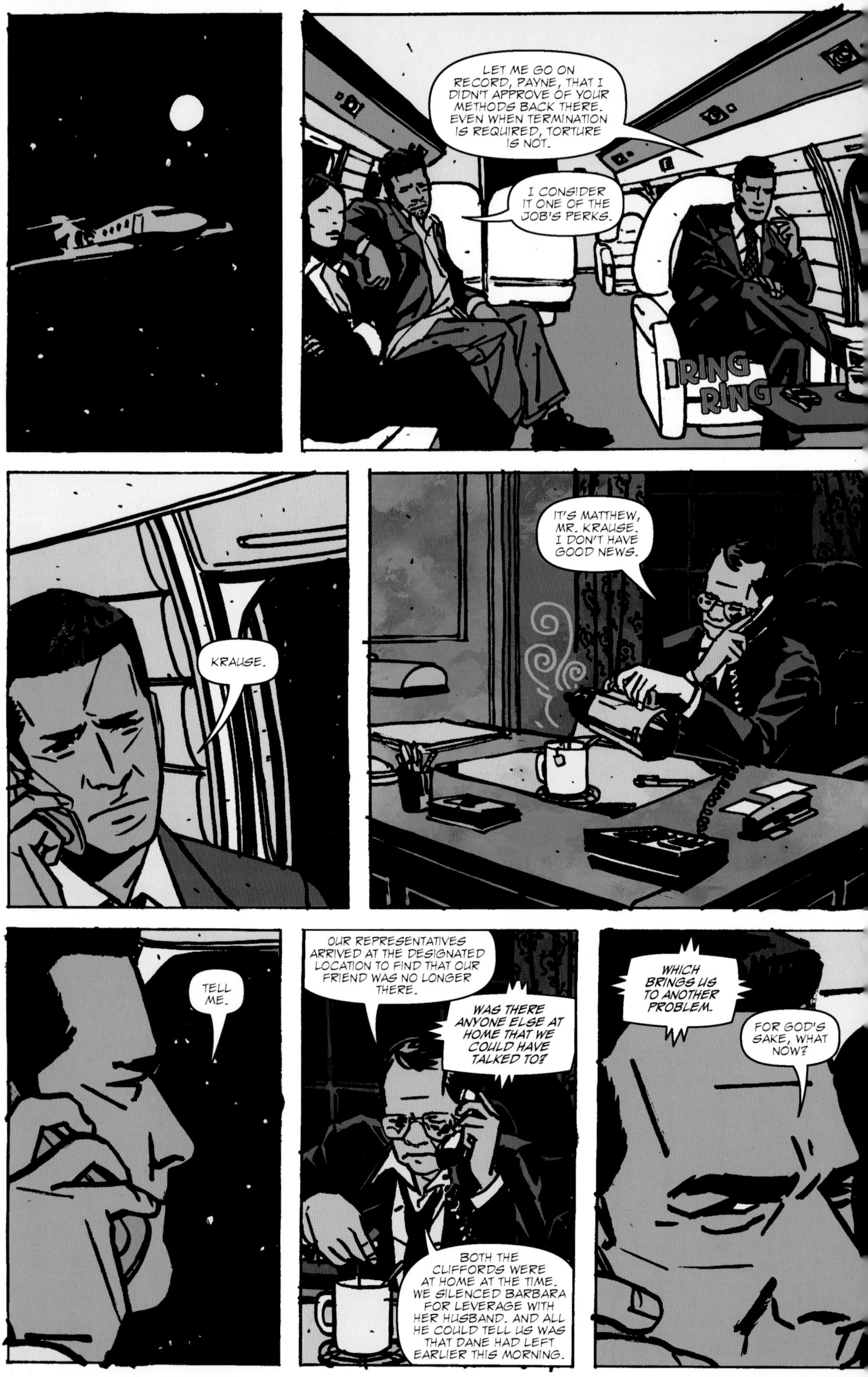
LET ME GO ON RECORD, PAYNE, THAT I DIDN'T APPROVE OF YOUR METHODS BACK THERE. EVEN WHEN TERMINATION IS REQUIRED, TORTURE IS NOT.
I CONSIDER IT ONE OF THE JOB'S PERKS.
RING RING
KRAUSE.
IT'S MATTHEW, MR. KRAUSE. I DON'T HAVE GOOD NEWS.
TELL ME.
OUR REPRESENTATIVES ARRIVED AT THE DESIGNATED LOCATION TO FIND THAT OUR FRIEND WAS NO LONGER THERE.
WAS THERE ANYONE ELSE AT HOME THAT WE COULD HAVE TALKED TO?
BOTH THE CLIFFORDS WERE AT HOME AT THE TIME. WE SILENCED BARBARA FOR LEVERAGE WITH HER HUSBAND. AND ALL HE COULD TELL US WAS THAT DANE HAD LEFT EARLIER THIS MORNING.
WHICH BRINGS US TO ANOTHER PROBLEM.
FOR GOD'S SAKE, WHAT NOW?

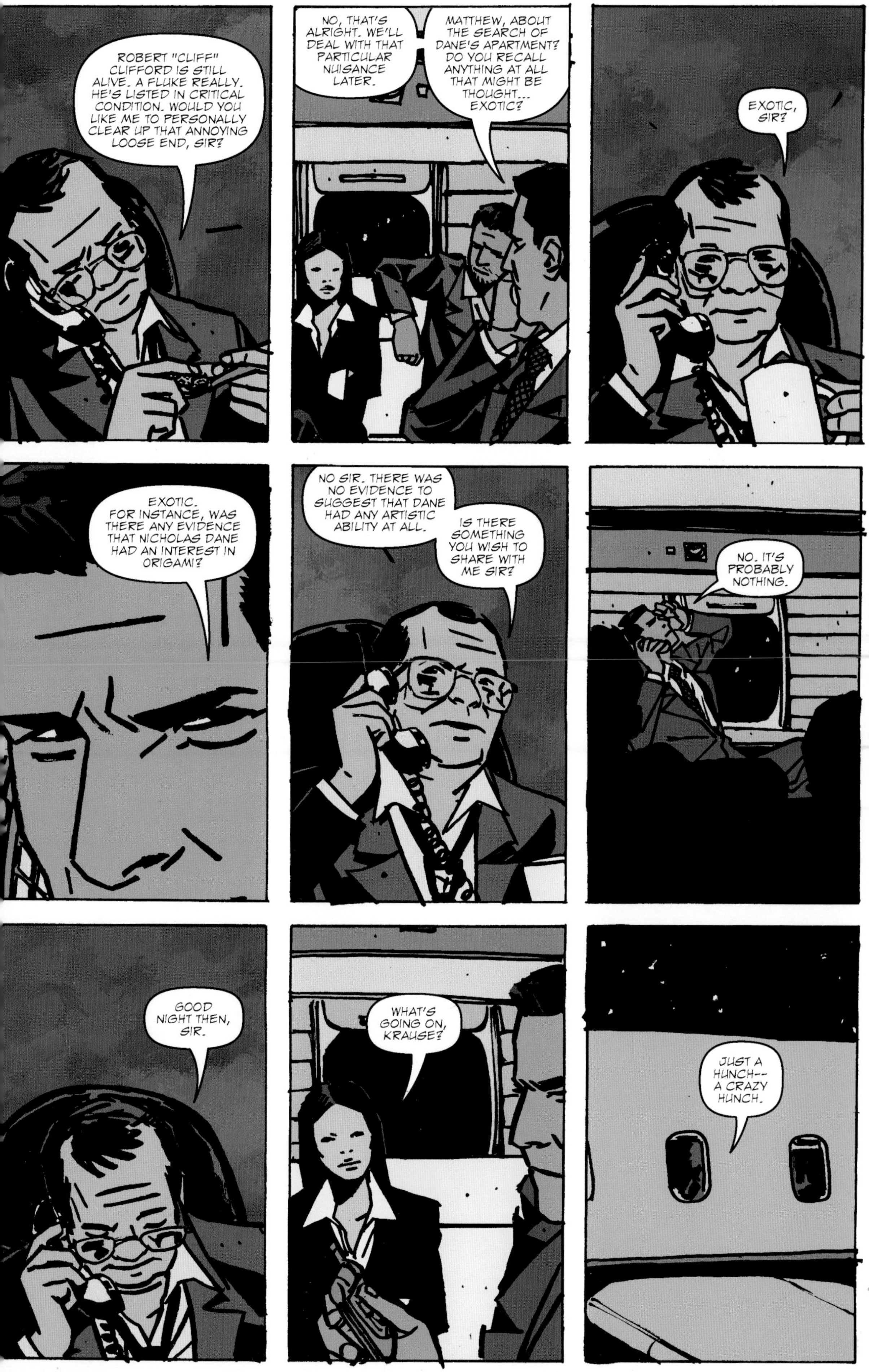
ROBERT "CLIFF" CLIFFORD IS STILL ALIVE. A FLUKE REALLY. HE'S LISTED IN CRITICAL CONDITION. WOULD YOU LIKE ME TO PERSONALLY CLEAR UP THAT ANNOYING LOOSE END, SIR?
NO, THAT'S ALRIGHT. WE'LL DEAL WITH THAT PARTICULAR NUISANCE LATER.
MATTHEW, ABOUT THE SEARCH OF DANE'S APARTMENT? DO YOU RECALL ANYTHING AT ALL THAT MIGHT BE THOUGHT... EXOTIC?
EXOTIC, SIR?
EXOTIC. FOR INSTANCE, WAS THERE ANY EVIDENCE THAT NICHOLAS DANE HAD AN INTEREST IN ORIGAMI?
NO SIR. THERE WAS NO EVIDENCE TO SUGGEST THAT DANE HAD ANY ARTISTIC ABILITY AT ALL.
IS THERE SOMETHING YOU WISH TO SHARE WITH ME SIR?
NO. IT'S PROBABLY NOTHING.
GOOD NIGHT THEN, SIR.
WHAT'S GOING ON, KRAUSE?
JUST A HUNCH-- A CRAZY HUNCH.

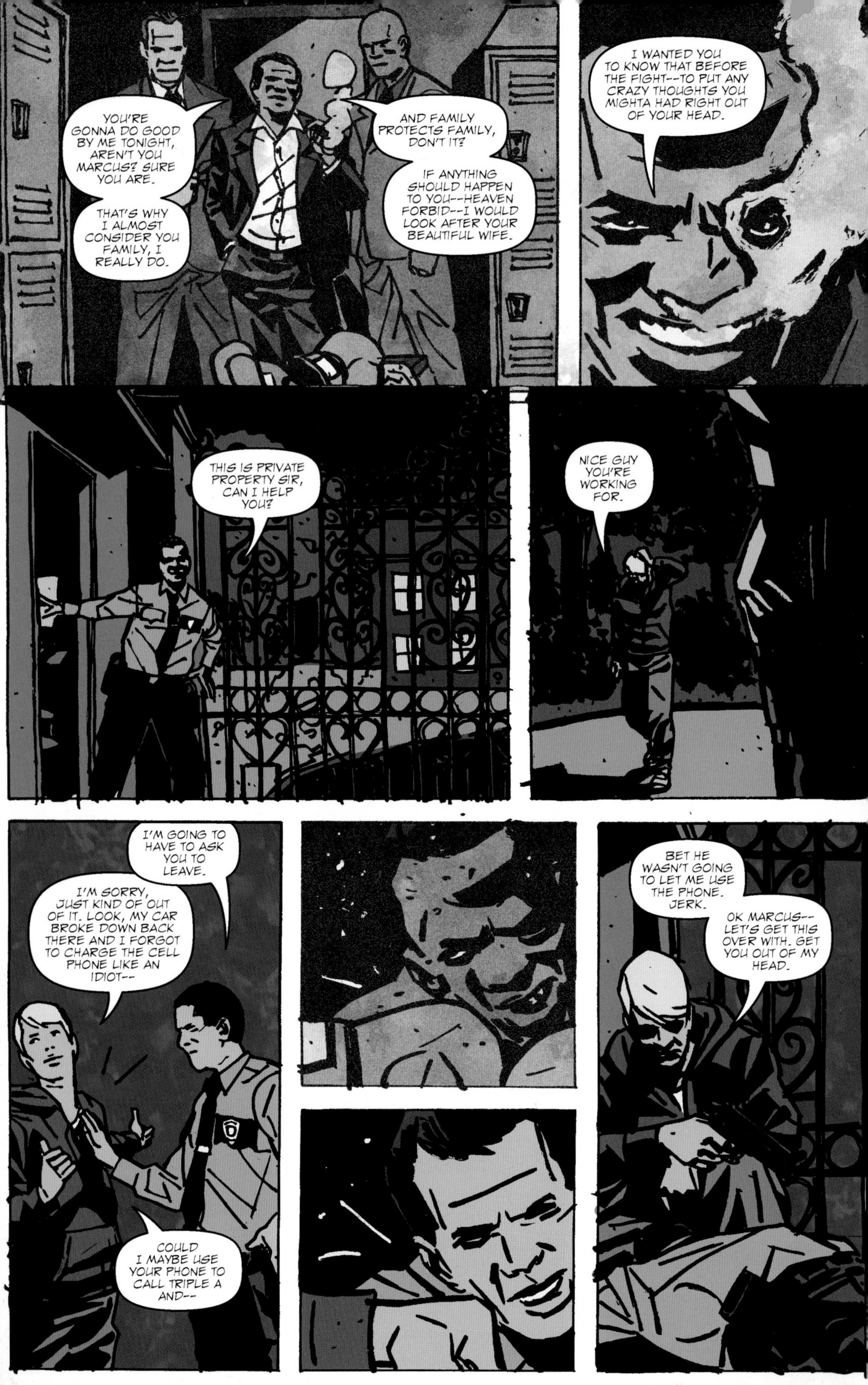
YOU'RE GONNA DO GOOD BY ME TONIGHT, AREN'T YOU MARCUS? SURE YOU ARE.
THAT'S WHY I ALMOST CONSIDER YOU FAMILY, I REALLY DO.
AND FAMILY PROTECTS FAMILY, DON'T IT?
IF ANYTHING SHOULD HAPPEN TO YOU--HEAVEN FORBID--I WOULD LOOK AFTER YOUR BEAUTIFUL WIFE.
I WANTED YOU TO KNOW THAT BEFORE THE FIGHT--TO PUT ANY CRAZY THOUGHTS YOU MIGHTA HAD RIGHT OUT OF YOUR HEAD.
THIS IS PRIVATE PROPERTY SIR, CAN I HELP YOU?
NICE GUY YOU'RE WORKING FOR.
I'M GOING TO HAVE TO ASK YOU TO LEAVE.
I'M SORRY, JUST KIND OF OUT OF IT. LOOK, MY CAR BROKE DOWN BACK THERE AND I FORGOT TO CHARGE THE CELL PHONE LIKE AN IDIOT--
COULD I MAYBE USE YOUR PHONE TO CALL TRIPLE A AND--
BET HE WASN'T GOING TO LET ME USE THE PHONE. JERK.
OK MARCUS--LET'S GET THIS OVER WITH. GET YOU OUT OF MY HEAD.

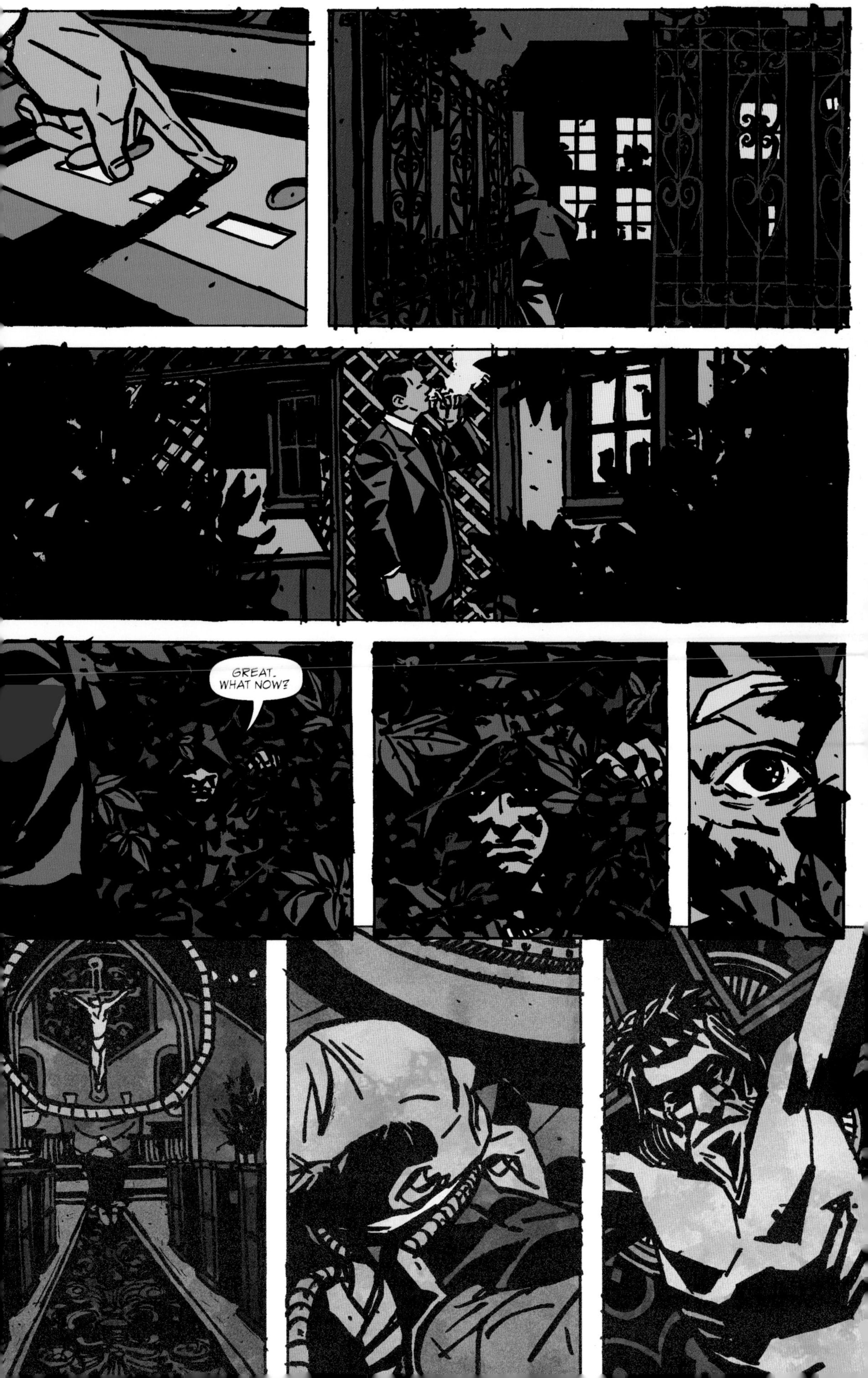
GREAT. WHAT NOW?

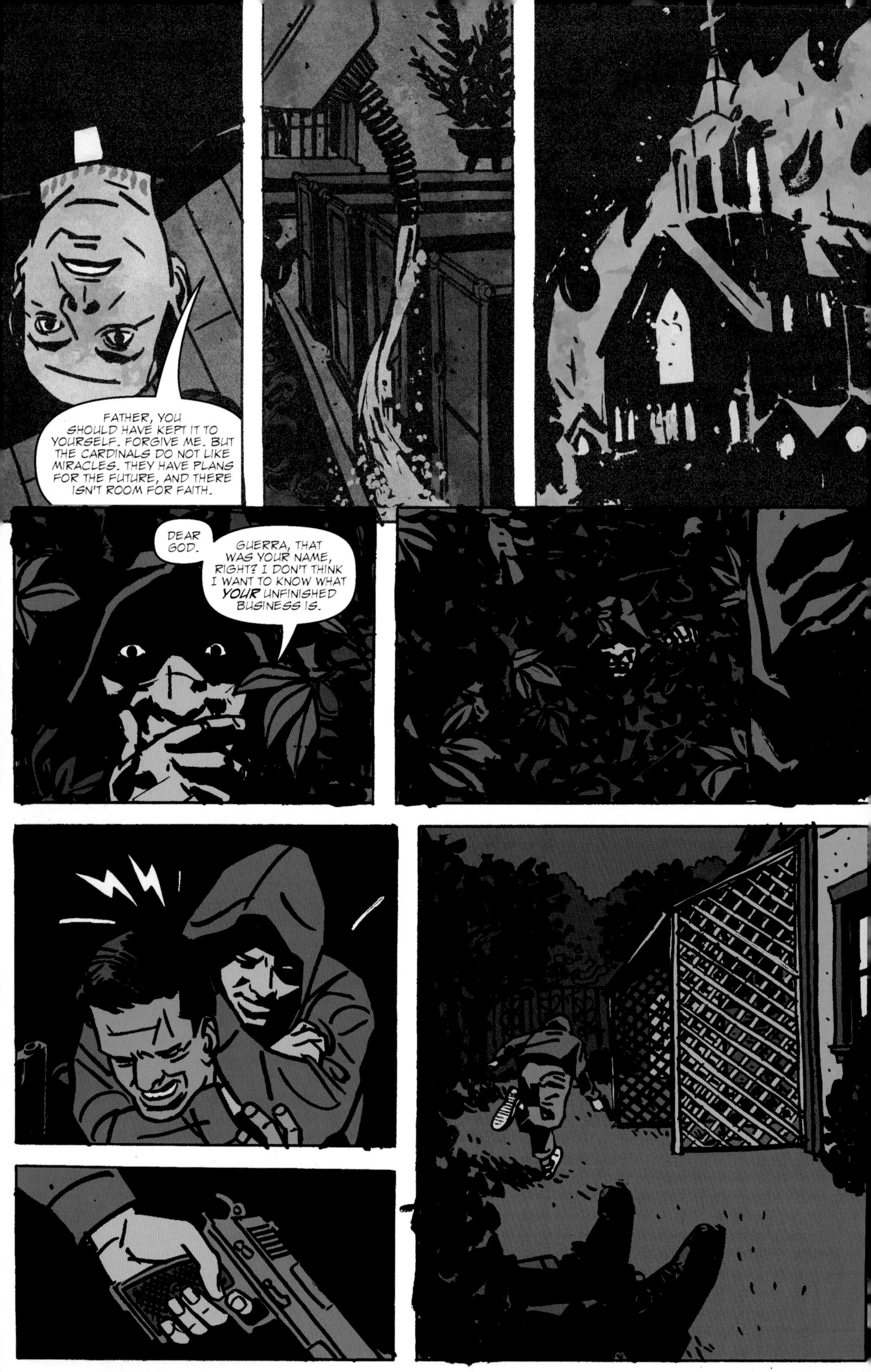
FATHER, YOU SHOULD HAVE KEPT IT TO YOURSELF. FORGIVE ME. BUT THE CARDINALS DO NOT LIKE MIRACLES. THEY HAVE PLANS FOR THE FUTURE, AND THERE ISN'T ROOM FOR FAITH.
DEAR GOD.
GUERRA, THAT WAS YOUR NAME, RIGHT? I DON'T THINK I WANT TO KNOW WHAT YOUR UNFINISHED BUSINESS IS.

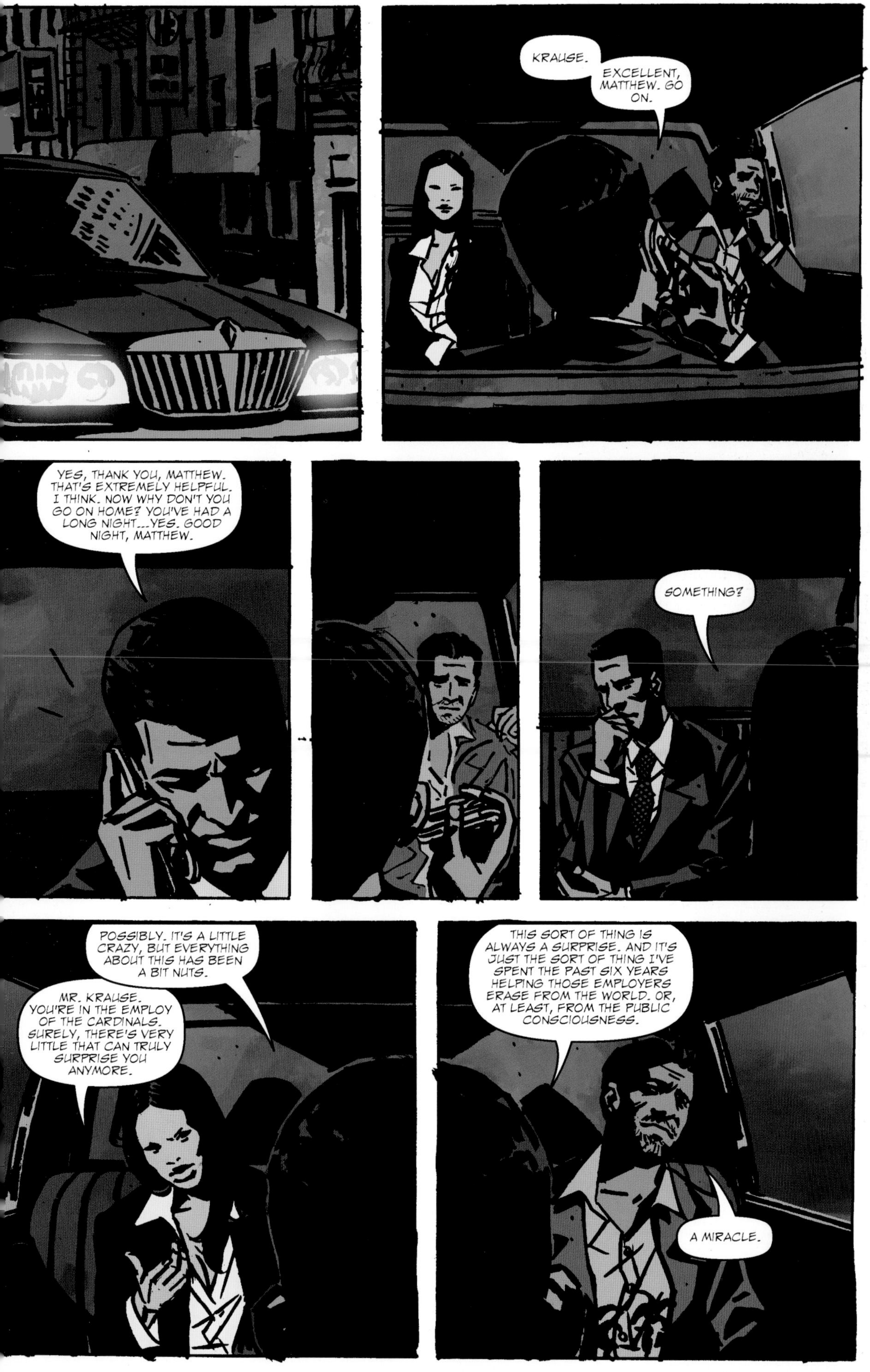
KRAUSE.
EXCELLENT, MATTHEW. GO ON.
YES, THANK YOU, MATTHEW. THAT'S EXTREMELY HELPFUL. I THINK. NOW WHY DON'T YOU GO ON HOME? YOU'VE HAD A LONG NIGHT...YES. GOOD NIGHT, MATTHEW.
SOMETHING?
POSSIBLY. IT'S A LITTLE CRAZY, BUT EVERYTHING ABOUT THIS HAS BEEN A BIT NUTS.
MR. KRAUSE. YOU'RE IN THE EMPLOY OF THE CARDINALS. SURELY, THERE'S VERY LITTLE THAT CAN TRULY SURPRISE YOU ANYMORE.
THIS SORT OF THING IS ALWAYS A SURPRISE. AND IT'S JUST THE SORT OF THING I'VE SPENT THE PAST SIX YEARS HELPING THOSE EMPLOYERS ERASE FROM THE WORLD. OR, AT LEAST, FROM THE PUBLIC CONSCIOUSNESS.
A MIRACLE.

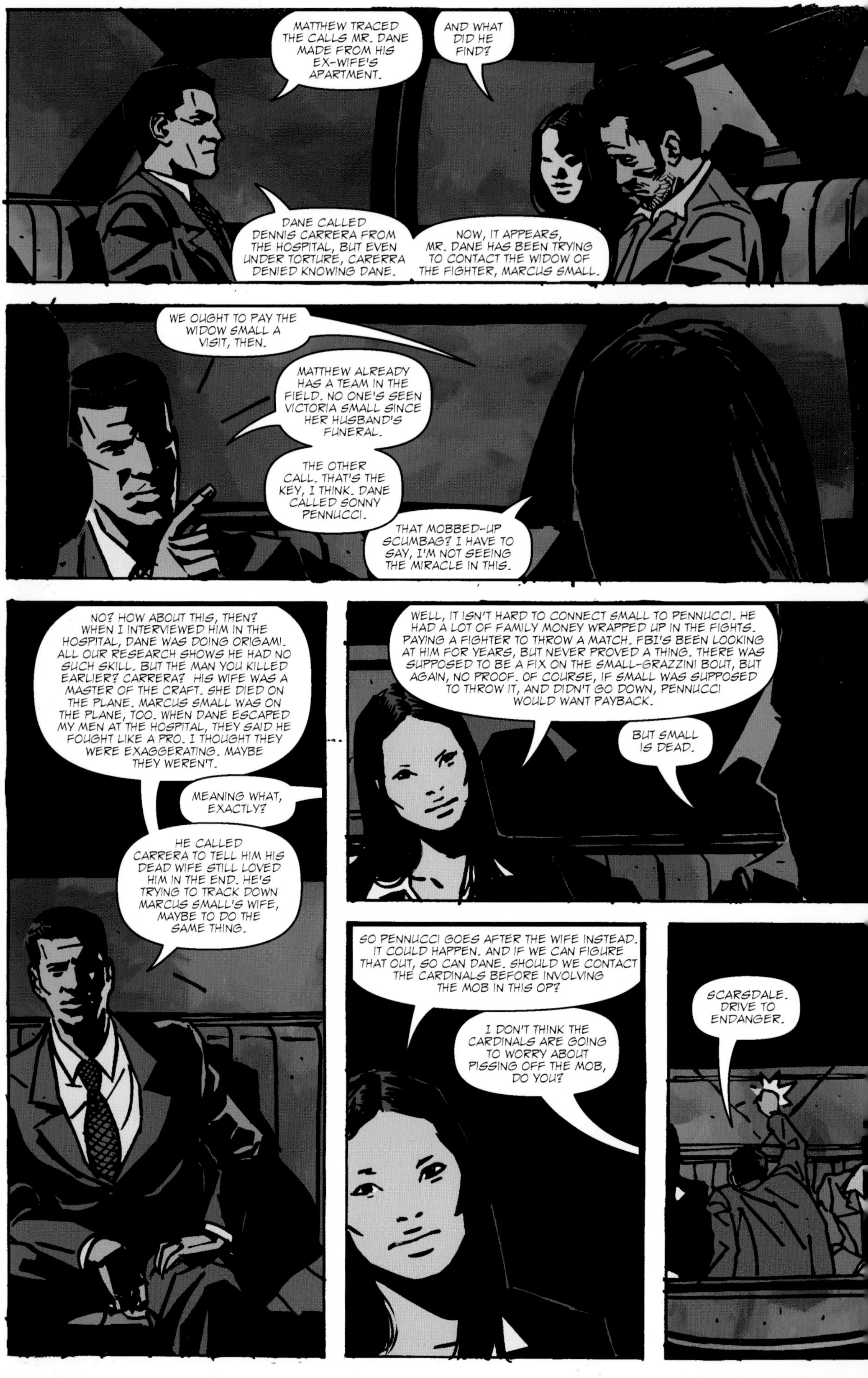
MATTHEW TRACED THE CALLS MR. DANE MADE FROM HIS EX-WIFE'S APARTMENT.
AND WHAT DID HE FIND?
DANE CALLED DENNIS CARRERA FROM THE HOSPITAL, BUT EVEN UNDER TORTURE, CARERRA DENIED KNOWING DANE.
NOW, IT APPEARS, MR. DANE HAS BEEN TRYING TO CONTACT THE WIDOW OF THE FIGHTER, MARCUS SMALL.
WE OUGHT TO PAY THE WIDOW SMALL A VISIT, THEN.
MATTHEW ALREADY HAS A TEAM IN THE FIELD. NO ONE'S SEEN VICTORIA SMALL SINCE HER HUSBAND'S FUNERAL.
THE OTHER CALL. THAT'S THE KEY, I THINK. DANE CALLED SONNY PENNUCCI.
THAT MOBBED-UP SCUMBAG? I HAVE TO SAY, I'M NOT SEEING THE MIRACLE IN THIS.
NO? HOW ABOUT THIS, THEN? WHEN I INTERVIEWED HIM IN THE HOSPITAL, DANE WAS DOING ORIGAMI. ALL OUR RESEARCH SHOWS HE HAD NO SUCH SKILL. BUT THE MAN YOU KILLED EARLIER? CARRERA? HIS WIFE WAS A MASTER OF THE CRAFT. SHE DIED ON THE PLANE. MARCUS SMALL WAS ON THE PLANE, TOO. WHEN DANE ESCAPED MY MEN AT THE HOSPITAL, THEY SAID HE FOUGHT LIKE A PRO. I THOUGHT THEY WERE EXAGGERATING. MAYBE THEY WEREN'T.
MEANING WHAT, EXACTLY?
HE CALLED CARRERA TO TELL HIM HIS DEAD WIFE STILL LOVED HIM IN THE END. HE'S TRYING TO TRACK DOWN MARCUS SMALL'S WIFE, MAYBE TO DO THE SAME THING.
WELL, IT ISN'T HARD TO CONNECT SMALL TO PENNUCCI. HE HAD A LOT OF FAMILY MONEY WRAPPED UP IN THE FIGHTS. PAYING A FIGHTER TO THROW A MATCH. FBI'S BEEN LOOKING AT HIM FOR YEARS, BUT NEVER PROVED A THING. THERE WAS SUPPOSED TO BE A FIX ON THE SMALL-GRAZZINI BOUT, BUT AGAIN, NO PROOF. OF COURSE, IF SMALL WAS SUPPOSED TO THROW IT, AND DIDN'T GO DOWN, PENNUCCI WOULD WANT PAYBACK.
BUT SMALL IS DEAD.
SO PENNUCCI GOES AFTER THE WIFE INSTEAD. IT COULD HAPPEN. AND IF WE CAN FIGURE THAT OUT, SO CAN DANE. SHOULD WE CONTACT THE CARDINALS BEFORE INVOLVING THE MOB IN THIS OP?
I DON'T THINK THE CARDINALS ARE GOING TO WORRY ABOUT PISSING OFF THE MOB, DO YOU?
SCARSDALE. DRIVE TO ENDANGER.

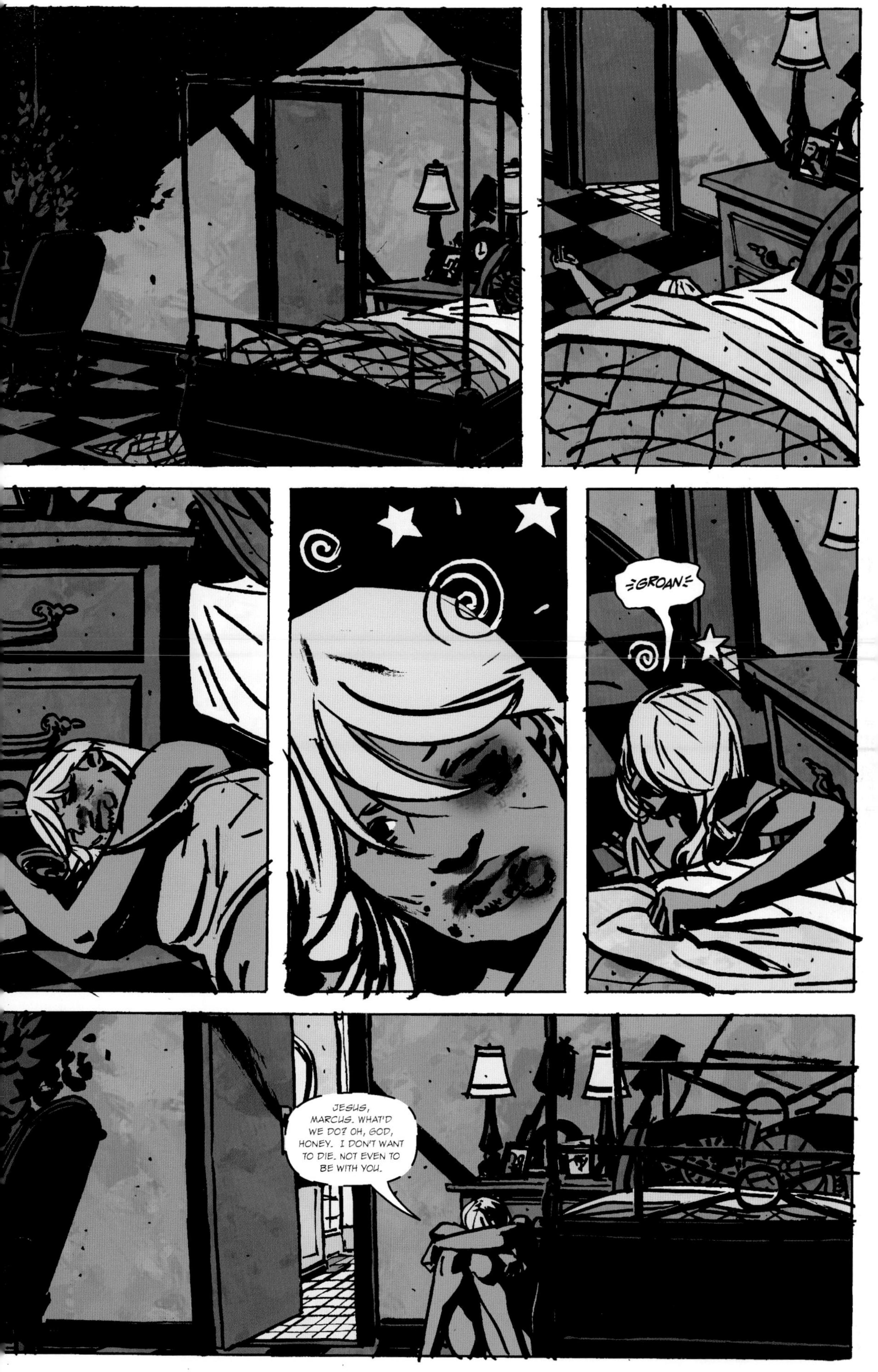
GROAN
JESUS, MARCUS. WHAT'D WE DO? OH, GOD, HONEY. I DON'T WANT TO DIE. NOT EVEN TO BE WITH YOU.

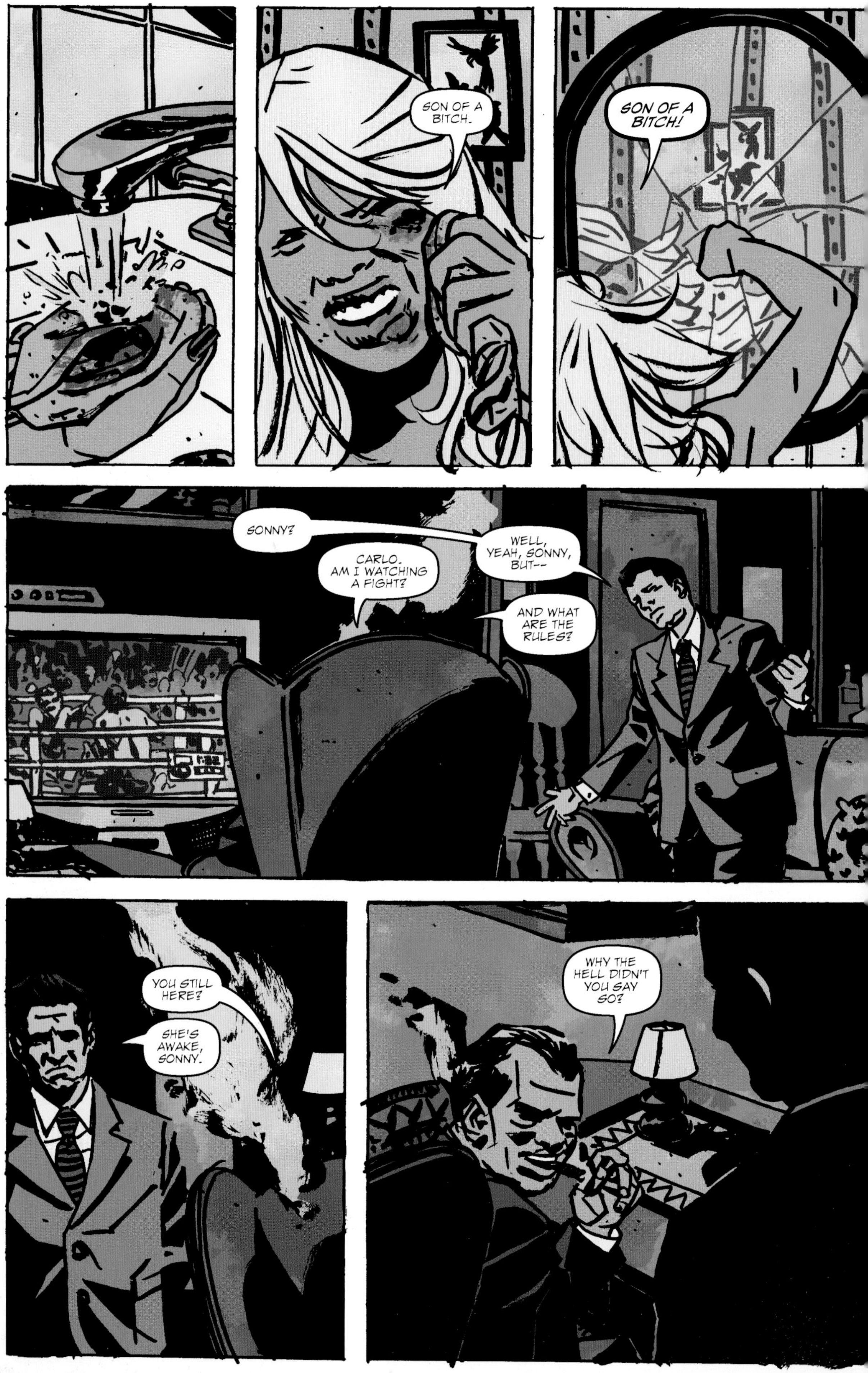
SON OF A BITCH.
SON OF A BITCH!
SONNY?
CARLO. AM I WATCHING A FIGHT?
WELL, YEAH, SONNY, BUT--
AND WHAT ARE THE RULES?
YOU STILL HERE?
SHE'S AWAKE, SONNY.
WHY THE HELL DIDN'T YOU SAY SO?

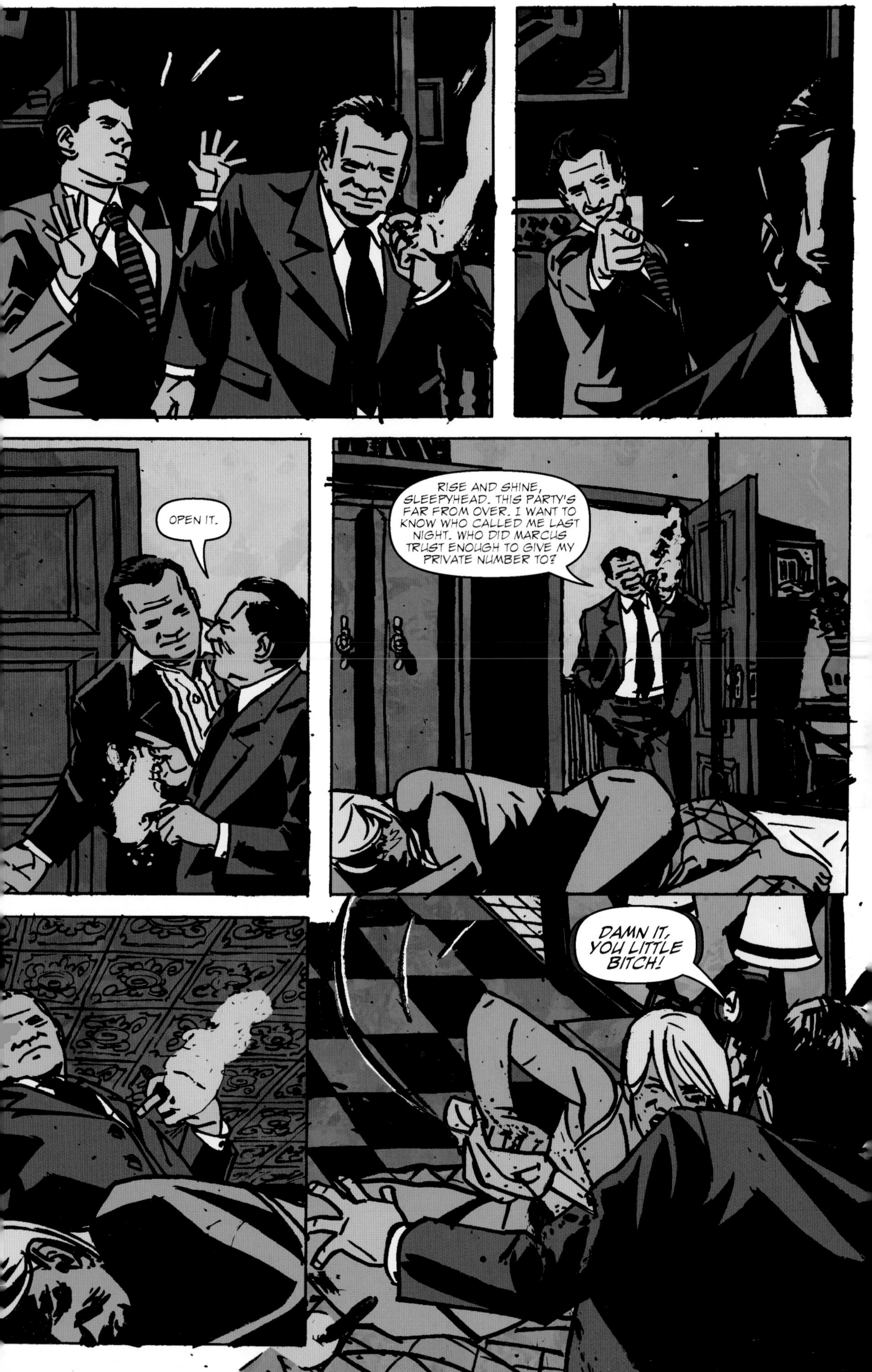
OPEN IT.
RISE AND SHINE, SLEEPYHEAD. THIS PARTY'S FAR FROM OVER. I WANT TO KNOW WHO CALLED ME LAST NIGHT. WHO DID MARCUS TRUST ENOUGH TO GIVE MY PRIVATE NUMBER TO?
DAMN IT, YOU LITTLE BITCH!

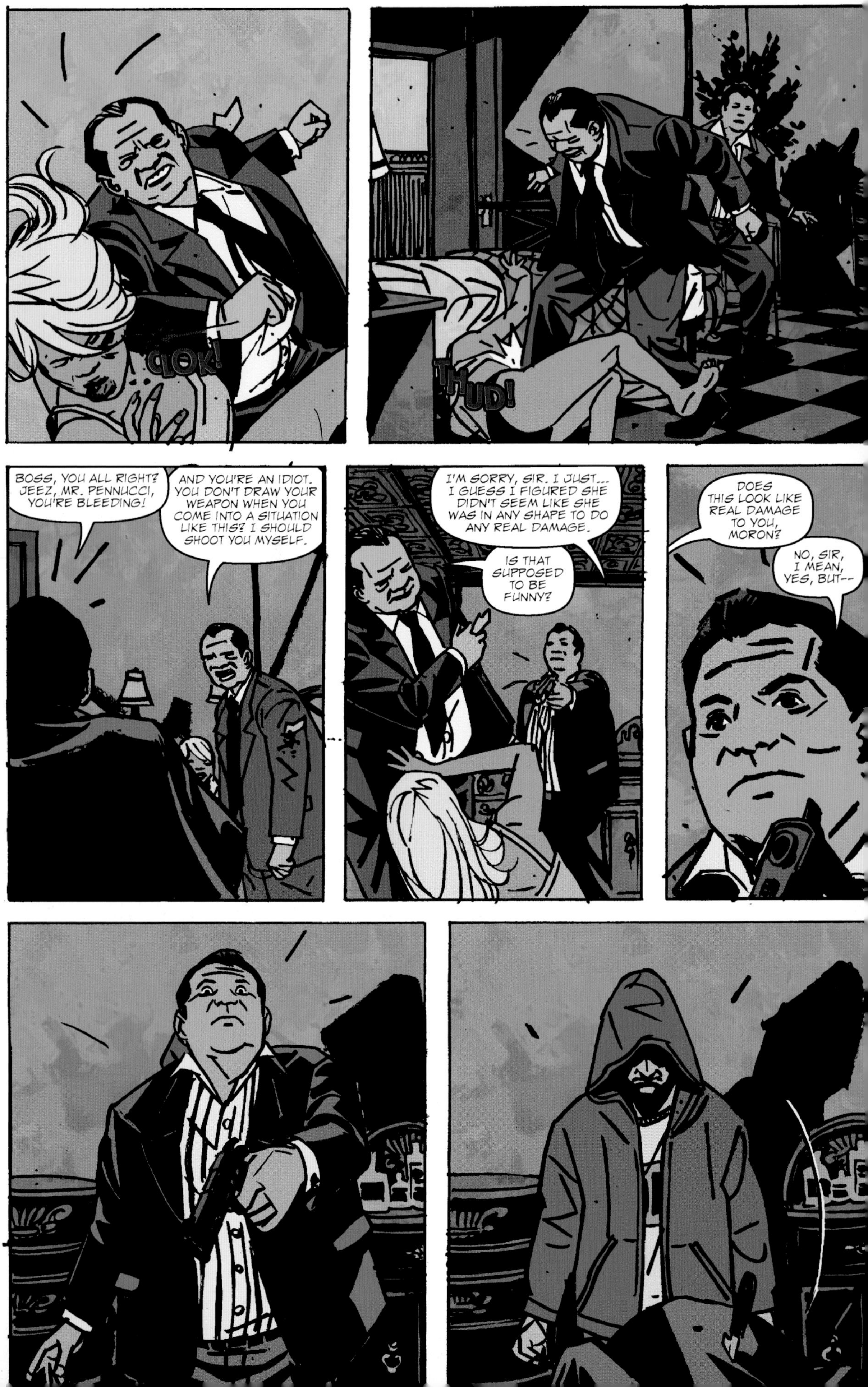
CLOK!
THUD!
BOSS, YOU ALL RIGHT? JEEZ, MR. PENNUCCI, YOU'RE BLEEDING!
AND YOU'RE AN IDIOT. YOU DON'T DRAW YOUR WEAPON WHEN YOU COME INTO A SITUATION LIKE THIS? I SHOULD SHOOT YOU MYSELF.
I'M SORRY, SIR. I JUST... I GUESS I FIGURED SHE DIDN'T SEEM LIKE SHE WAS IN ANY SHAPE TO DO ANY REAL DAMAGE.
IS THAT SUPPOSED TO BE FUNNY?
DOES THIS LOOK LIKE REAL DAMAGE TO YOU, MORON?
NO, SIR, I MEAN, YES, BUT--

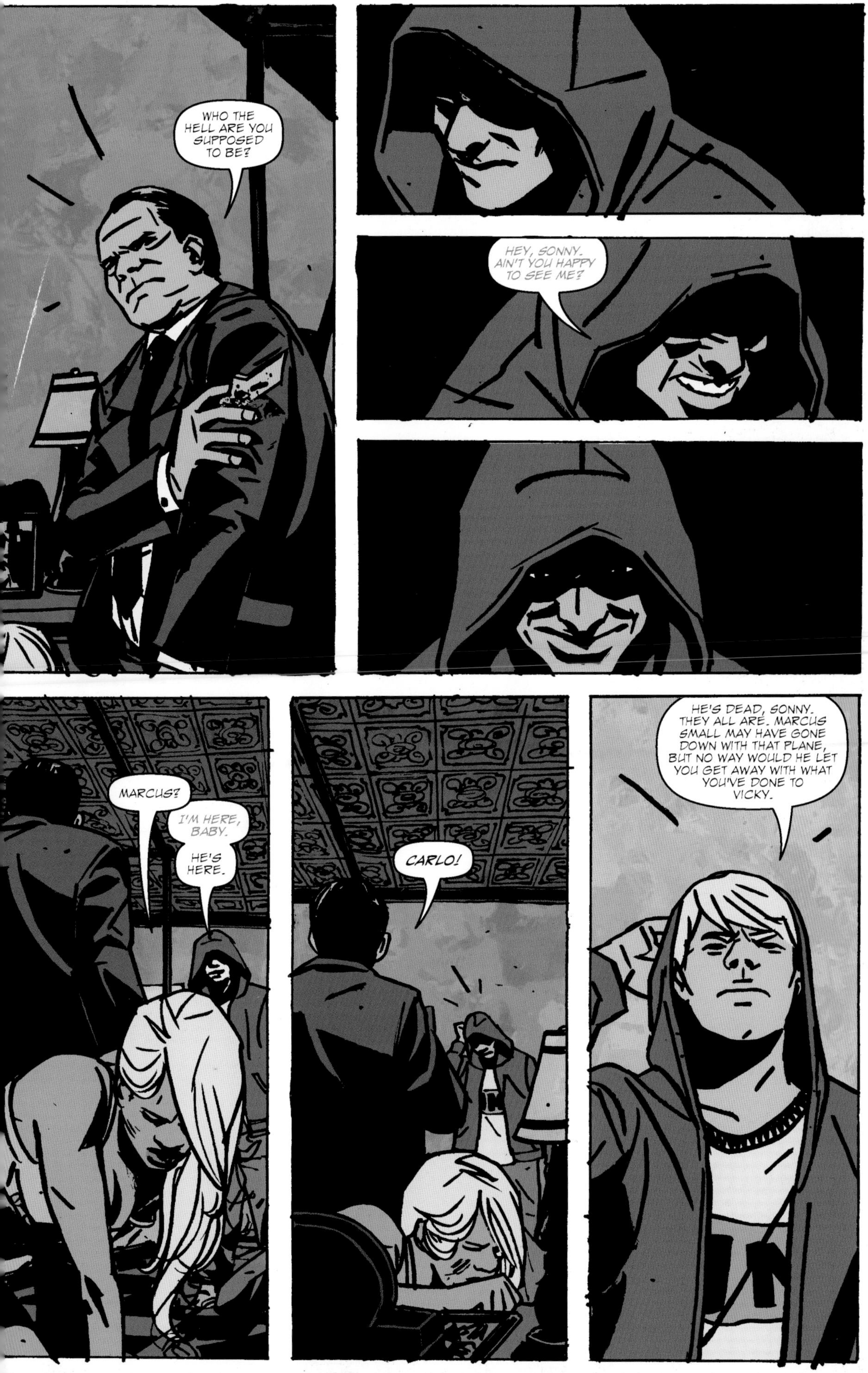

WHO THE HELL ARE YOU SUPPOSED TO BE?
HEY, SONNY. AIN'T YOU HAPPY TO SEE ME?
MARCUS?
I'M HERE, BABY.
HE'S HERE.
CARLO!
HE'S DEAD, SONNY. THEY ALL ARE. MARCUS SMALL MAY HAVE GONE DOWN WITH THAT PLANE, BUT NO WAY WOULD HE LET YOU GET AWAY WITH WHAT YOU'VE DONE TO VICKY.

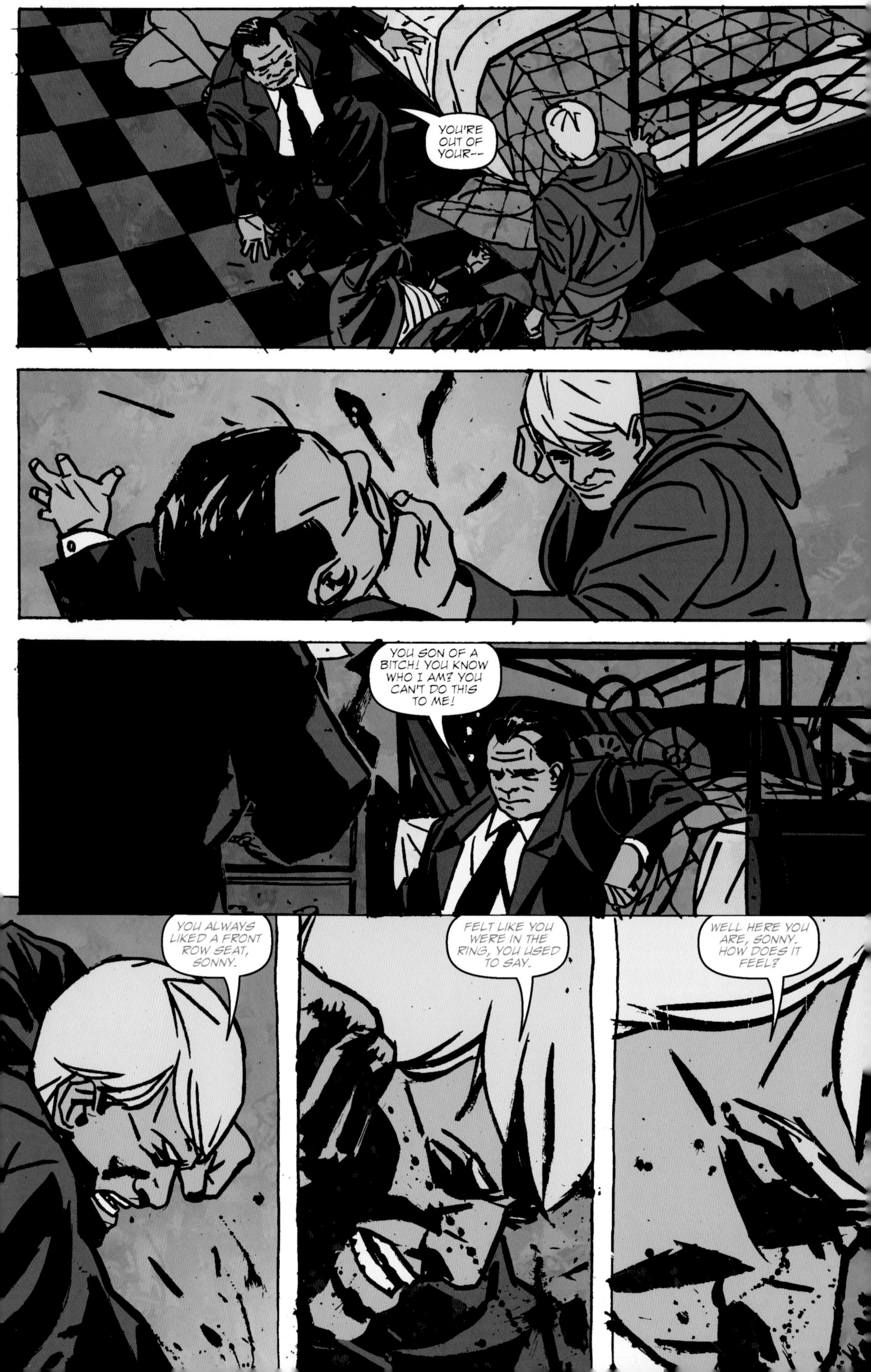
YOU'RE OUT OF YOUR--
YOU SON OF A BITCH! YOU KNOW WHO I AM? YOU CAN'T DO THIS TO ME!
YOU ALWAYS LIKED A FRONT ROW SEAT, SONNY.
FELT LIKE YOU WERE IN THE RING, YOU USED TO SAY.
WELL HERE YOU ARE, SONNY. HOW DOES IT FEEL?

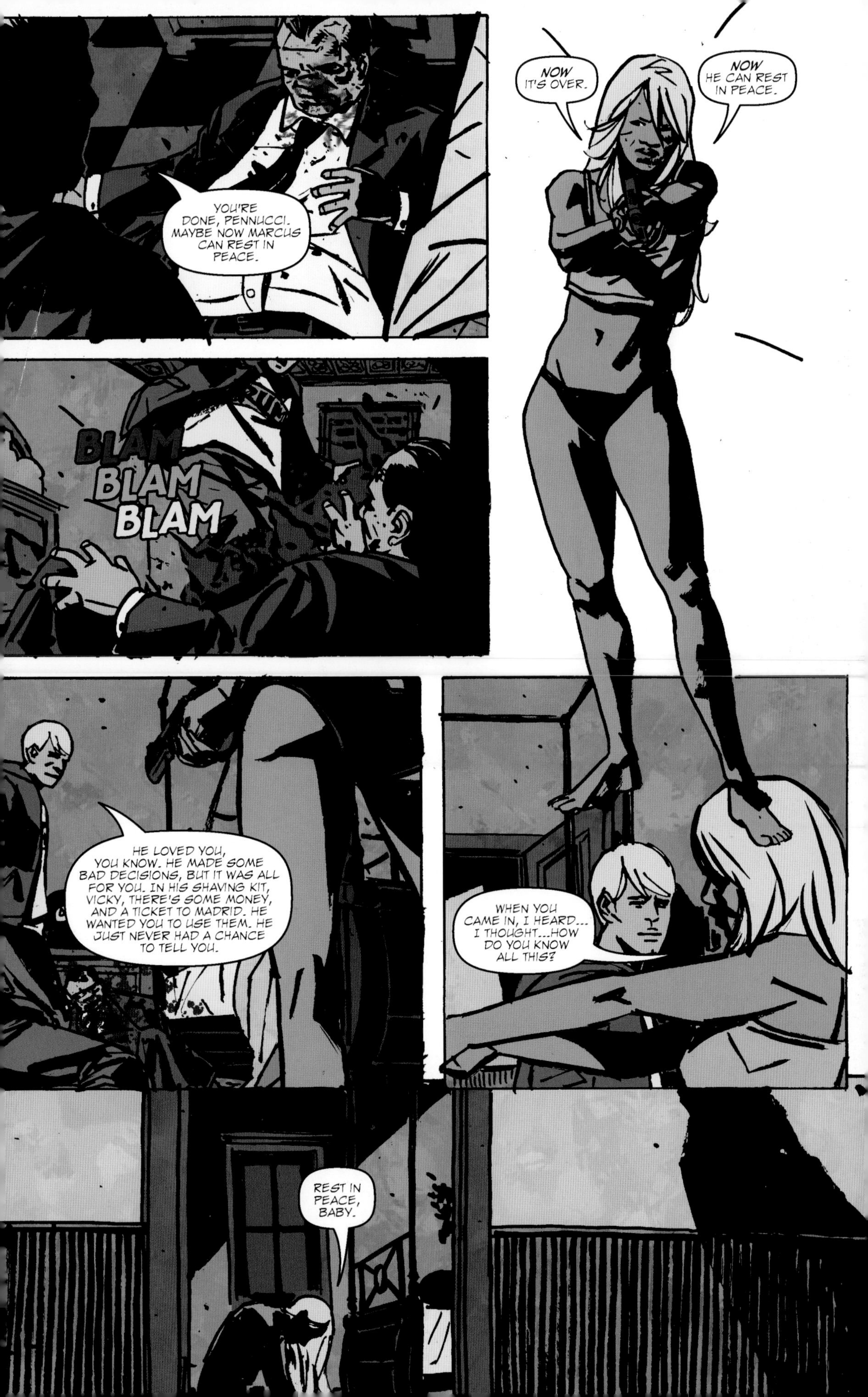
YOU'RE DONE, PENNUCCI. MAYBE NOW MARCUS CAN REST IN PEACE.
NOW IT'S OVER.
NOW HE CAN REST IN PEACE.
BLAM BLAM BLAM
HE LOVED YOU, YOU KNOW. HE MADE SOME BAD DECISIONS, BUT IT WAS ALL FOR YOU. IN HIS SHAVING KIT, VICKY, THERE'S SOME MONEY, AND A TICKET TO MADRID. HE WANTED YOU TO USE THEM. HE JUST NEVER HAD A CHANCE TO TELL YOU.
WHEN YOU CAME IN, I HEARD... I THOUGHT...HOW DO YOU KNOW ALL THIS?
REST IN PEACE, BABY.

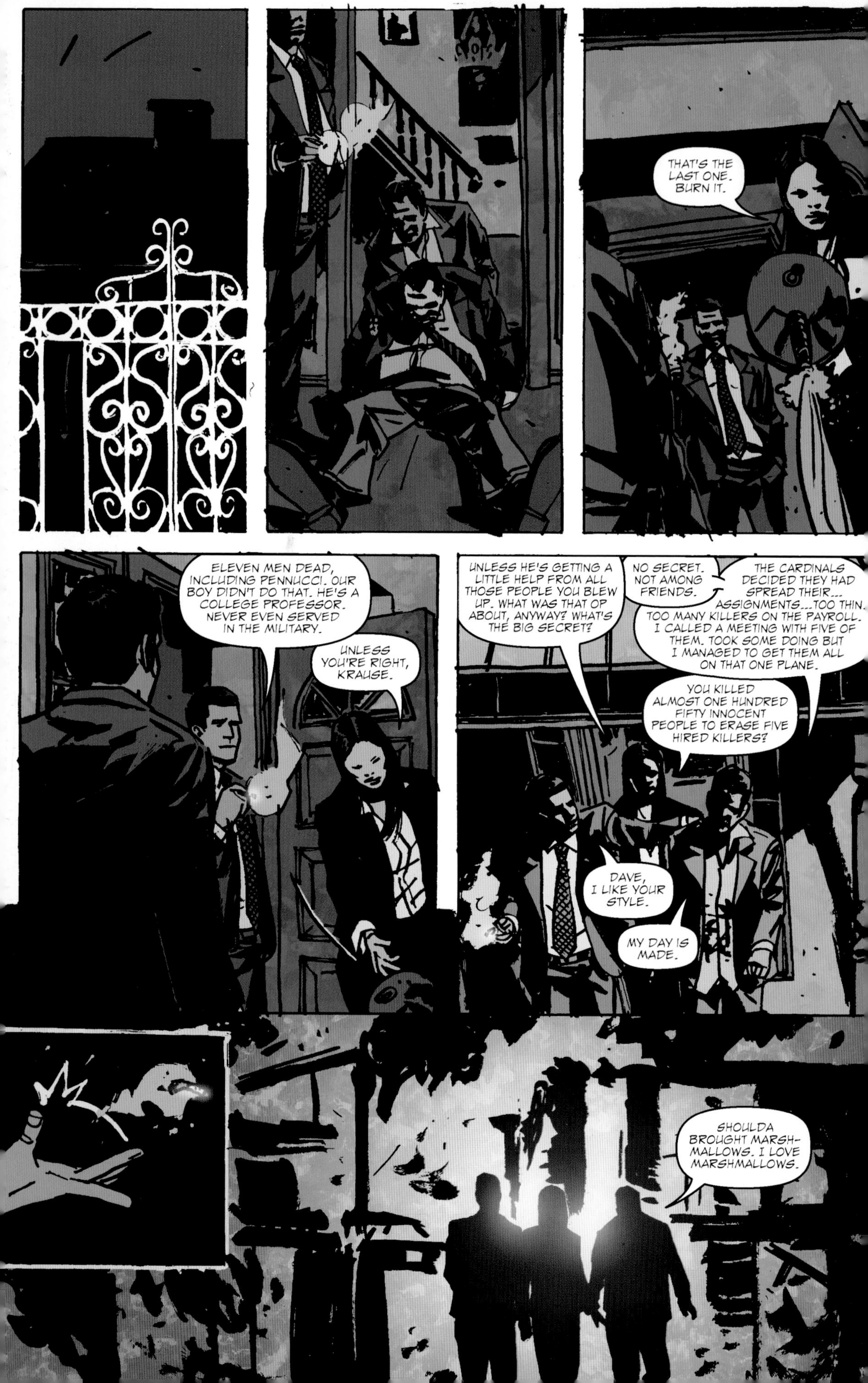
THAT'S THE LAST ONE. BURN IT.
ELEVEN MEN DEAD, INCLUDING PENNUCCI. OUR BOY DIDN'T DO THAT. HE'S A COLLEGE PROFESSOR. NEVER EVEN SERVED IN THE MILITARY.
UNLESS YOU'RE RIGHT, KRAUSE.
UNLESS HE'S GETTING A LITTLE HELP FROM ALL THOSE PEOPLE YOU BLEW UP. WHAT WAS THAT OP ABOUT, ANYWAY? WHAT'S THE BIG SECRET?
NO SECRET. NOT AMONG FRIENDS.
THE CARDINALS DECIDED THEY HAD SPREAD THEIR... ASSIGNMENTS...TOO THIN. TOO MANY KILLERS ON THE PAYROLL. I CALLED A MEETING WITH FIVE OF THEM. TOOK SOME DOING BUT I MANAGED TO GET THEM ALL ON THAT ONE PLANE.
YOU KILLED ALMOST ONE HUNDRED FIFTY INNOCENT PEOPLE TO ERASE FIVE HIRED KILLERS?
DAVE, I LIKE YOUR STYLE.
MY DAY IS MADE.
SHOULDA BROUGHT MARSH-MALLOWS. I LOVE MARSHMALLOWS.

**PAUL AZACETA**
original series cover

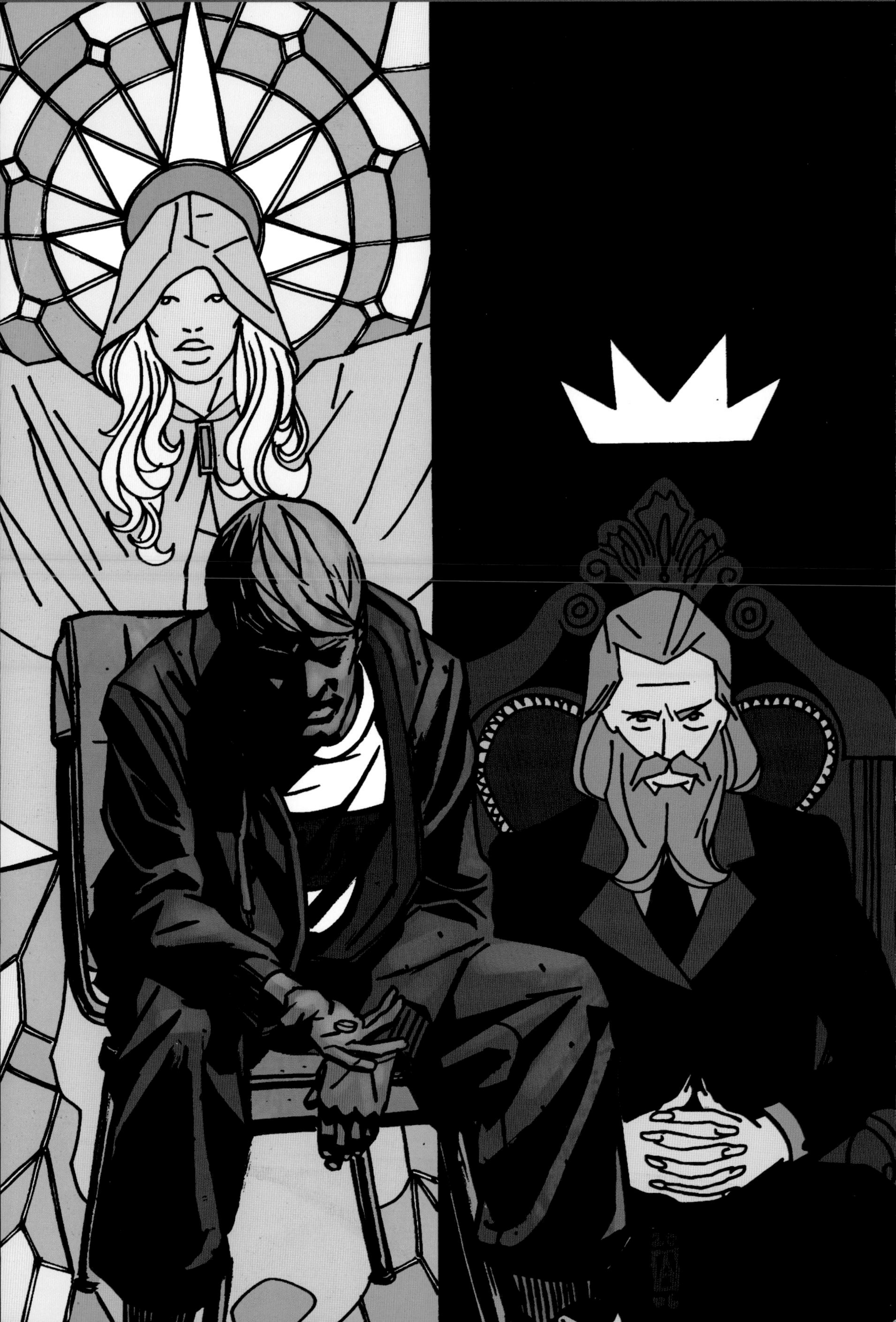

# CHAPTER FOUR 4

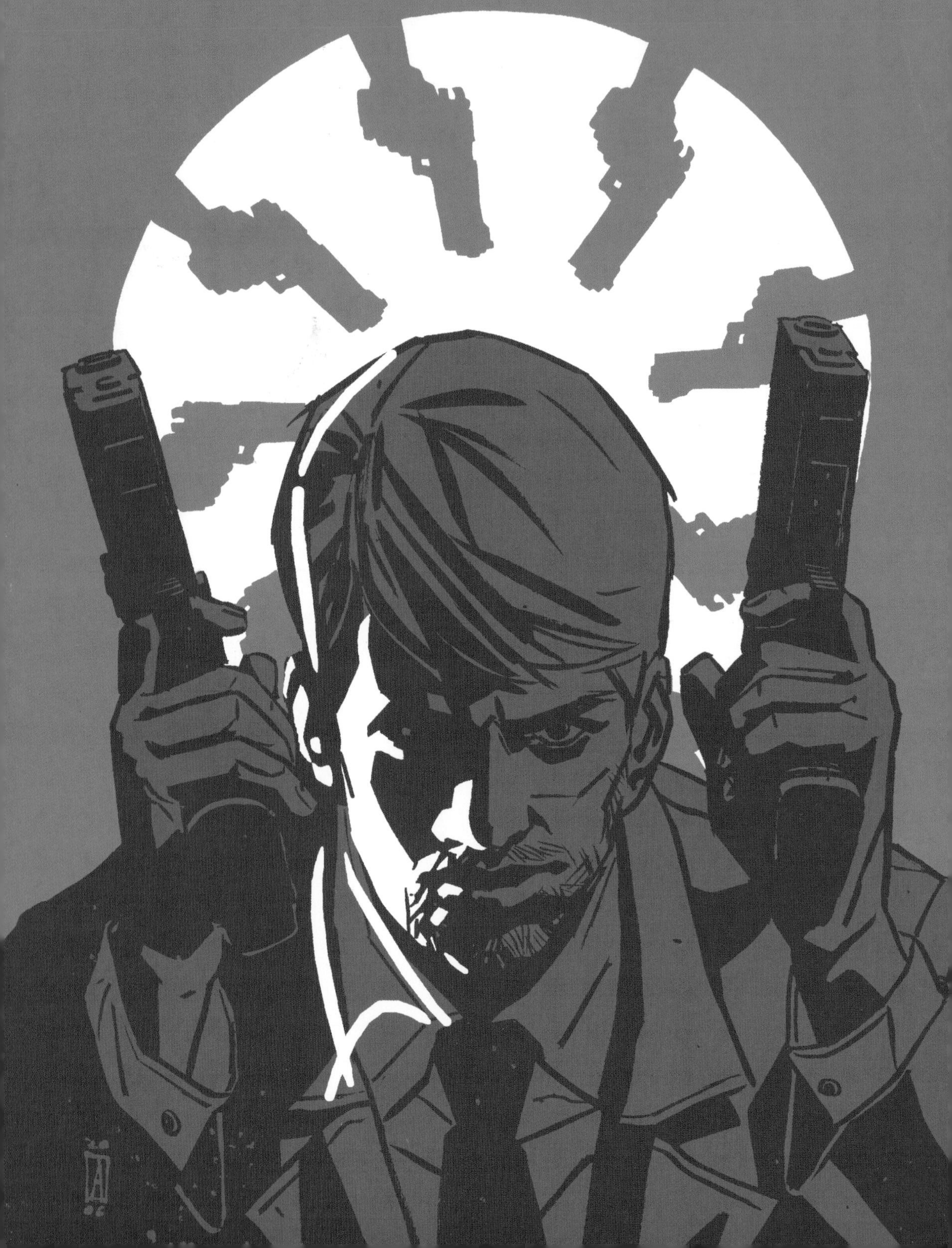

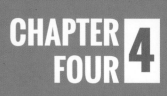

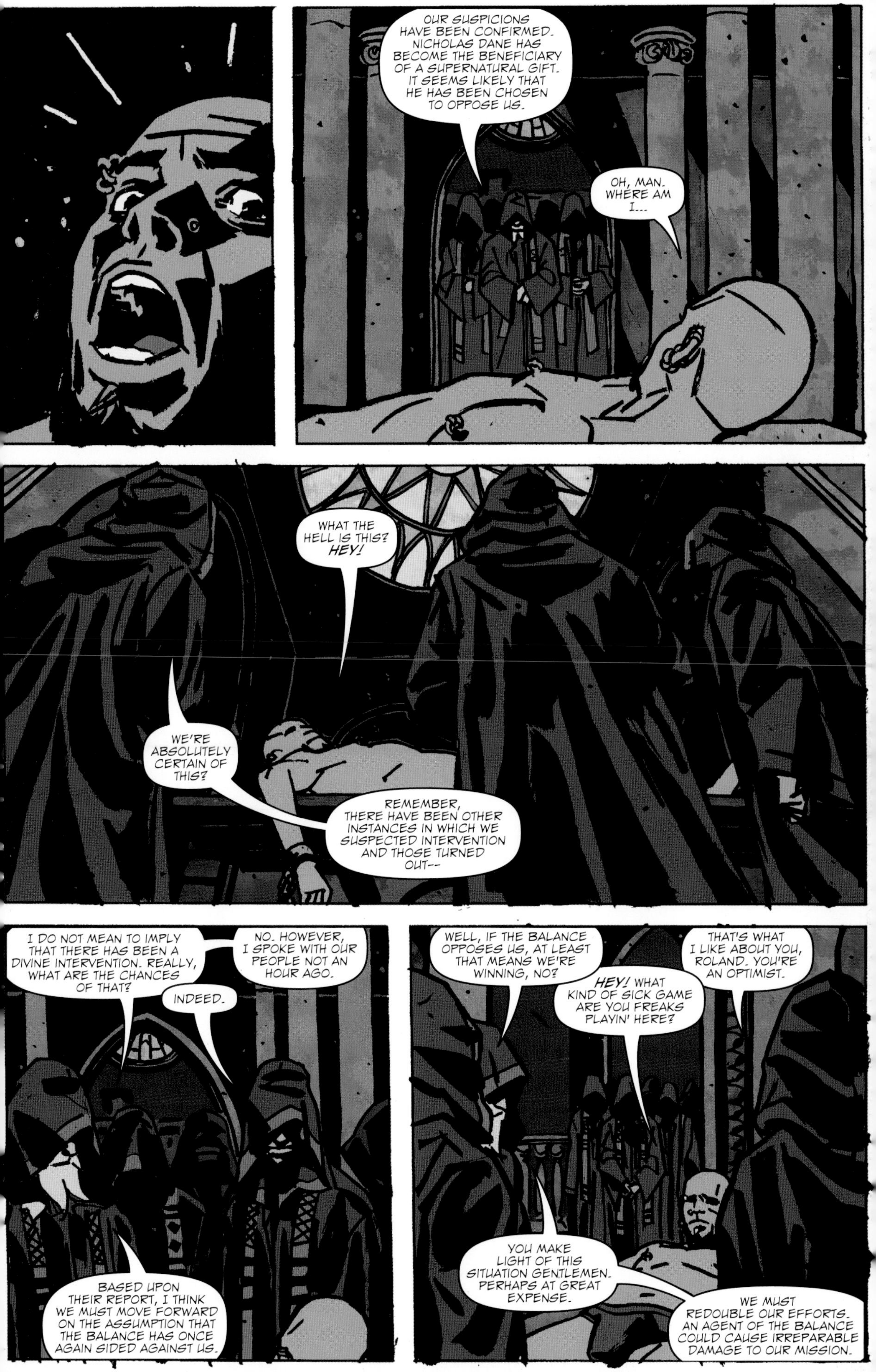
OUR SUSPICIONS HAVE BEEN CONFIRMED. NICHOLAS DANE HAS BECOME THE BENEFICIARY OF A SUPERNATURAL GIFT. IT SEEMS LIKELY THAT HE HAS BEEN CHOSEN TO OPPOSE US.
OH, MAN. WHERE AM I...
WHAT THE HELL IS THIS? *HEY!*
WE'RE ABSOLUTELY CERTAIN OF THIS?
REMEMBER, THERE HAVE BEEN OTHER INSTANCES IN WHICH WE SUSPECTED INTERVENTION AND THOSE TURNED OUT--
I DO NOT MEAN TO IMPLY THAT THERE HAS BEEN A DIVINE INTERVENTION. REALLY, WHAT ARE THE CHANCES OF THAT?
NO. HOWEVER, I SPOKE WITH OUR PEOPLE NOT AN HOUR AGO.
INDEED.
BASED UPON THEIR REPORT, I THINK WE MUST MOVE FORWARD ON THE ASSUMPTION THAT THE BALANCE HAS ONCE AGAIN SIDED AGAINST US.
WELL, IF THE BALANCE OPPOSES US, AT LEAST THAT MEANS WE'RE WINNING, NO?
THAT'S WHAT I LIKE ABOUT YOU, ROLAND. YOU'RE AN OPTIMIST.
*HEY!* WHAT KIND OF SICK GAME ARE YOU FREAKS PLAYIN' HERE?
YOU MAKE LIGHT OF THIS SITUATION GENTLEMEN. PERHAPS AT GREAT EXPENSE.
WE MUST REDOUBLE OUR EFFORTS. AN AGENT OF THE BALANCE COULD CAUSE IRREPARABLE DAMAGE TO OUR MISSION.

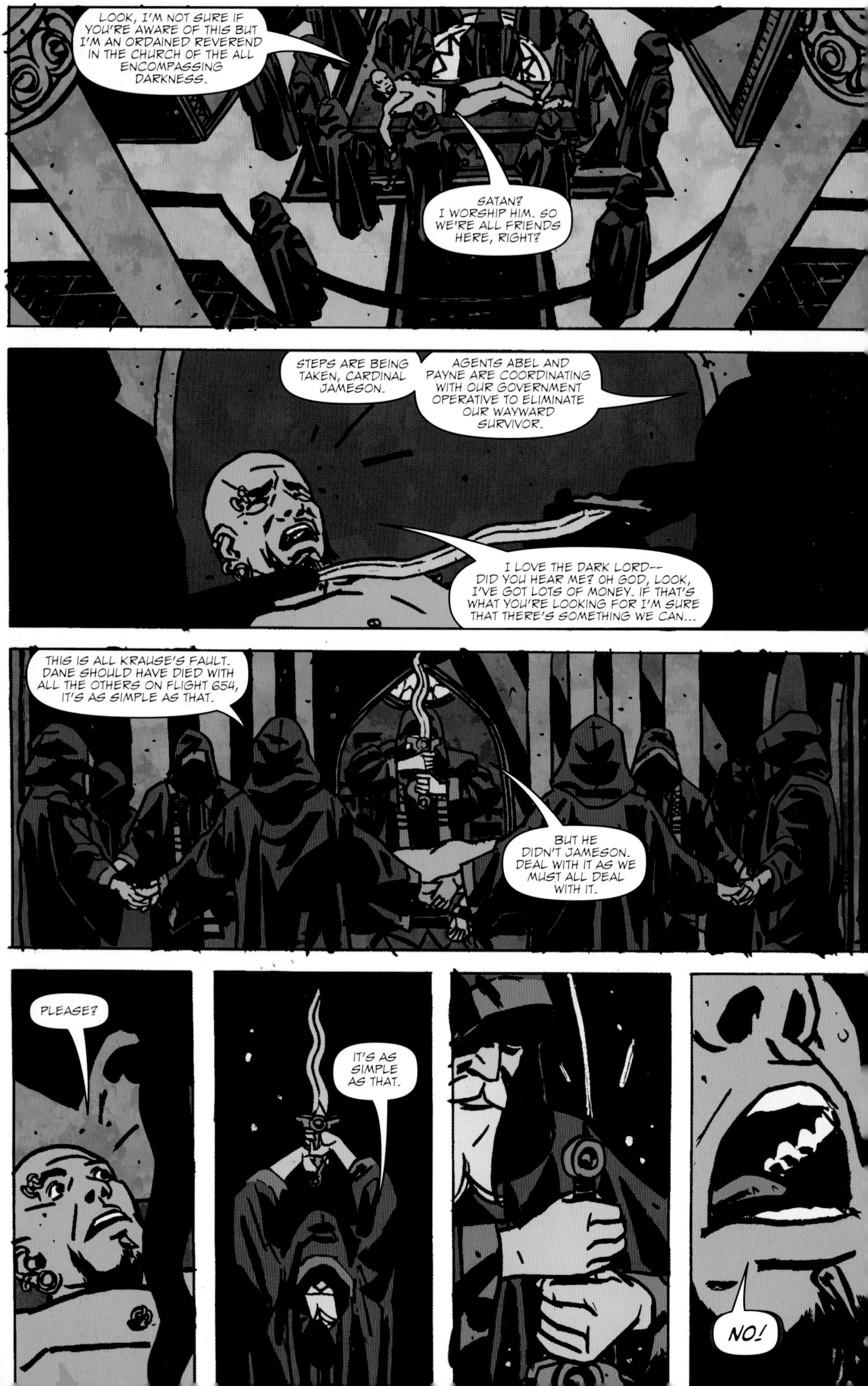
LOOK, I'M NOT SURE IF YOU'RE AWARE OF THIS BUT I'M AN ORDAINED REVEREND IN THE CHURCH OF THE ALL ENCOMPASSING DARKNESS.
SATAN? I WORSHIP HIM. SO WE'RE ALL FRIENDS HERE, RIGHT?
STEPS ARE BEING TAKEN, CARDINAL JAMESON.
AGENTS ABEL AND PAYNE ARE COORDINATING WITH OUR GOVERNMENT OPERATIVE TO ELIMINATE OUR WAYWARD SURVIVOR.
I LOVE THE DARK LORD-- DID YOU HEAR ME? OH GOD, LOOK, I'VE GOT LOTS OF MONEY. IF THAT'S WHAT YOU'RE LOOKING FOR I'M SURE THAT THERE'S SOMETHING WE CAN...
THIS IS ALL KRAUSE'S FAULT. DANE SHOULD HAVE DIED WITH ALL THE OTHERS ON FLIGHT 654, IT'S AS SIMPLE AS THAT.
BUT HE DIDN'T JAMESON. DEAL WITH IT AS WE MUST ALL DEAL WITH IT.
PLEASE?
IT'S AS SIMPLE AS THAT.
NO!

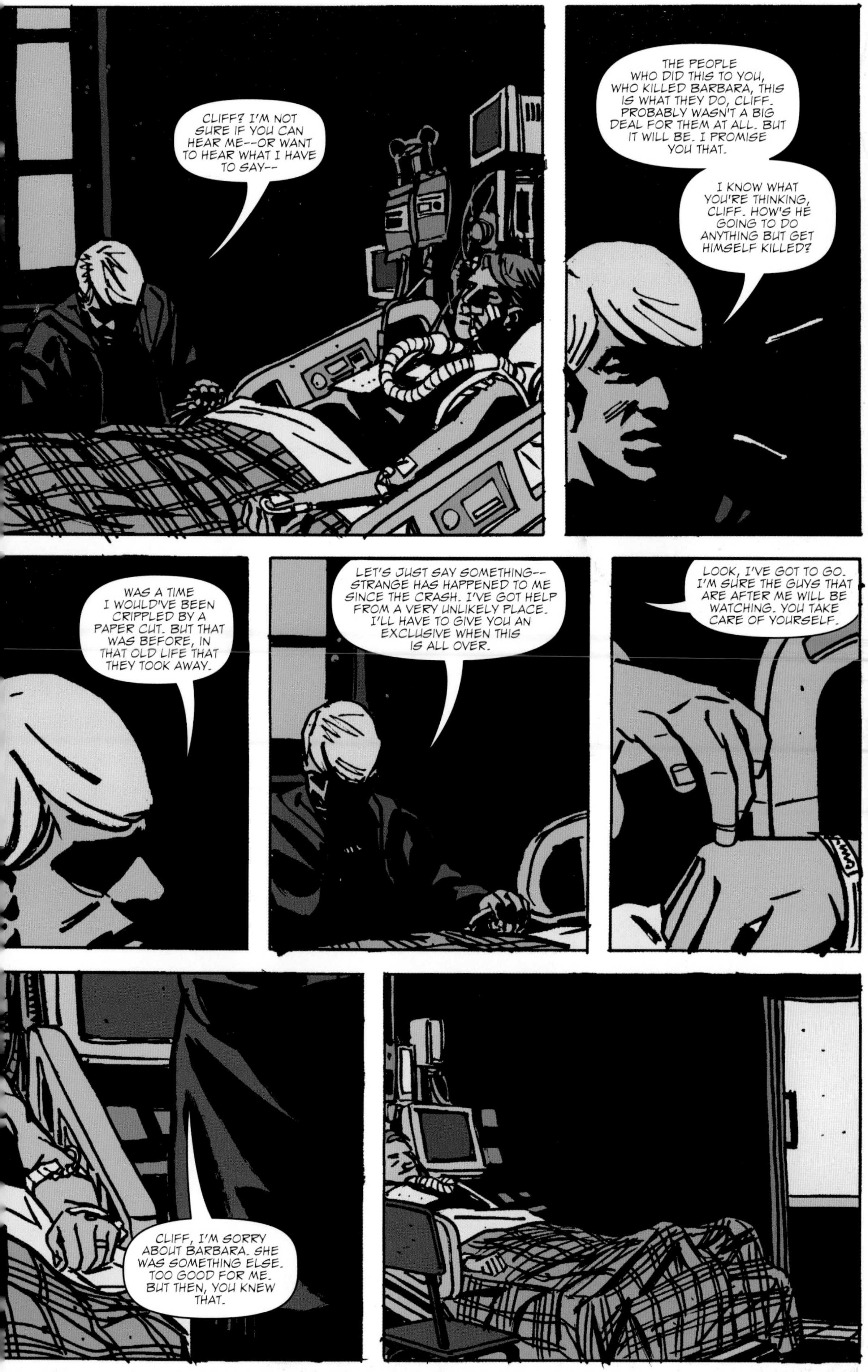
CLIFF? I'M NOT SURE IF YOU CAN HEAR ME--OR WANT TO HEAR WHAT I HAVE TO SAY--
THE PEOPLE WHO DID THIS TO YOU, WHO KILLED BARBARA, THIS IS WHAT THEY DO, CLIFF. PROBABLY WASN'T A BIG DEAL FOR THEM AT ALL. BUT IT WILL BE. I PROMISE YOU THAT.
I KNOW WHAT YOU'RE THINKING, CLIFF. HOW'S HE GOING TO DO ANYTHING BUT GET HIMSELF KILLED?
WAS A TIME I WOULD'VE BEEN CRIPPLED BY A PAPER CUT. BUT THAT WAS BEFORE, IN THAT OLD LIFE THAT THEY TOOK AWAY.
LET'S JUST SAY SOMETHING-- STRANGE HAS HAPPENED TO ME SINCE THE CRASH. I'VE GOT HELP FROM A VERY UNLIKELY PLACE. I'LL HAVE TO GIVE YOU AN EXCLUSIVE WHEN THIS IS ALL OVER.
LOOK, I'VE GOT TO GO. I'M SURE THE GUYS THAT ARE AFTER ME WILL BE WATCHING. YOU TAKE CARE OF YOURSELF.
CLIFF, I'M SORRY ABOUT BARBARA. SHE WAS SOMETHING ELSE. TOO GOOD FOR ME. BUT THEN, YOU KNEW THAT.

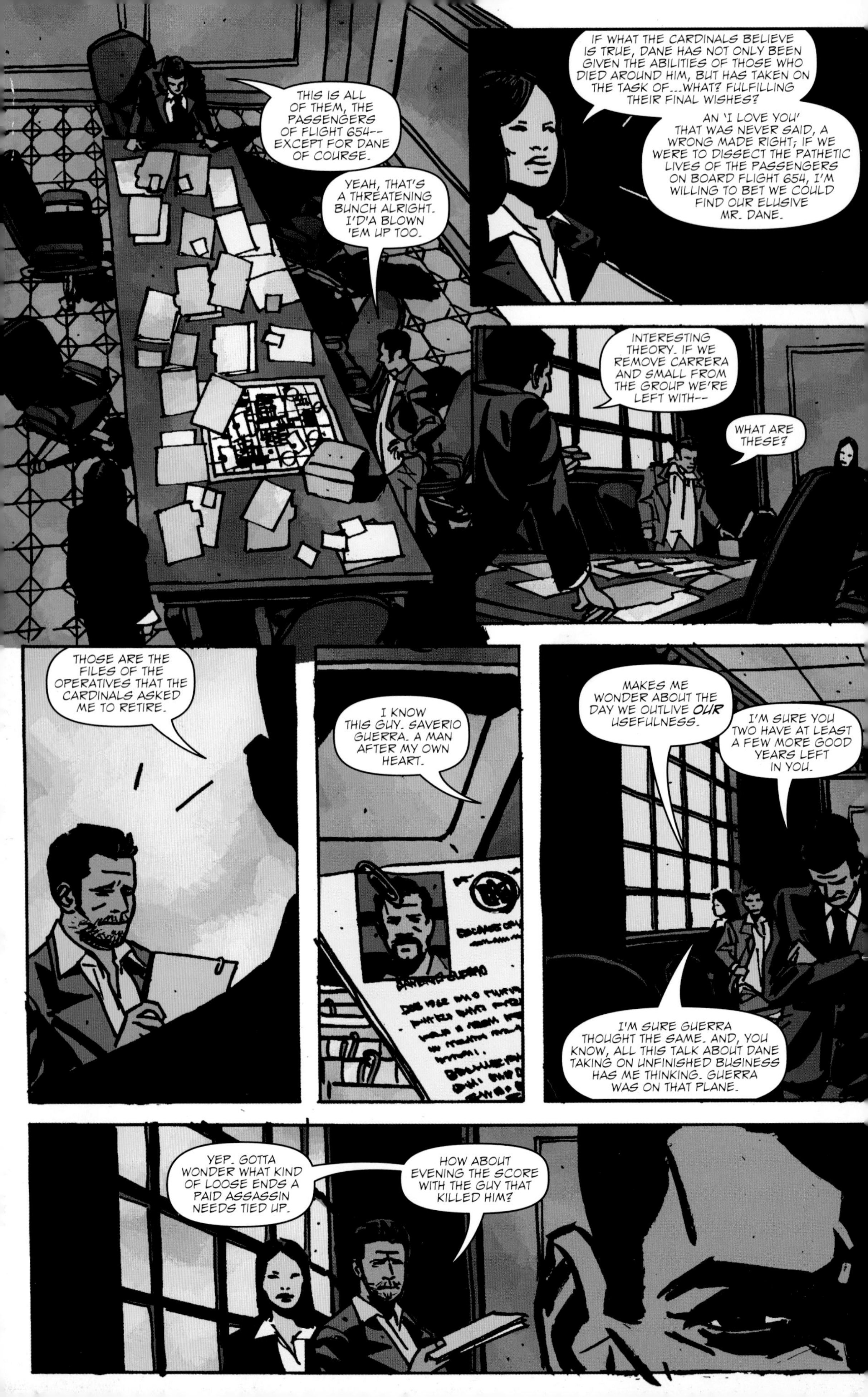
THIS IS ALL OF THEM, THE PASSENGERS OF FLIGHT 654-- EXCEPT FOR DANE OF COURSE.
YEAH, THAT'S A THREATENING BUNCH ALRIGHT. I'D'A BLOWN 'EM UP TOO.
IF WHAT THE CARDINALS BELIEVE IS TRUE, DANE HAS NOT ONLY BEEN GIVEN THE ABILITIES OF THOSE WHO DIED AROUND HIM, BUT HAS TAKEN ON THE TASK OF...WHAT? FULFILLING THEIR FINAL WISHES?
AN 'I LOVE YOU' THAT WAS NEVER SAID, A WRONG MADE RIGHT; IF WE WERE TO DISSECT THE PATHETIC LIVES OF THE PASSENGERS ON BOARD FLIGHT 654, I'M WILLING TO BET WE COULD FIND OUR ELUSIVE MR. DANE.
INTERESTING THEORY. IF WE REMOVE CARRERA AND SMALL FROM THE GROUP WE'RE LEFT WITH--
WHAT ARE THESE?
THOSE ARE THE FILES OF THE OPERATIVES THAT THE CARDINALS ASKED ME TO RETIRE.
I KNOW THIS GUY. SAVERIO GUERRA. A MAN AFTER MY OWN HEART.
MAKES ME WONDER ABOUT THE DAY WE OUTLIVE ***OUR*** USEFULNESS.
I'M SURE YOU TWO HAVE AT LEAST A FEW MORE GOOD YEARS LEFT IN YOU.
I'M SURE GUERRA THOUGHT THE SAME. AND, YOU KNOW, ALL THIS TALK ABOUT DANE TAKING ON UNFINISHED BUSINESS HAS ME THINKING. GUERRA WAS ON THAT PLANE.
YEP. GOTTA WONDER WHAT KIND OF LOOSE ENDS A PAID ASSASSIN NEEDS TIED UP.
HOW ABOUT EVENING THE SCORE WITH THE GUY THAT KILLED HIM?

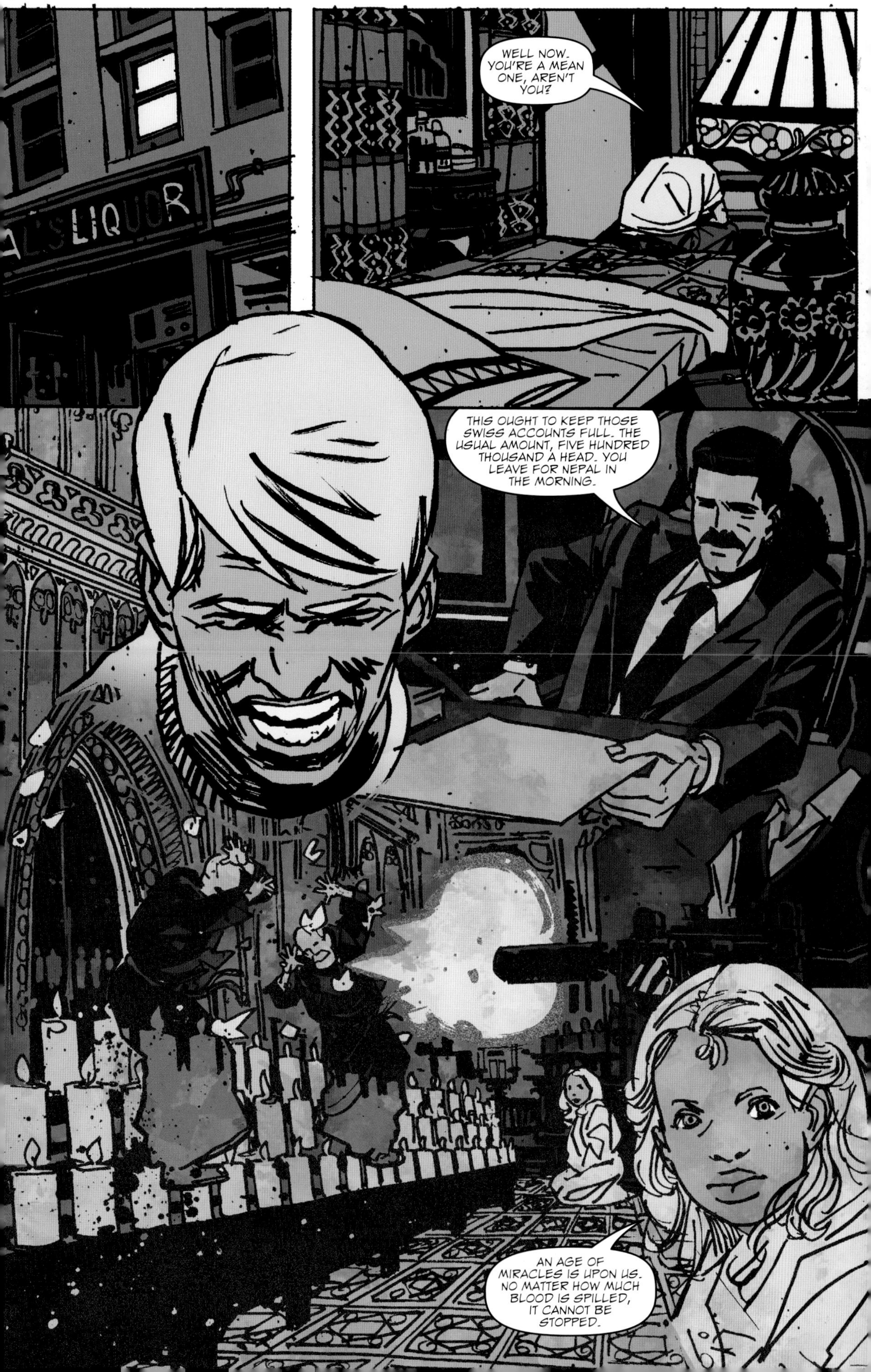
AL'S LIQUOR
WELL NOW. YOU'RE A MEAN ONE, AREN'T YOU?
THIS OUGHT TO KEEP THOSE SWISS ACCOUNTS FULL. THE USUAL AMOUNT, FIVE HUNDRED THOUSAND A HEAD. YOU LEAVE FOR NEPAL IN THE MORNING.
AN AGE OF MIRACLES IS UPON US. NO MATTER HOW MUCH BLOOD IS SPILLED, IT CANNOT BE STOPPED.

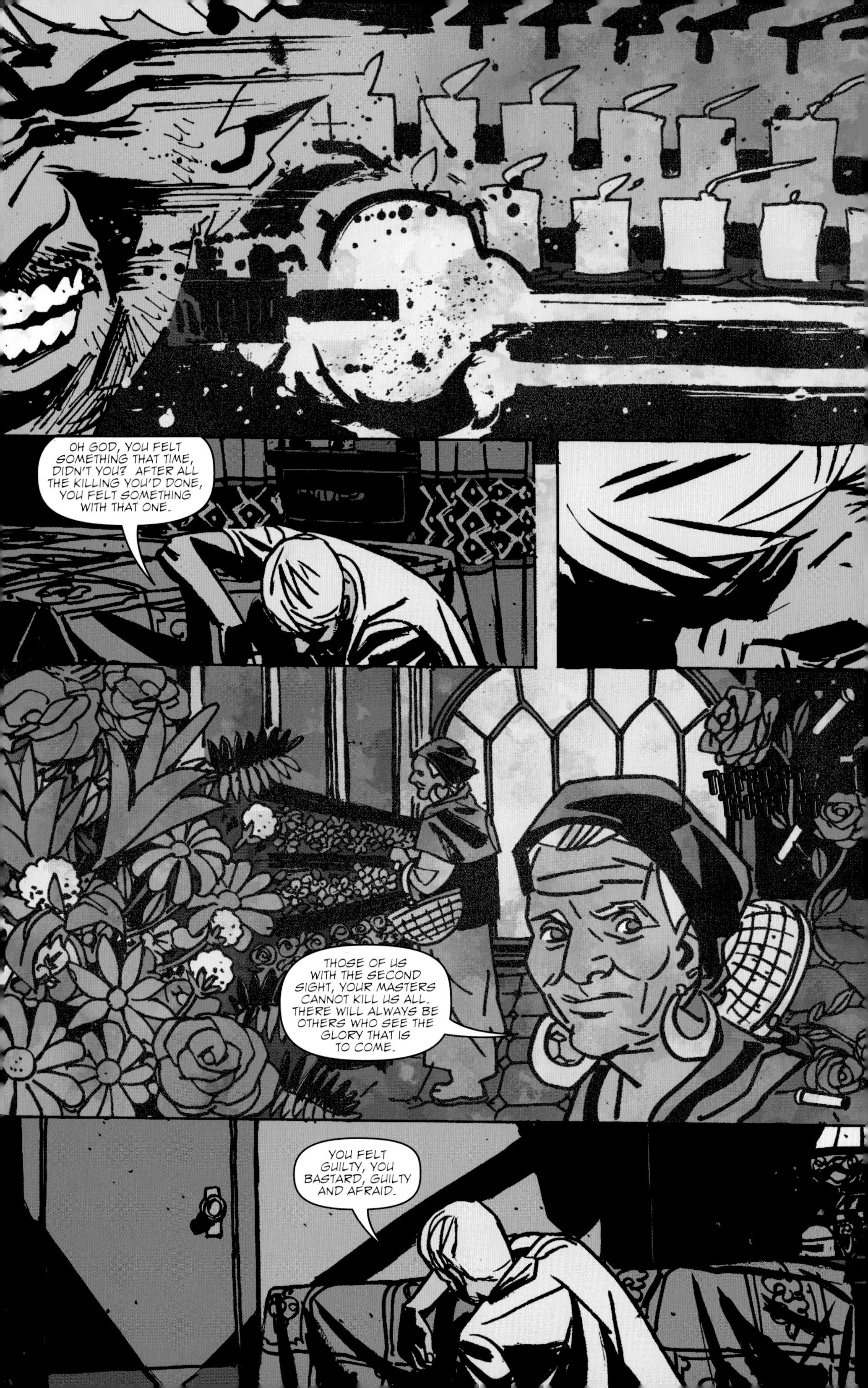
OH GOD, YOU FELT SOMETHING THAT TIME, DIDN'T YOU? AFTER ALL THE KILLING YOU'D DONE, YOU FELT SOMETHING WITH THAT ONE.
THOSE OF US WITH THE SECOND SIGHT, YOUR MASTERS CANNOT KILL US ALL. THERE WILL ALWAYS BE OTHERS WHO SEE THE GLORY THAT IS TO COME.
YOU FELT GUILTY, YOU BASTARD, GUILTY AND AFRAID.

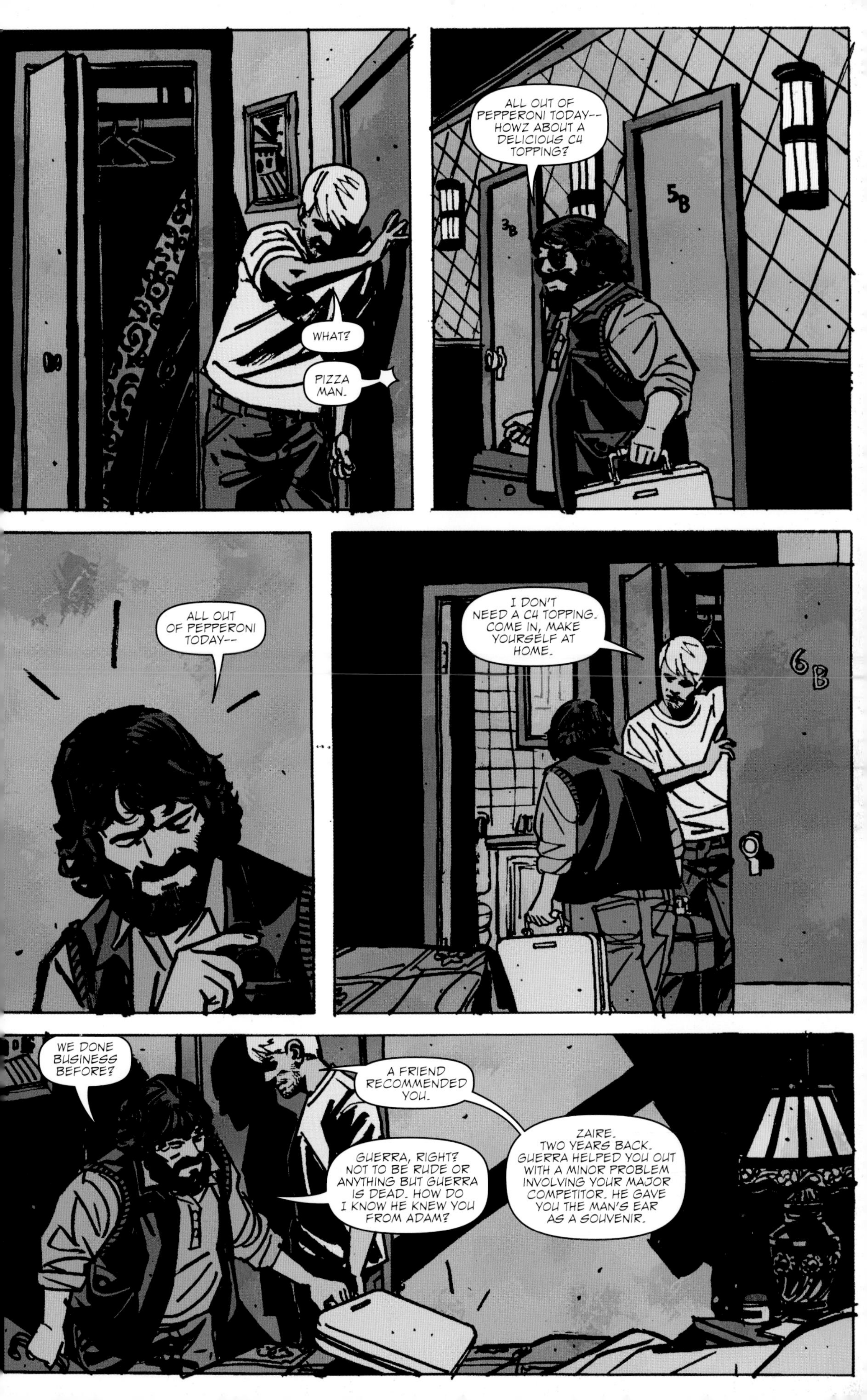
WHAT?
PIZZA MAN.
ALL OUT OF PEPPERONI TODAY-- HOWZ ABOUT A DELICIOUS C4 TOPPING?
5B
3B
ALL OUT OF PEPPERONI TODAY--
I DON'T NEED A C4 TOPPING. COME IN, MAKE YOURSELF AT HOME.
6B
WE DONE BUSINESS BEFORE?
A FRIEND RECOMMENDED YOU.
GUERRA, RIGHT? NOT TO BE RUDE OR ANYTHING BUT GUERRA IS DEAD. HOW DO I KNOW HE KNEW YOU FROM ADAM?
ZAIRE. TWO YEARS BACK. GUERRA HELPED YOU OUT WITH A MINOR PROBLEM INVOLVING YOUR MAJOR COMPETITOR. HE GAVE YOU THE MAN'S EAR AS A SOUVENIR.

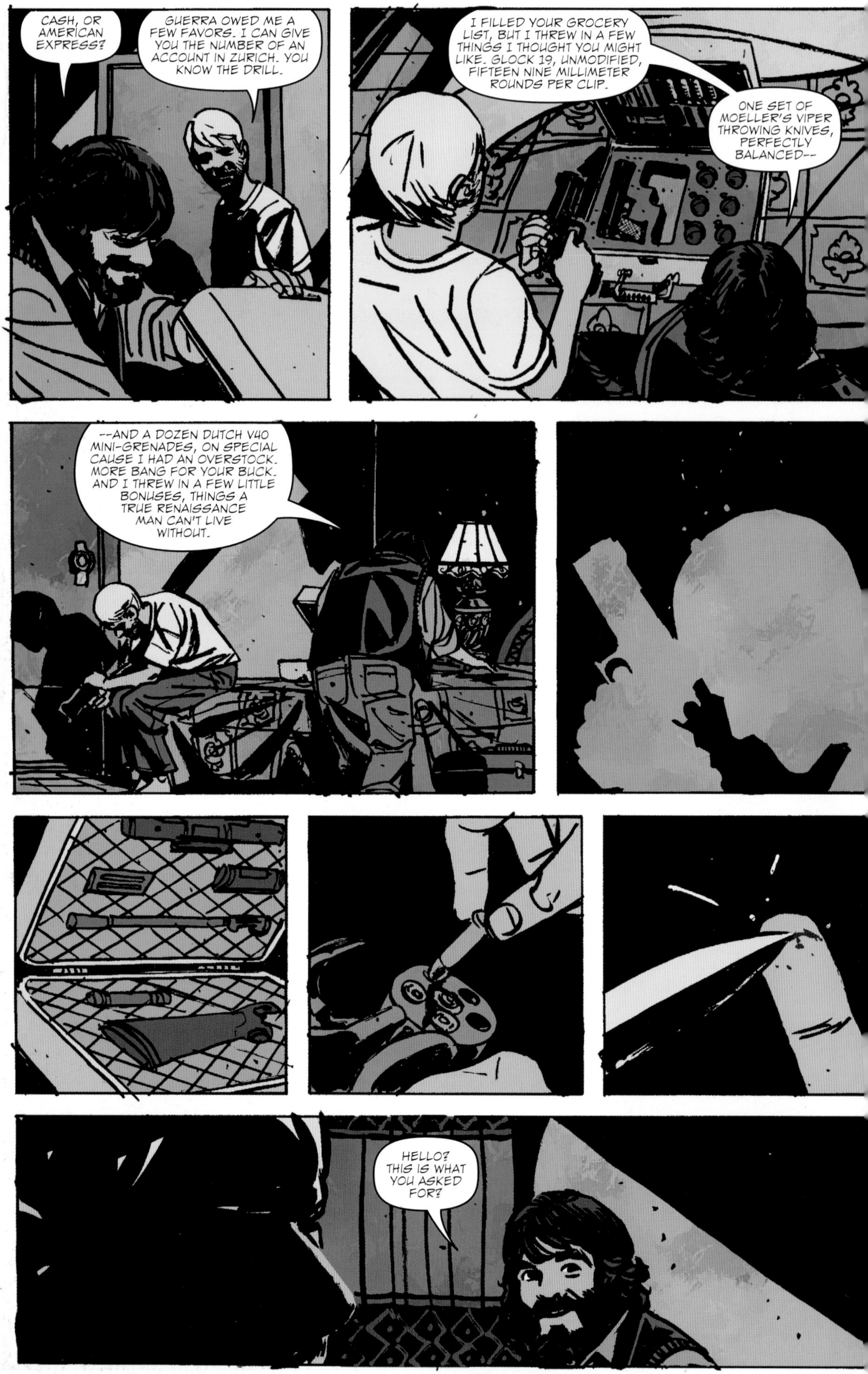
CASH, OR AMERICAN EXPRESS?
GUERRA OWED ME A FEW FAVORS. I CAN GIVE YOU THE NUMBER OF AN ACCOUNT IN ZURICH. YOU KNOW THE DRILL.
I FILLED YOUR GROCERY LIST, BUT I THREW IN A FEW THINGS I THOUGHT YOU MIGHT LIKE. GLOCK 19, UNMODIFIED, FIFTEEN NINE MILLIMETER ROUNDS PER CLIP.
ONE SET OF MOELLER'S VIPER THROWING KNIVES, PERFECTLY BALANCED--
--AND A DOZEN DUTCH V40 MINI-GRENADES, ON SPECIAL CAUSE I HAD AN OVERSTOCK. MORE BANG FOR YOUR BUCK. AND I THREW IN A FEW LITTLE BONUSES, THINGS A TRUE RENAISSANCE MAN CAN'T LIVE WITHOUT.
HELLO? THIS IS WHAT YOU ASKED FOR?

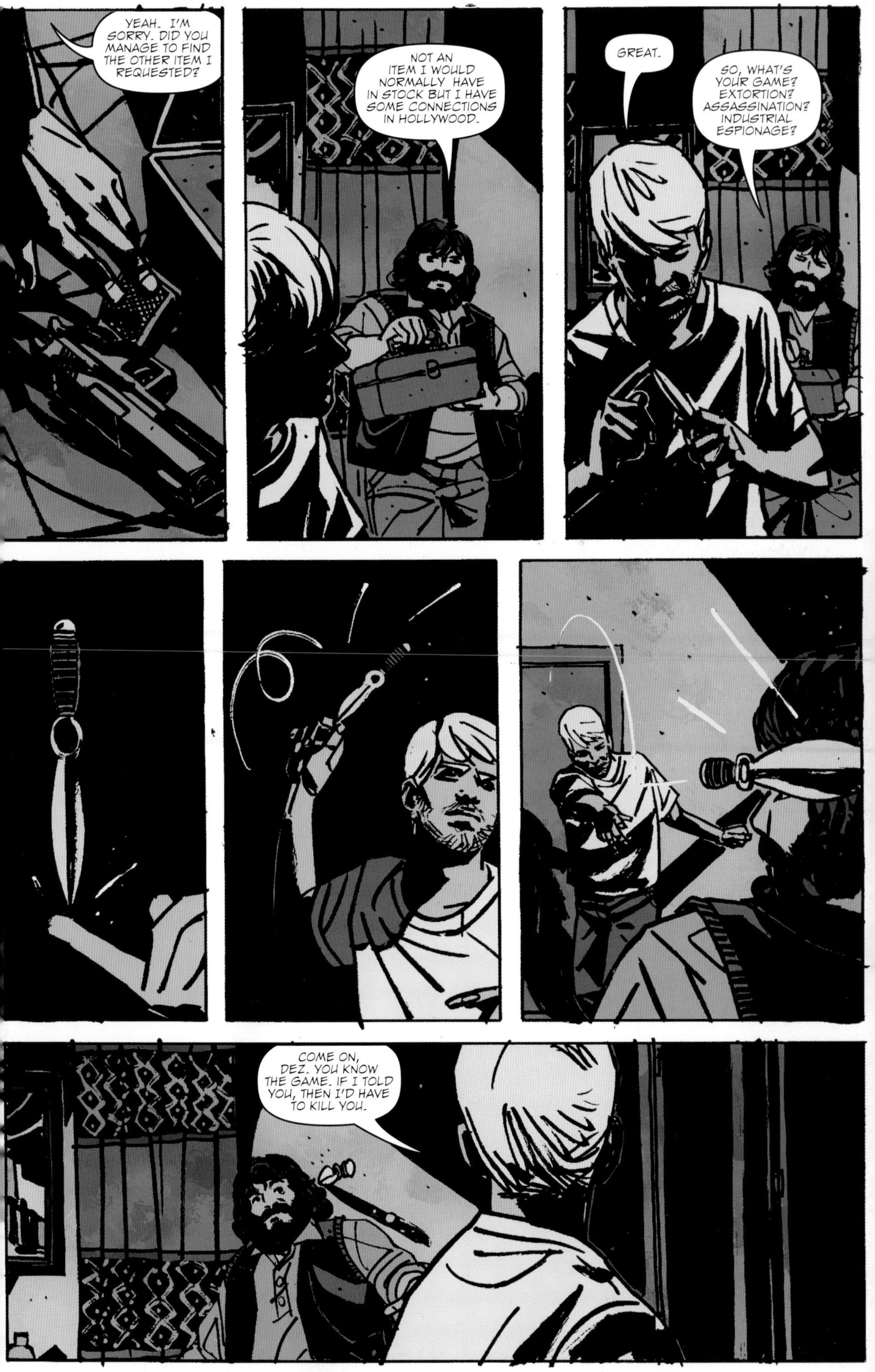
YEAH. I'M SORRY. DID YOU MANAGE TO FIND THE OTHER ITEM I REQUESTED?
NOT AN ITEM I WOULD NORMALLY HAVE IN STOCK BUT I HAVE SOME CONNECTIONS IN HOLLYWOOD.
GREAT.
SO, WHAT'S YOUR GAME? EXTORTION? ASSASSINATION? INDUSTRIAL ESPIONAGE?
COME ON, DEZ. YOU KNOW THE GAME. IF I TOLD YOU, THEN I'D HAVE TO KILL YOU.

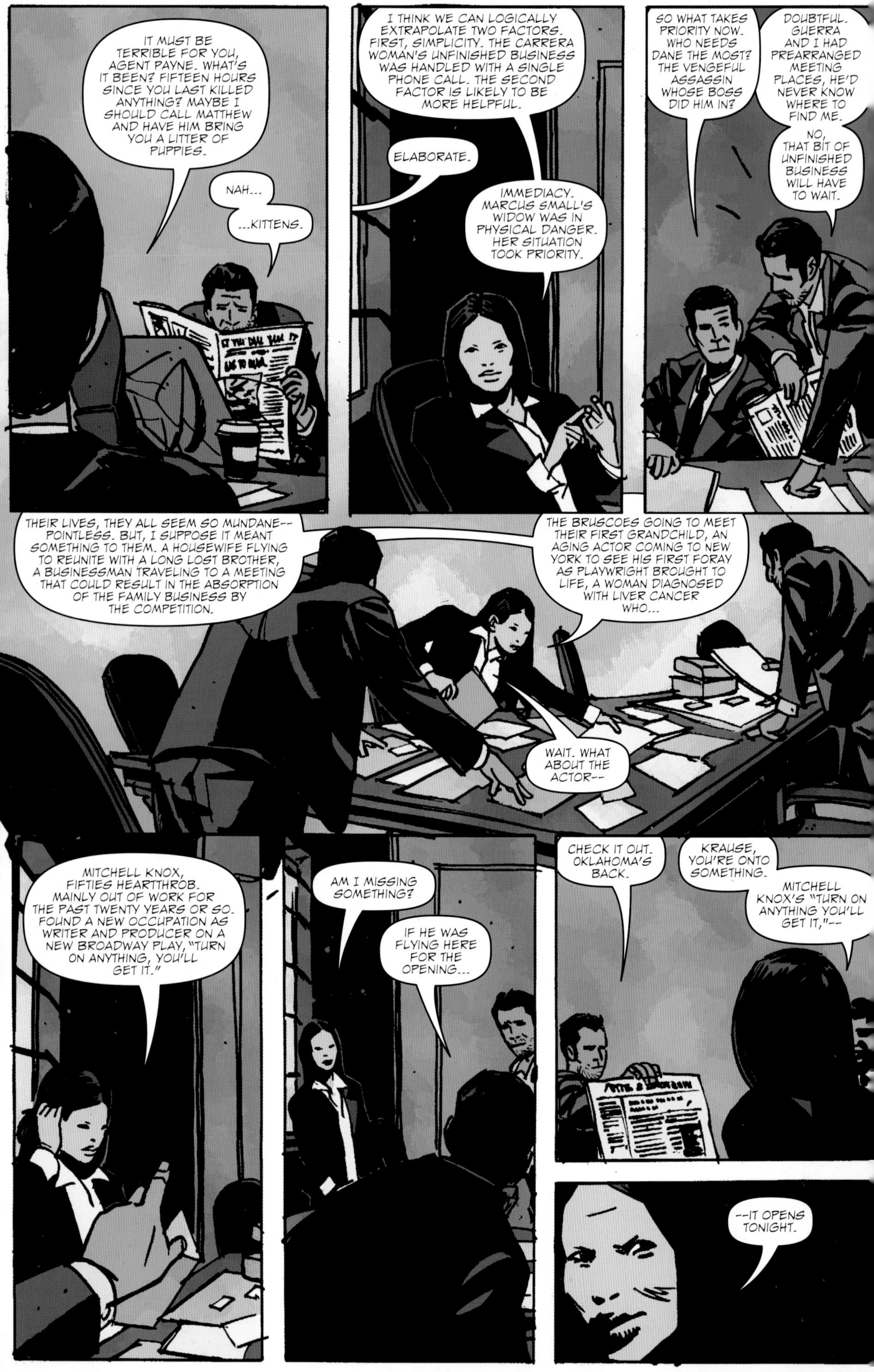
IT MUST BE TERRIBLE FOR YOU, AGENT PAYNE. WHAT'S IT BEEN? FIFTEEN HOURS SINCE YOU LAST KILLED ANYTHING? MAYBE I SHOULD CALL MATTHEW AND HAVE HIM BRING YOU A LITTER OF PUPPIES.
NAH...
...KITTENS.
I THINK WE CAN LOGICALLY EXTRAPOLATE TWO FACTORS. FIRST, SIMPLICITY. THE CARRERA WOMAN'S UNFINISHED BUSINESS WAS HANDLED WITH A SINGLE PHONE CALL. THE SECOND FACTOR IS LIKELY TO BE MORE HELPFUL.
ELABORATE.
IMMEDIACY. MARCUS SMALL'S WIDOW WAS IN PHYSICAL DANGER. HER SITUATION TOOK PRIORITY.
SO WHAT TAKES PRIORITY NOW. WHO NEEDS DANE THE MOST? THE VENGEFUL ASSASSIN WHOSE BOSS DID HIM IN?
DOUBTFUL. GUERRA AND I HAD PREARRANGED MEETING PLACES, HE'D NEVER KNOW WHERE TO FIND ME.
NO, THAT BIT OF UNFINISHED BUSINESS WILL HAVE TO WAIT.
THEIR LIVES, THEY ALL SEEM SO MUNDANE--POINTLESS. BUT, I SUPPOSE IT MEANT SOMETHING TO THEM. A HOUSEWIFE FLYING TO REUNITE WITH A LONG LOST BROTHER, A BUSINESSMAN TRAVELING TO A MEETING THAT COULD RESULT IN THE ABSORPTION OF THE FAMILY BUSINESS BY THE COMPETITION.
THE BRUSCOES GOING TO MEET THEIR FIRST GRANDCHILD, AN AGING ACTOR COMING TO NEW YORK TO SEE HIS FIRST FORAY AS PLAYWRIGHT BROUGHT TO LIFE, A WOMAN DIAGNOSED WITH LIVER CANCER WHO...
WAIT. WHAT ABOUT THE ACTOR--
MITCHELL KNOX, FIFTIES HEARTTHROB. MAINLY OUT OF WORK FOR THE PAST TWENTY YEARS OR SO. FOUND A NEW OCCUPATION AS WRITER AND PRODUCER ON A NEW BROADWAY PLAY, "TURN ON ANYTHING, YOU'LL GET IT."
AM I MISSING SOMETHING?
IF HE WAS FLYING HERE FOR THE OPENING...
CHECK IT OUT. OKLAHOMA'S BACK.
KRAUSE, YOU'RE ONTO SOMETHING.
MITCHELL KNOX'S "TURN ON ANYTHING YOU'LL GET IT,"--
--IT OPENS TONIGHT.

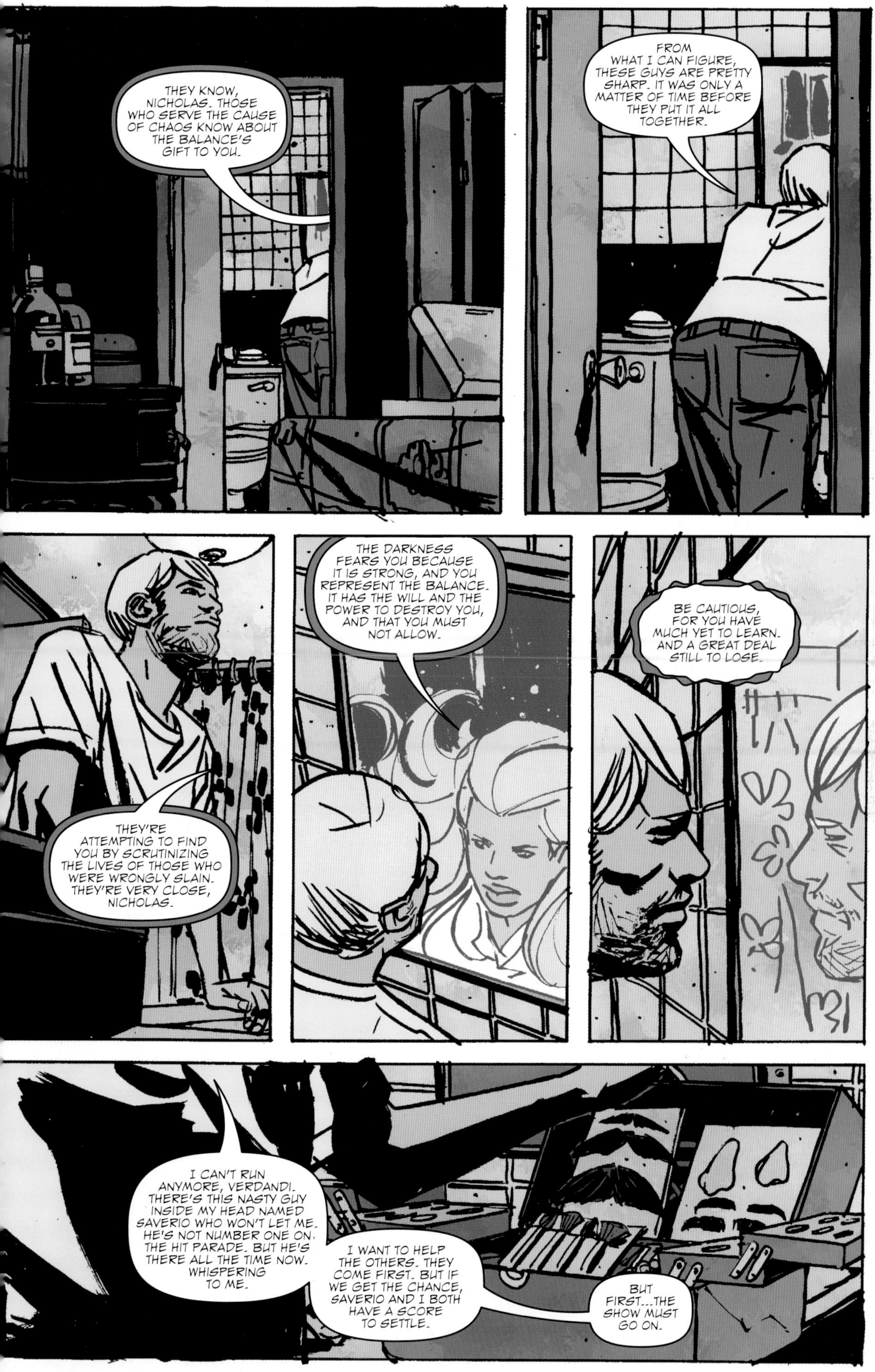
THEY KNOW, NICHOLAS. THOSE WHO SERVE THE CAUSE OF CHAOS KNOW ABOUT THE BALANCE'S GIFT TO YOU.
FROM WHAT I CAN FIGURE, THESE GUYS ARE PRETTY SHARP. IT WAS ONLY A MATTER OF TIME BEFORE THEY PUT IT ALL TOGETHER.
THEY'RE ATTEMPTING TO FIND YOU BY SCRUTINIZING THE LIVES OF THOSE WHO WERE WRONGLY SLAIN. THEY'RE VERY CLOSE, NICHOLAS.
THE DARKNESS FEARS YOU BECAUSE IT IS STRONG, AND YOU REPRESENT THE BALANCE. IT HAS THE WILL AND THE POWER TO DESTROY YOU, AND THAT YOU MUST NOT ALLOW.
BE CAUTIOUS, FOR YOU HAVE MUCH YET TO LEARN. AND A GREAT DEAL STILL TO LOSE.
I CAN'T RUN ANYMORE, VERDANDI. THERE'S THIS NASTY GUY INSIDE MY HEAD NAMED SAVERIO WHO WON'T LET ME. HE'S NOT NUMBER ONE ON THE HIT PARADE. BUT HE'S THERE ALL THE TIME NOW. WHISPERING TO ME.
I WANT TO HELP THE OTHERS. THEY COME FIRST. BUT IF WE GET THE CHANCE, SAVERIO AND I BOTH HAVE A SCORE TO SETTLE.
BUT FIRST...THE SHOW MUST GO ON.

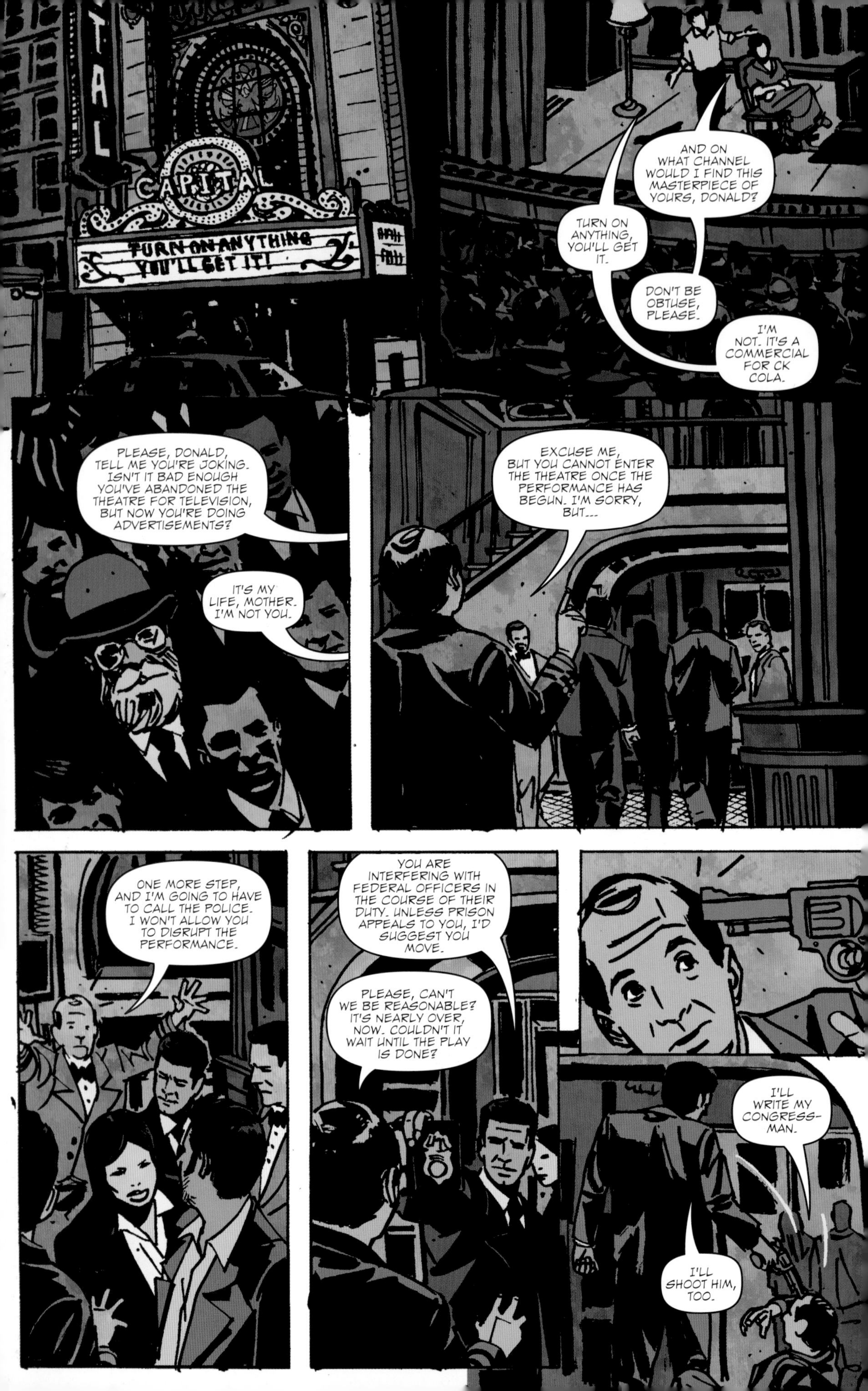
CAPITAL
TURN ON ANYTHING YOU'LL GET IT!
AND ON WHAT CHANNEL WOULD I FIND THIS MASTERPIECE OF YOURS, DONALD?
TURN ON ANYTHING, YOU'LL GET IT.
DON'T BE OBTUSE, PLEASE.
I'M NOT. IT'S A COMMERCIAL FOR CK COLA.
PLEASE, DONALD, TELL ME YOU'RE JOKING. ISN'T IT BAD ENOUGH YOU'VE ABANDONED THE THEATRE FOR TELEVISION, BUT NOW YOU'RE DOING ADVERTISEMENTS?
IT'S MY LIFE, MOTHER. I'M NOT YOU.
EXCUSE ME, BUT YOU CANNOT ENTER THE THEATRE ONCE THE PERFORMANCE HAS BEGUN. I'M SORRY, BUT...
ONE MORE STEP, AND I'M GOING TO HAVE TO CALL THE POLICE. I WON'T ALLOW YOU TO DISRUPT THE PERFORMANCE.
YOU ARE INTERFERING WITH FEDERAL OFFICERS IN THE COURSE OF THEIR DUTY. UNLESS PRISON APPEALS TO YOU, I'D SUGGEST YOU MOVE.
PLEASE, CAN'T WE BE REASONABLE? IT'S NEARLY OVER, NOW. COULDN'T IT WAIT UNTIL THE PLAY IS DONE?
I'LL WRITE MY CONGRESS-MAN.
I'LL SHOOT HIM, TOO.

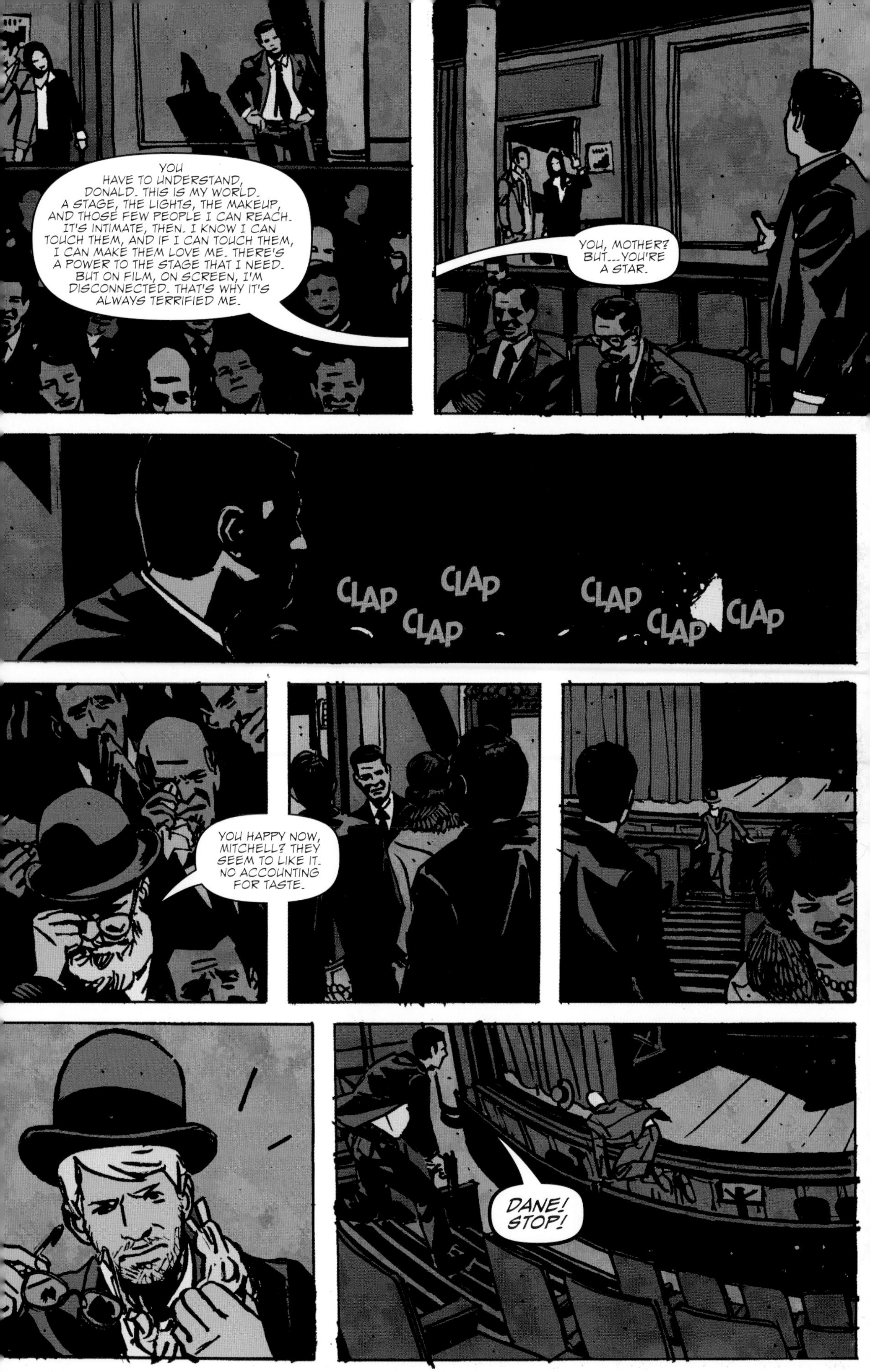
YOU HAVE TO UNDERSTAND, DONALD. THIS IS MY WORLD. A STAGE, THE LIGHTS, THE MAKEUP, AND THOSE FEW PEOPLE I CAN REACH. IT'S INTIMATE, THEN. I KNOW I CAN TOUCH THEM, AND IF I CAN TOUCH THEM, I CAN MAKE THEM LOVE ME. THERE'S A POWER TO THE STAGE THAT I NEED. BUT ON FILM, ON SCREEN, I'M DISCONNECTED. THAT'S WHY IT'S ALWAYS TERRIFIED ME.
YOU, MOTHER? BUT... YOU'RE A STAR.
CLAP CLAP CLAP CLAP CLAP CLAP
YOU HAPPY NOW, MITCHELL? THEY SEEM TO LIKE IT. NO ACCOUNTING FOR TASTE.
DANE! STOP!

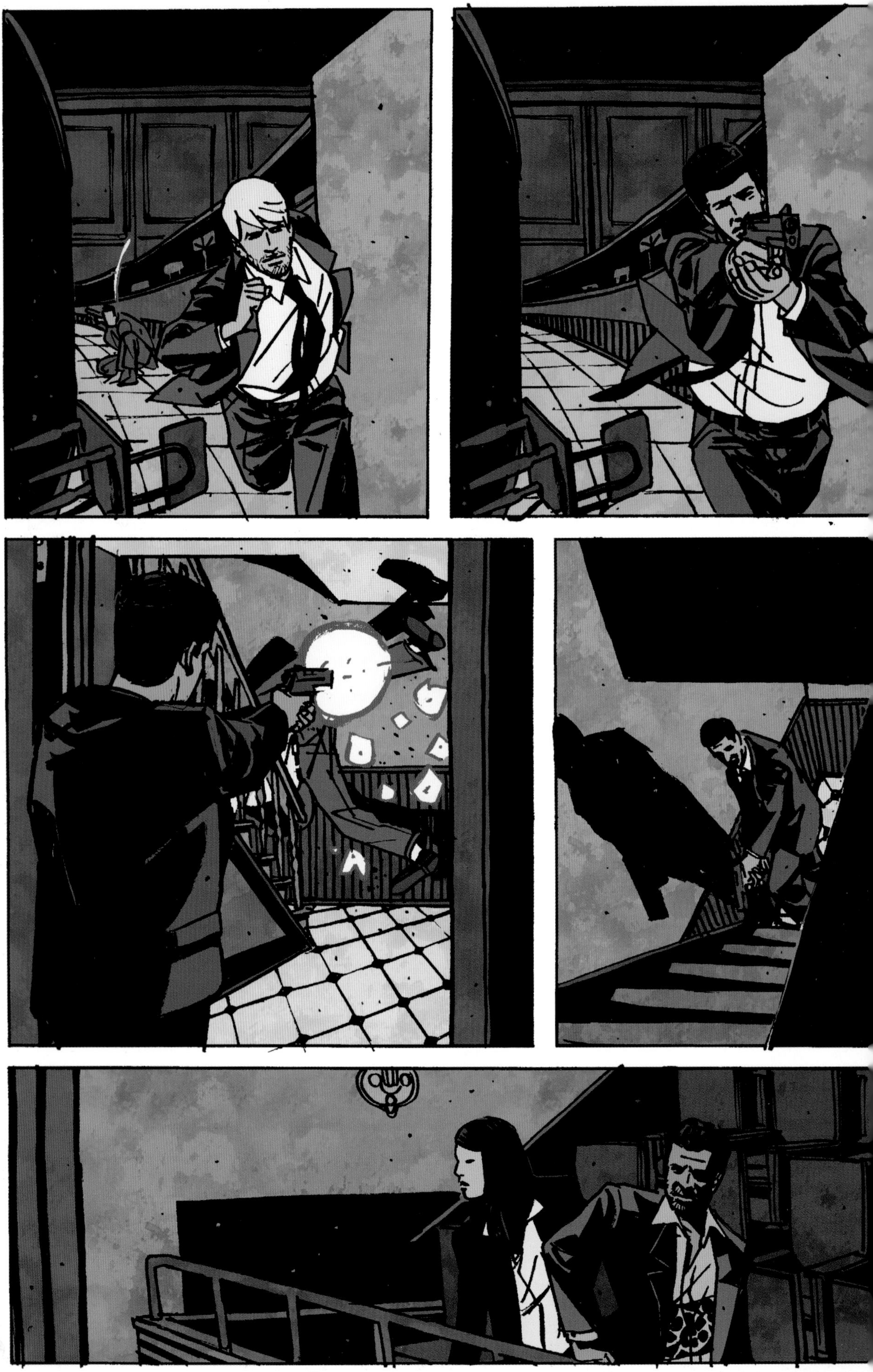

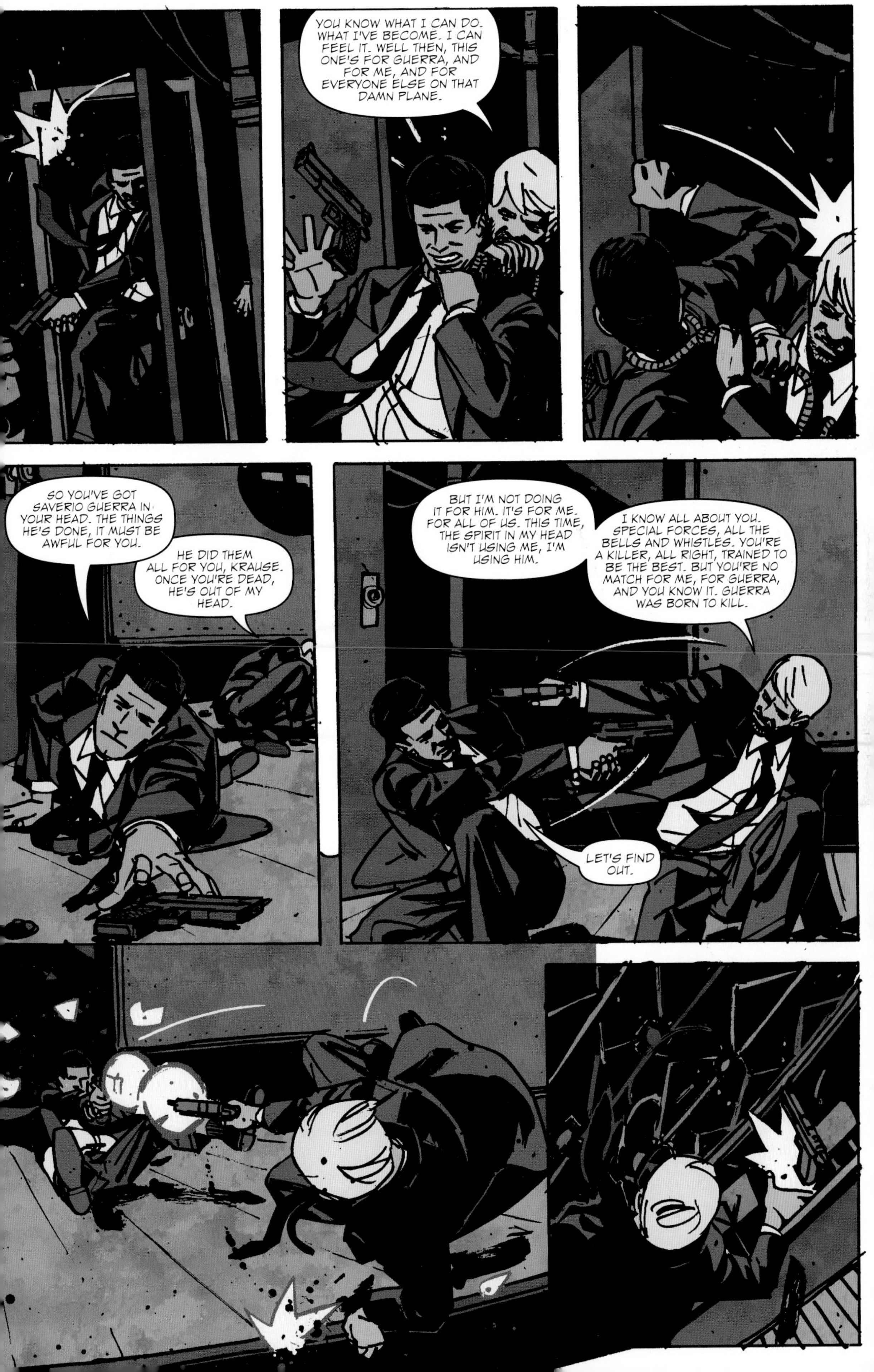
YOU KNOW WHAT I CAN DO. WHAT I'VE BECOME. I CAN FEEL IT. WELL THEN, THIS ONE'S FOR GUERRA, AND FOR ME, AND FOR EVERYONE ELSE ON THAT DAMN PLANE.
SO YOU'VE GOT SAVERIO GUERRA IN YOUR HEAD. THE THINGS HE'S DONE, IT MUST BE AWFUL FOR YOU.
HE DID THEM ALL FOR YOU, KRAUSE. ONCE YOU'RE DEAD, HE'S OUT OF MY HEAD.
BUT I'M NOT DOING IT FOR HIM. IT'S FOR ME. FOR ALL OF US. THIS TIME, THE SPIRIT IN MY HEAD ISN'T USING ME, I'M USING HIM.
I KNOW ALL ABOUT YOU. SPECIAL FORCES, ALL THE BELLS AND WHISTLES. YOU'RE A KILLER, ALL RIGHT, TRAINED TO BE THE BEST. BUT YOU'RE NO MATCH FOR ME, FOR GUERRA, AND YOU KNOW IT. GUERRA WAS BORN TO KILL.
LET'S FIND OUT.

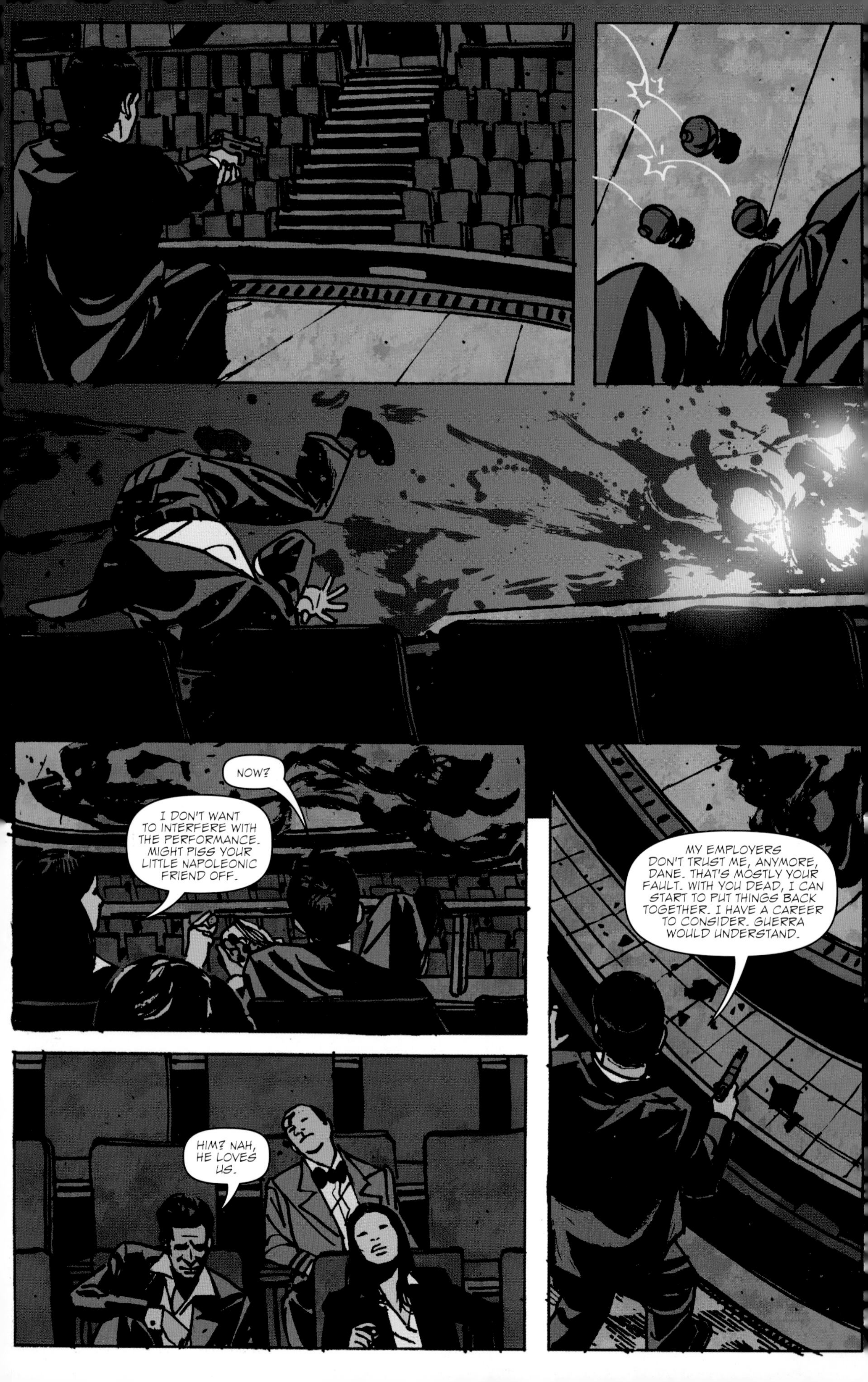
NOW?
I DON'T WANT TO INTERFERE WITH THE PERFORMANCE. MIGHT PISS YOUR LITTLE NAPOLEONIC FRIEND OFF.
MY EMPLOYERS DON'T TRUST ME, ANYMORE, DANE. THAT'S MOSTLY YOUR FAULT. WITH YOU DEAD, I CAN START TO PUT THINGS BACK TOGETHER. I HAVE A CAREER TO CONSIDER. GUERRA WOULD UNDERSTAND.
HIM? NAH, HE LOVES US.

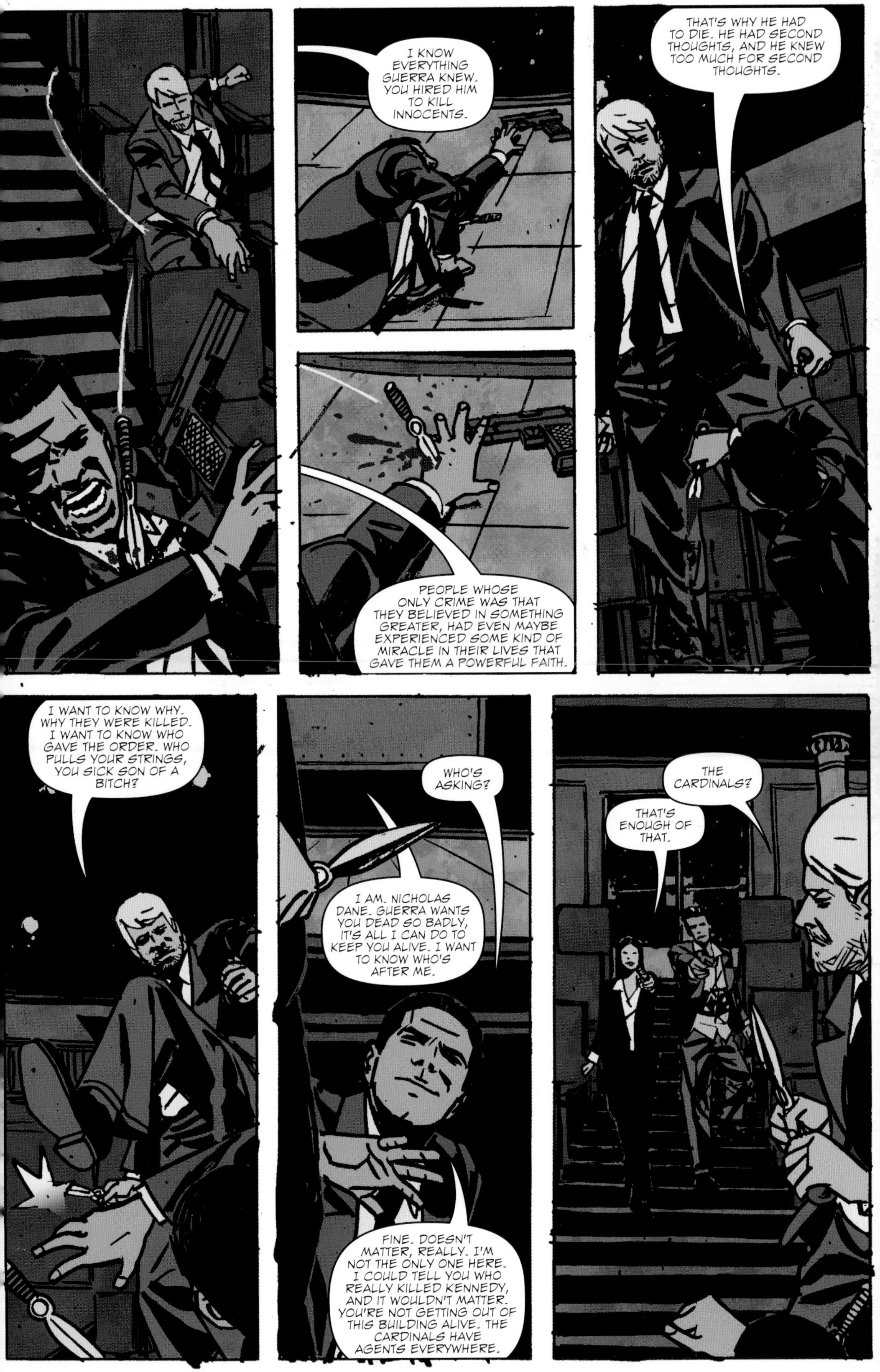
I KNOW EVERYTHING GUERRA KNEW. YOU HIRED HIM TO KILL INNOCENTS.
PEOPLE WHOSE ONLY CRIME WAS THAT THEY BELIEVED IN SOMETHING GREATER, HAD EVEN MAYBE EXPERIENCED SOME KIND OF MIRACLE IN THEIR LIVES THAT GAVE THEM A POWERFUL FAITH.
THAT'S WHY HE HAD TO DIE. HE HAD SECOND THOUGHTS, AND HE KNEW TOO MUCH FOR SECOND THOUGHTS.
I WANT TO KNOW WHY. WHY THEY WERE KILLED. I WANT TO KNOW WHO GAVE THE ORDER. WHO PULLS YOUR STRINGS, YOU SICK SON OF A BITCH?
WHO'S ASKING?
I AM. NICHOLAS DANE. GUERRA WANTS YOU DEAD SO BADLY, IT'S ALL I CAN DO TO KEEP YOU ALIVE. I WANT TO KNOW WHO'S AFTER ME.
FINE. DOESN'T MATTER, REALLY. I'M NOT THE ONLY ONE HERE. I COULD TELL YOU WHO REALLY KILLED KENNEDY, AND IT WOULDN'T MATTER. YOU'RE NOT GETTING OUT OF THIS BUILDING ALIVE. THE CARDINALS HAVE AGENTS EVERYWHERE.
THE CARDINALS?
THAT'S ENOUGH OF THAT.

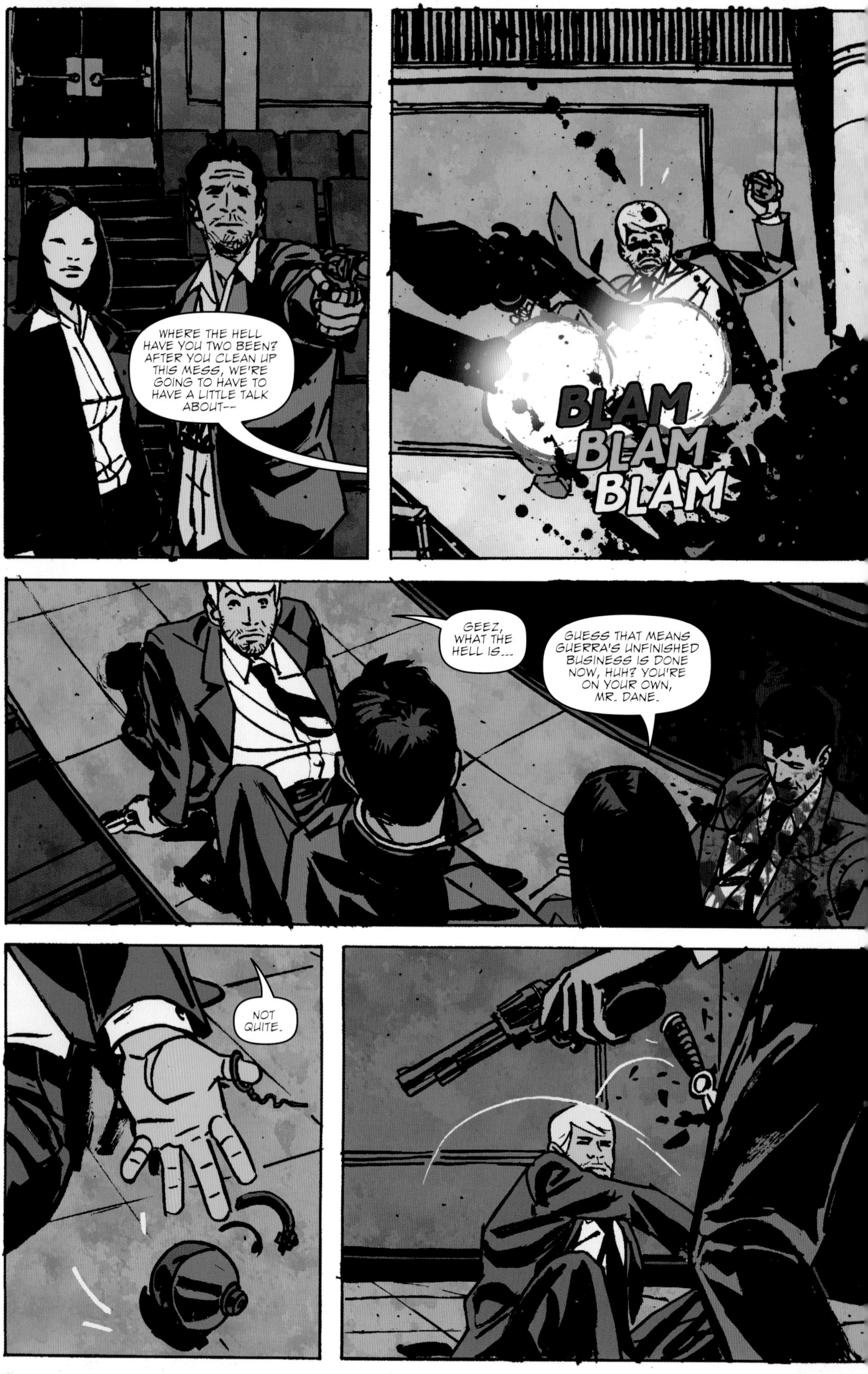
WHERE THE HELL HAVE YOU TWO BEEN? AFTER YOU CLEAN UP THIS MESS, WE'RE GOING TO HAVE TO HAVE A LITTLE TALK ABOUT--
BLAM
BLAM
BLAM
GEEZ, WHAT THE HELL IS...
GUESS THAT MEANS GUERRA'S UNFINISHED BUSINESS IS DONE NOW, HUH? YOU'RE ON YOUR OWN, MR. DANE.
NOT QUITE.

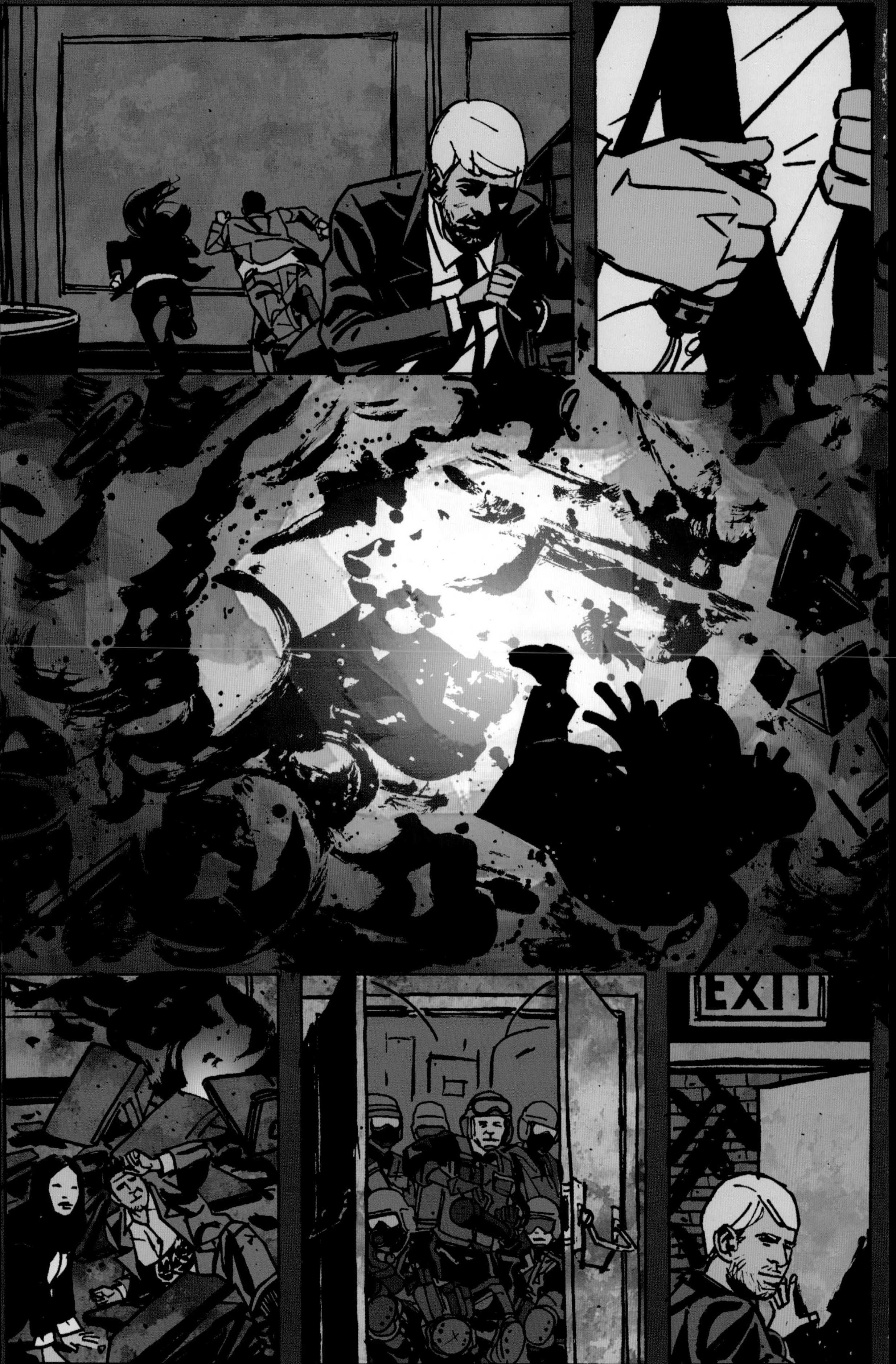
EXIT

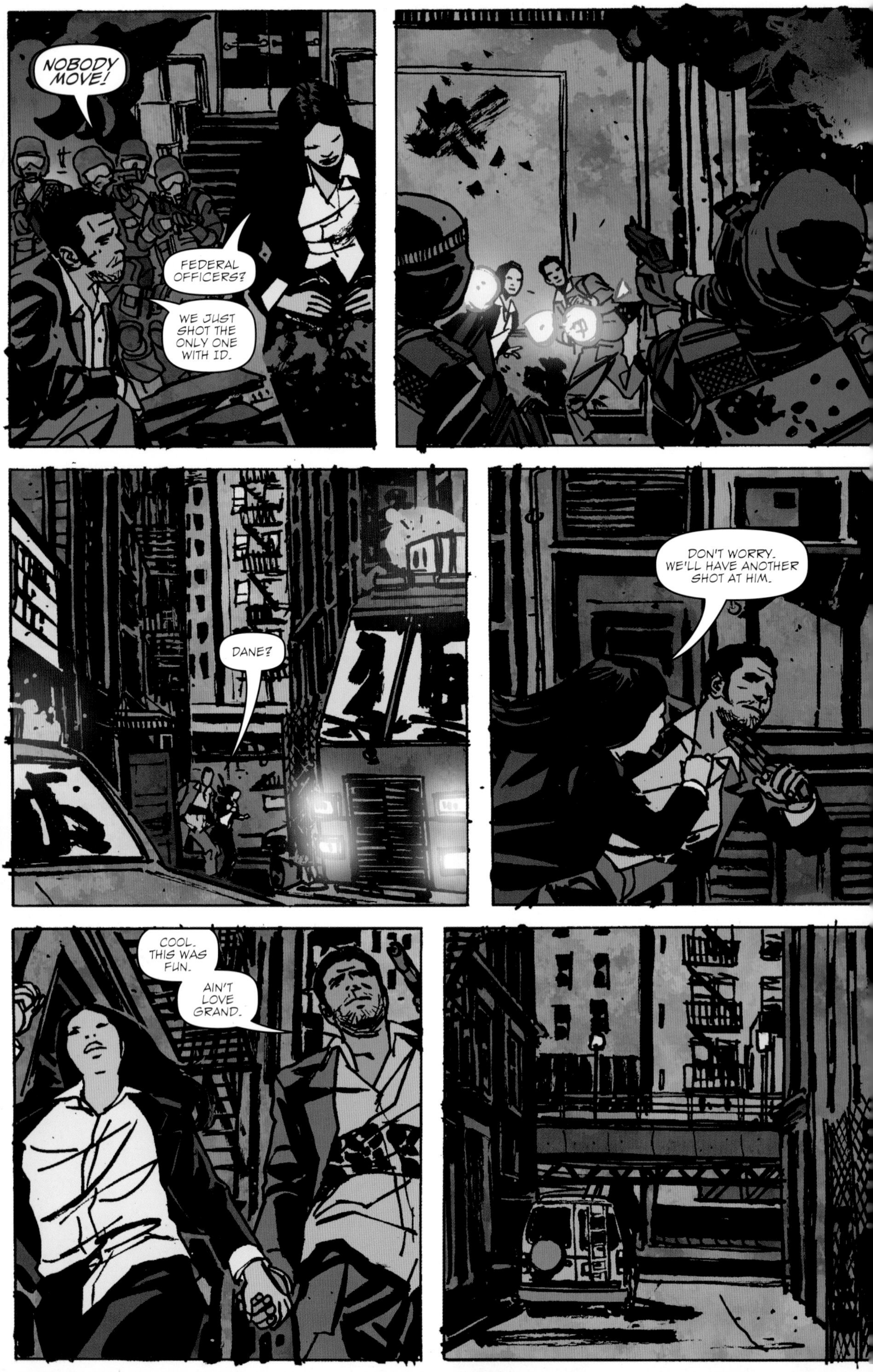

NOBODY MOVE!
FEDERAL OFFICERS?
WE JUST SHOT THE ONLY ONE WITH ID.
DANE?
DON'T WORRY. WE'LL HAVE ANOTHER SHOT AT HIM.
COOL. THIS WAS FUN.
AIN'T LOVE GRAND.

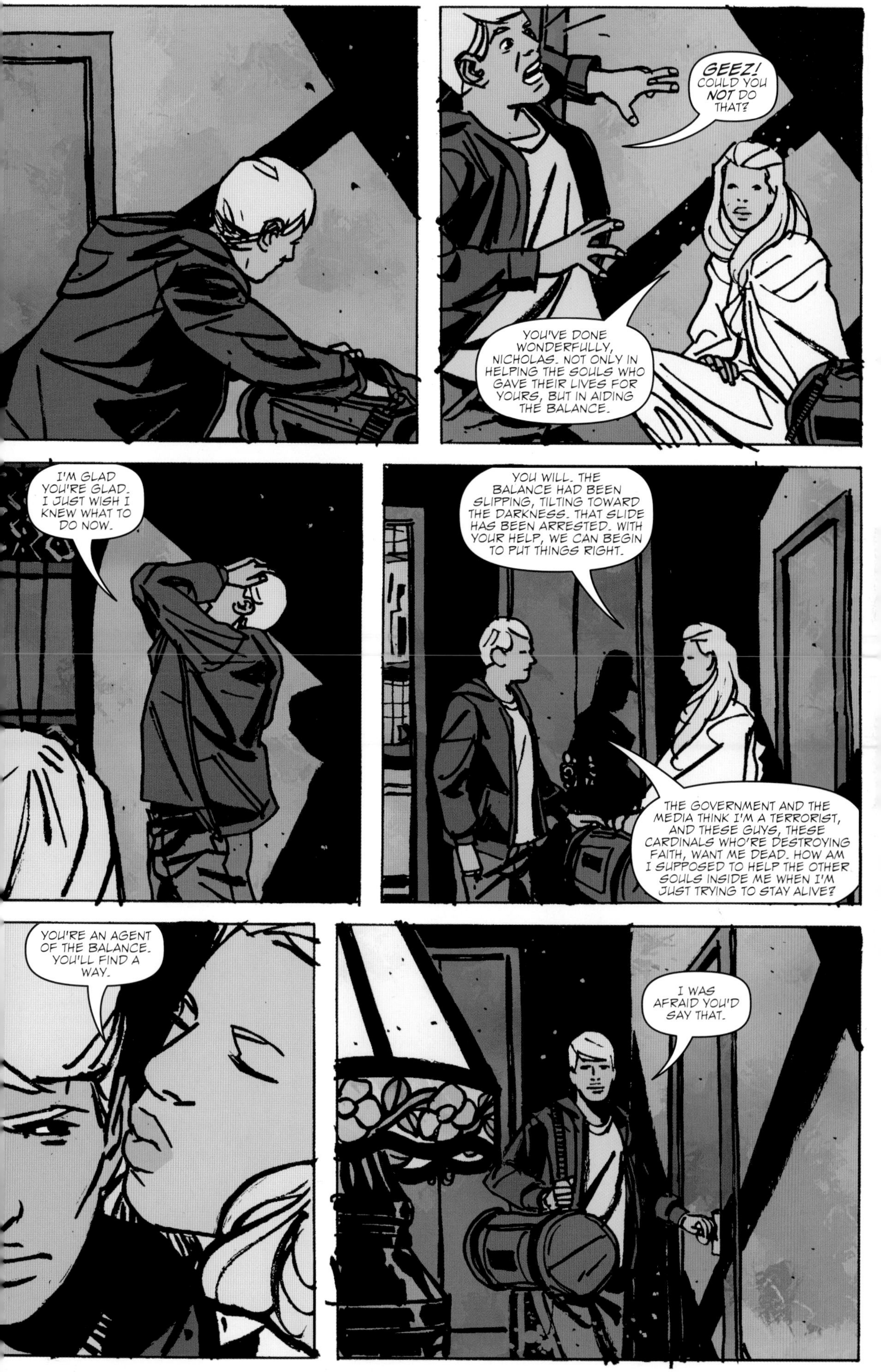
GEEZ! COULD YOU NOT DO THAT?
YOU'VE DONE WONDERFULLY, NICHOLAS. NOT ONLY IN HELPING THE SOULS WHO GAVE THEIR LIVES FOR YOURS, BUT IN AIDING THE BALANCE.
I'M GLAD YOU'RE GLAD. I JUST WISH I KNEW WHAT TO DO NOW.
YOU WILL. THE BALANCE HAD BEEN SLIPPING, TILTING TOWARD THE DARKNESS. THAT SLIDE HAS BEEN ARRESTED. WITH YOUR HELP, WE CAN BEGIN TO PUT THINGS RIGHT.
THE GOVERNMENT AND THE MEDIA THINK I'M A TERRORIST, AND THESE GUYS, THESE CARDINALS WHO'RE DESTROYING FAITH, WANT ME DEAD. HOW AM I SUPPOSED TO HELP THE OTHER SOULS INSIDE ME WHEN I'M JUST TRYING TO STAY ALIVE?
YOU'RE AN AGENT OF THE BALANCE. YOU'LL FIND A WAY.
I WAS AFRAID YOU'D SAY THAT.

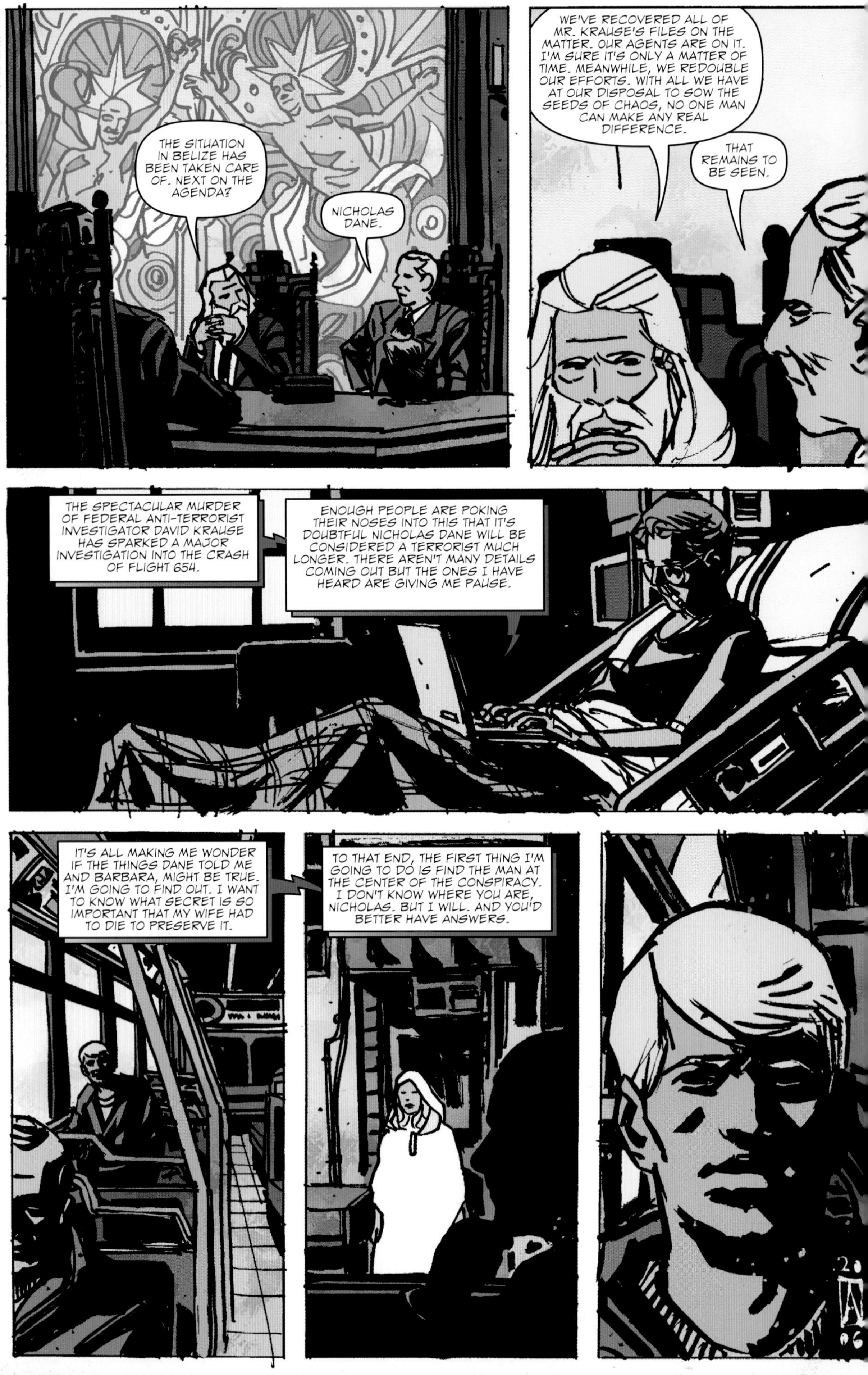
THE SITUATION IN BELIZE HAS BEEN TAKEN CARE OF. NEXT ON THE AGENDA?
NICHOLAS DANE.
WE'VE RECOVERED ALL OF MR. KRAUSE'S FILES ON THE MATTER. OUR AGENTS ARE ON IT. I'M SURE IT'S ONLY A MATTER OF TIME. MEANWHILE, WE REDOUBLE OUR EFFORTS. WITH ALL WE HAVE AT OUR DISPOSAL TO SOW THE SEEDS OF CHAOS, NO ONE MAN CAN MAKE ANY REAL DIFFERENCE.
THAT REMAINS TO BE SEEN.
THE SPECTACULAR MURDER OF FEDERAL ANTI-TERRORIST INVESTIGATOR DAVID KRAUSE HAS SPARKED A MAJOR INVESTIGATION INTO THE CRASH OF FLIGHT 654.
ENOUGH PEOPLE ARE POKING THEIR NOSES INTO THIS THAT IT'S DOUBTFUL NICHOLAS DANE WILL BE CONSIDERED A TERRORIST MUCH LONGER. THERE AREN'T MANY DETAILS COMING OUT BUT THE ONES I HAVE HEARD ARE GIVING ME PAUSE.
IT'S ALL MAKING ME WONDER IF THE THINGS DANE TOLD ME AND BARBARA, MIGHT BE TRUE. I'M GOING TO FIND OUT. I WANT TO KNOW WHAT SECRET IS SO IMPORTANT THAT MY WIFE HAD TO DIE TO PRESERVE IT.
TO THAT END, THE FIRST THING I'M GOING TO DO IS FIND THE MAN AT THE CENTER OF THE CONSPIRACY. I DON'T KNOW WHERE YOU ARE, NICHOLAS. BUT I WILL. AND YOU'D BETTER HAVE ANSWERS.

**PAUL AZACETA**
original series cover

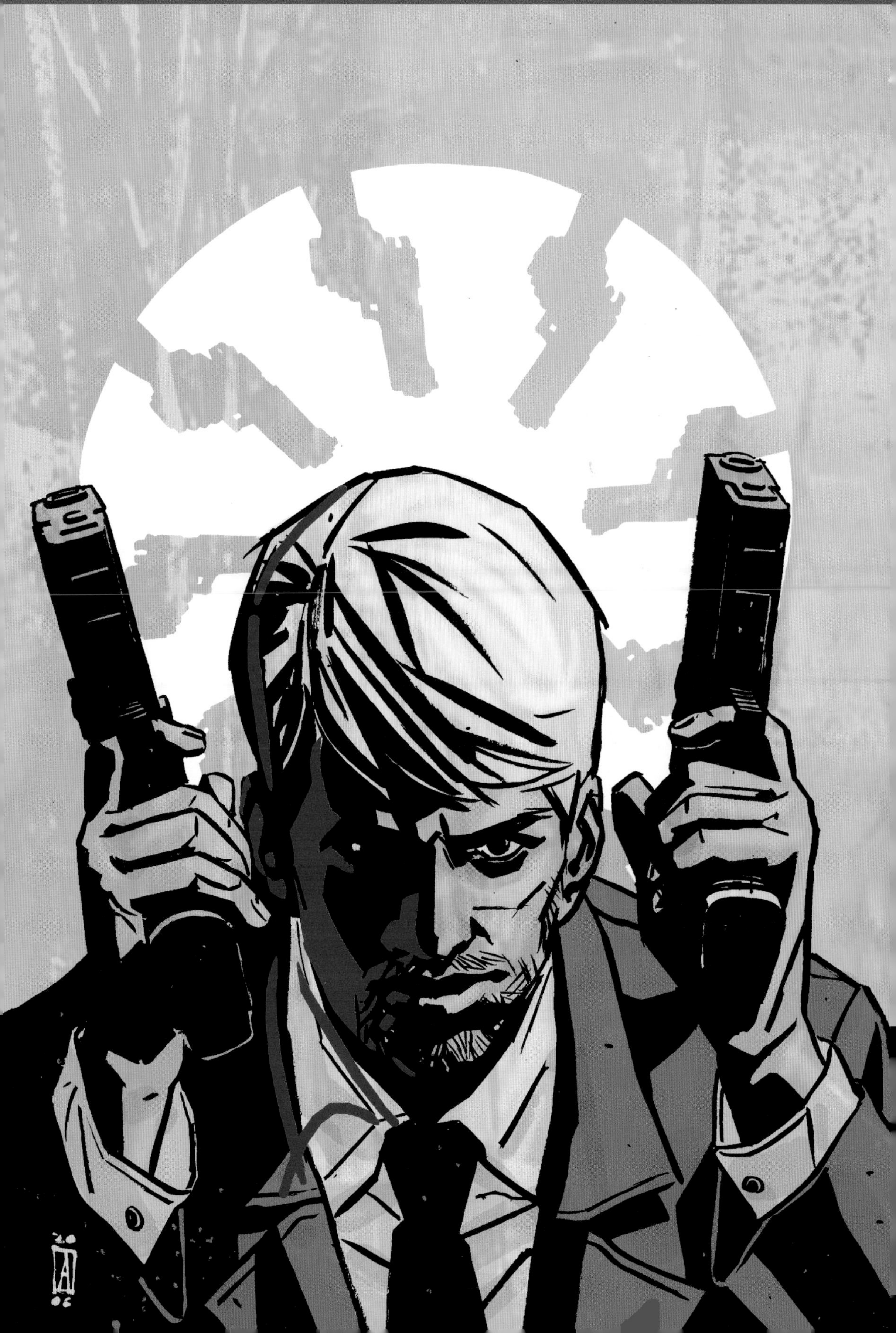

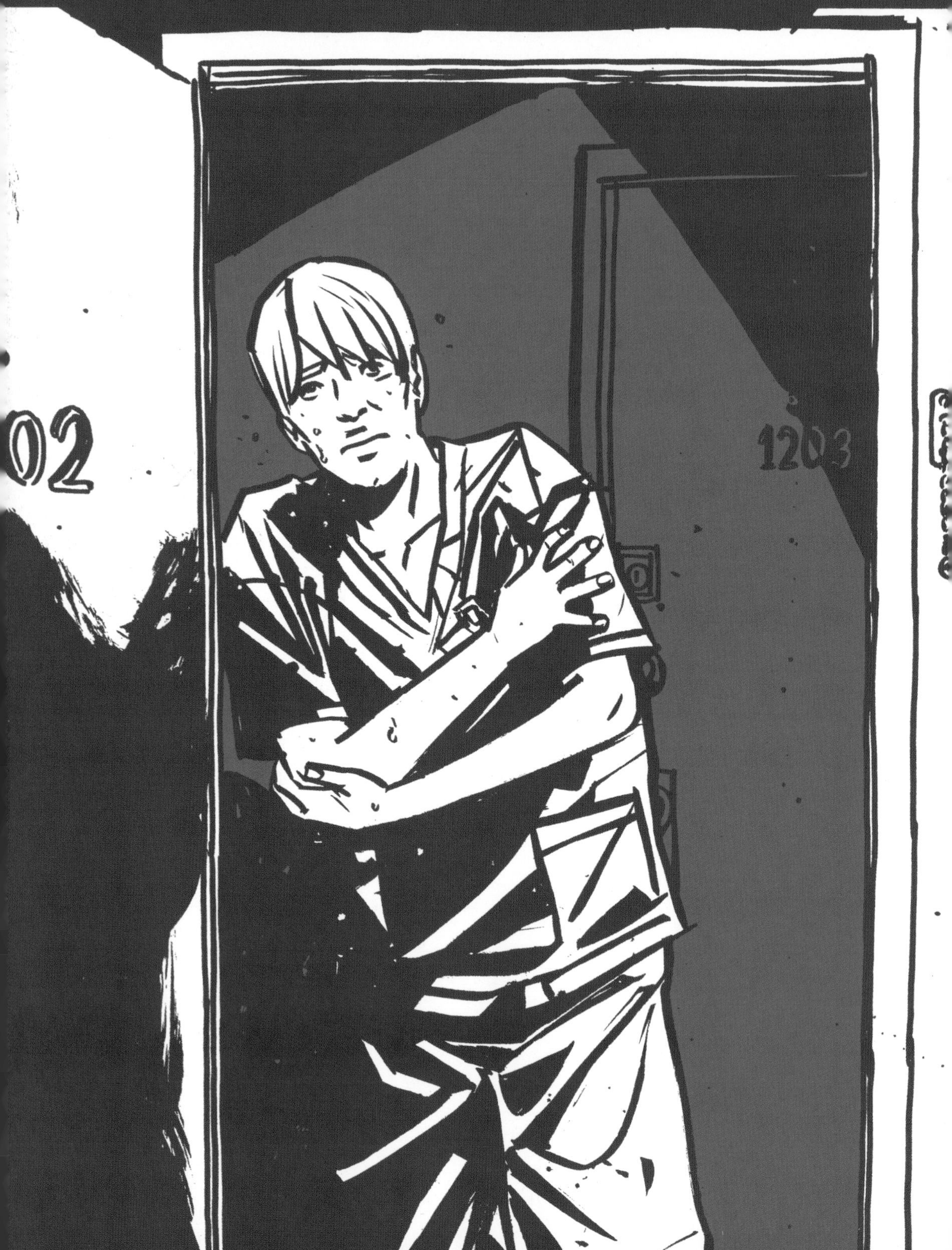
02
1203

# GALLERY

BY PAUL AZACETA

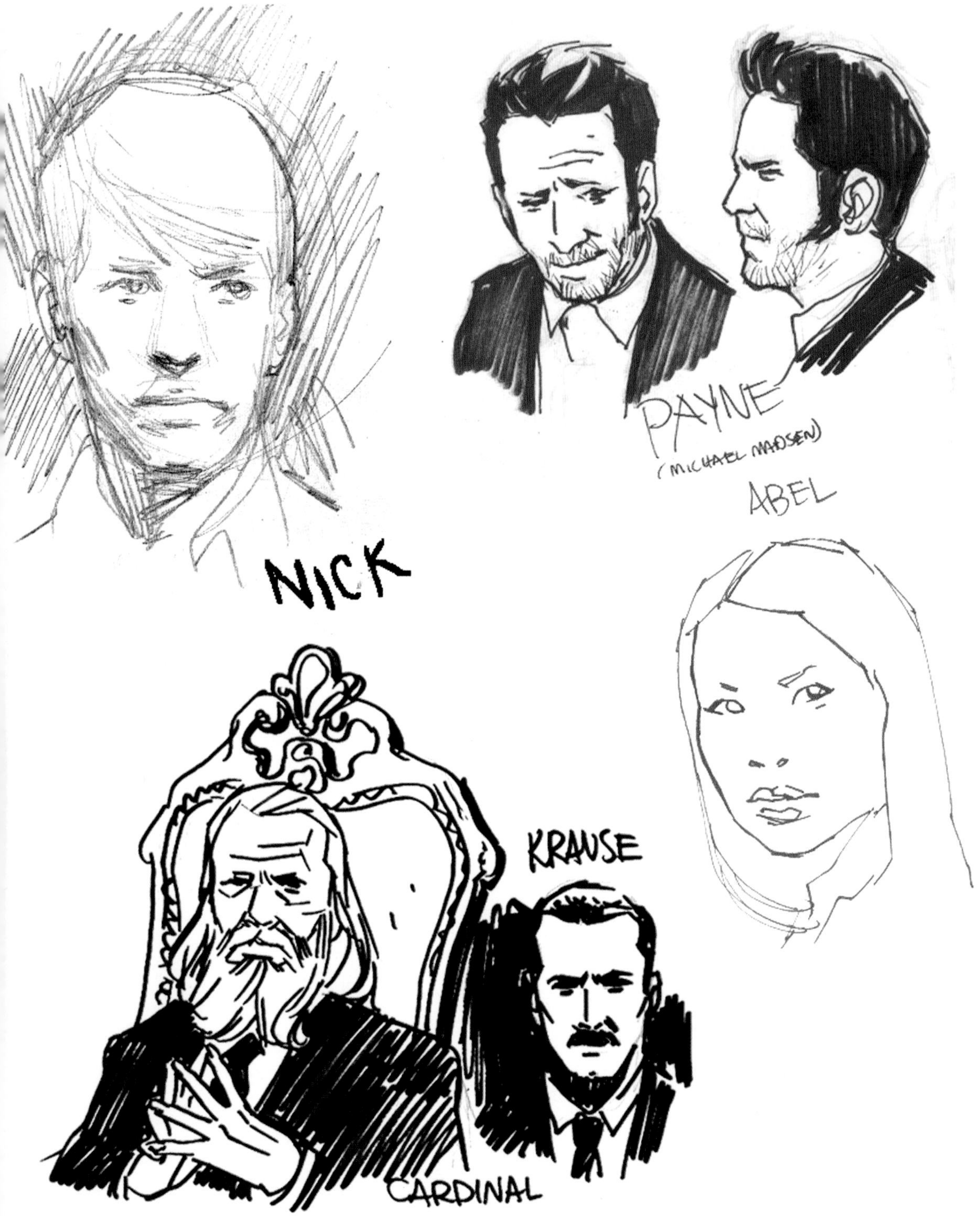
NICK
PAYNE
(MICHAEL MADSEN)
ABEL
KRAUSE
CARDINAL
MONTAGUE

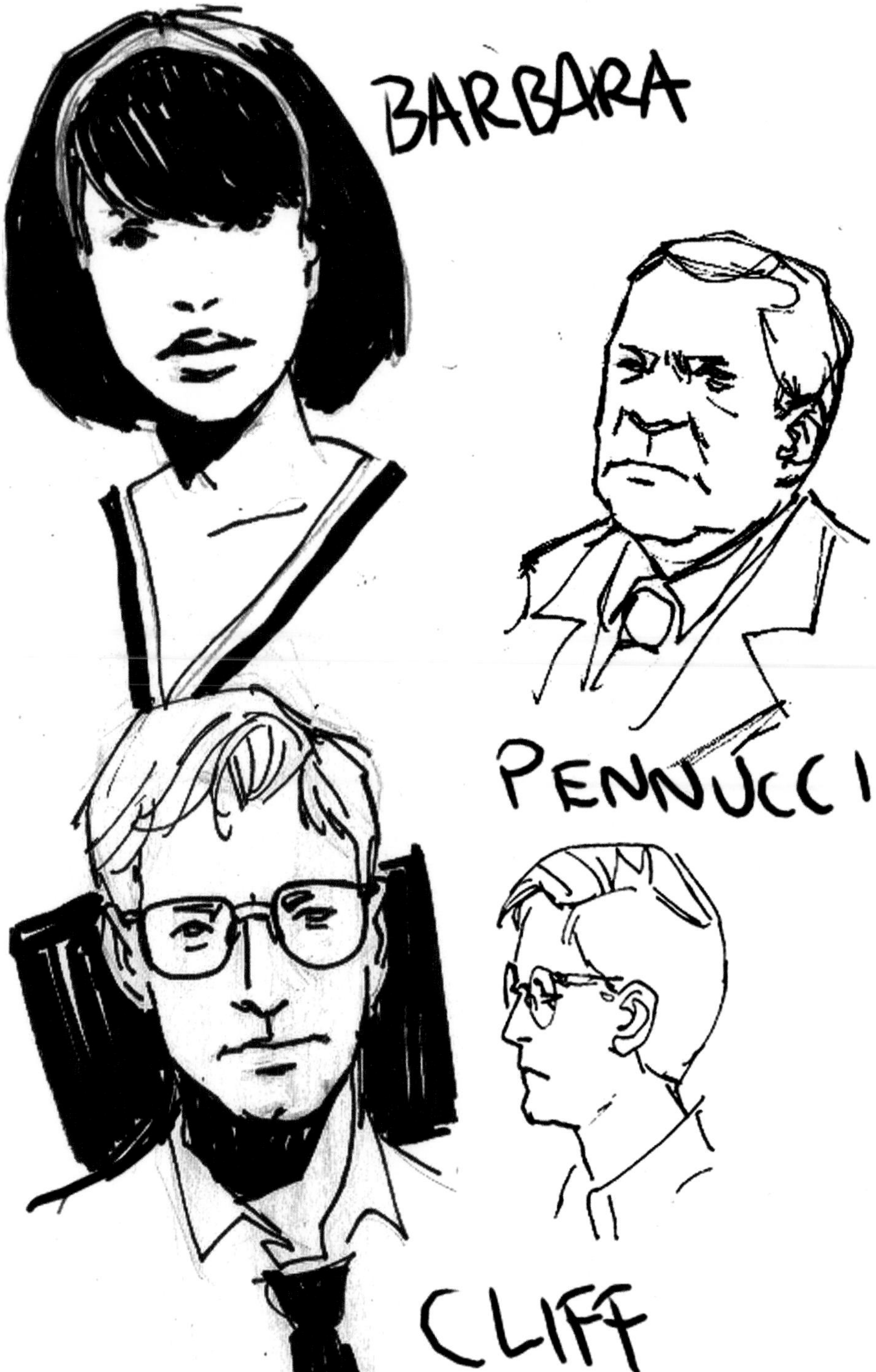
BARBARA
PENNUCCI
CLIFF

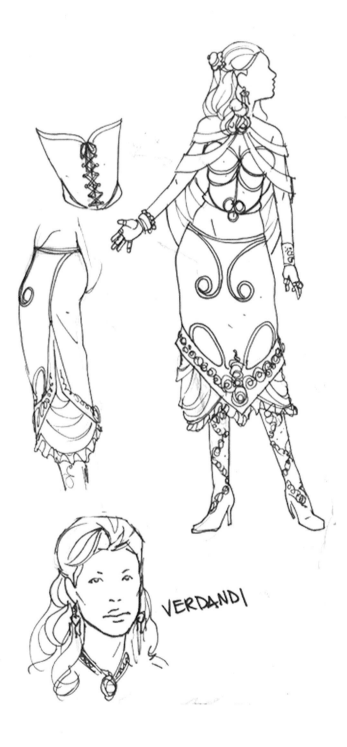

VERDANDI

VERDANDI

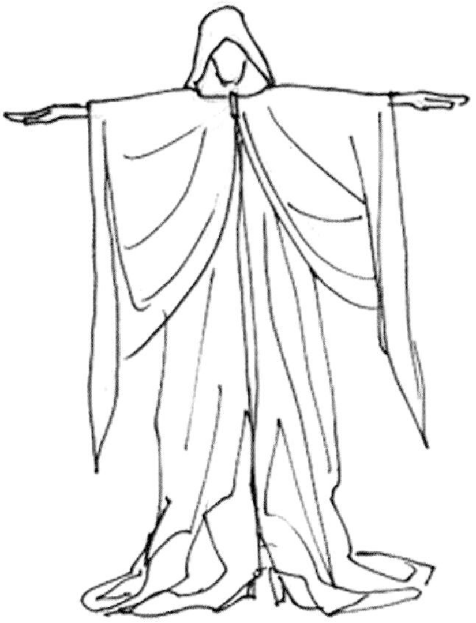

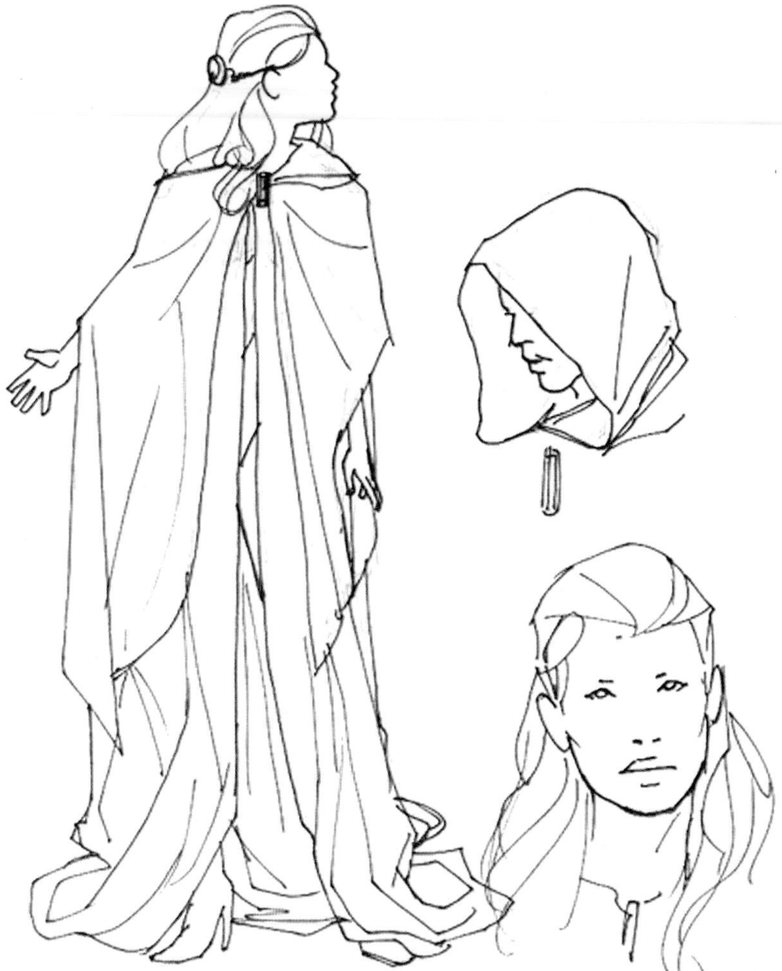

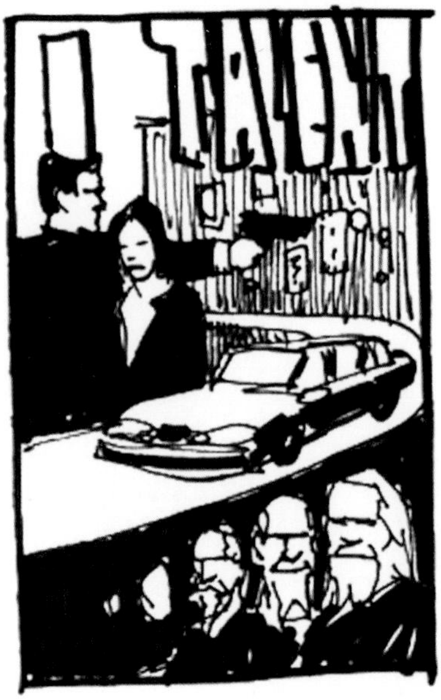

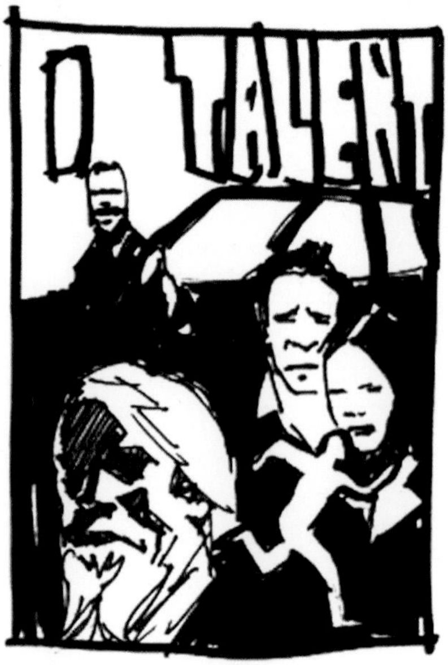

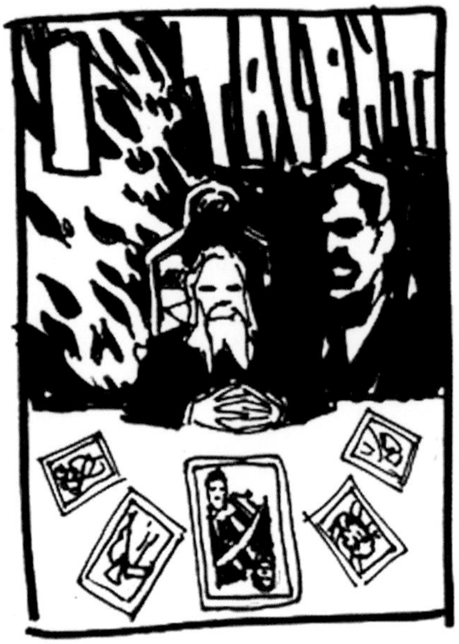

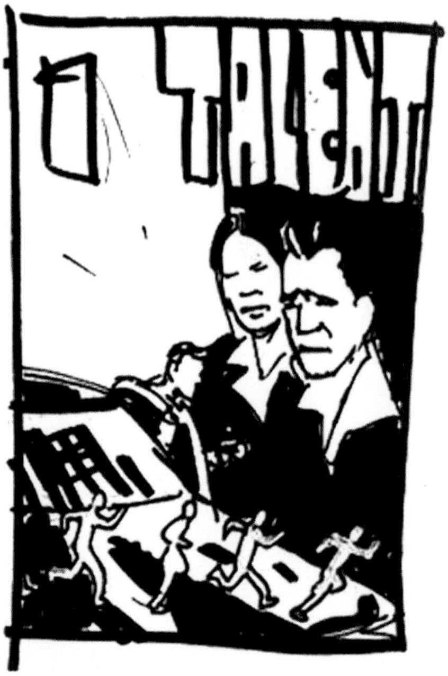

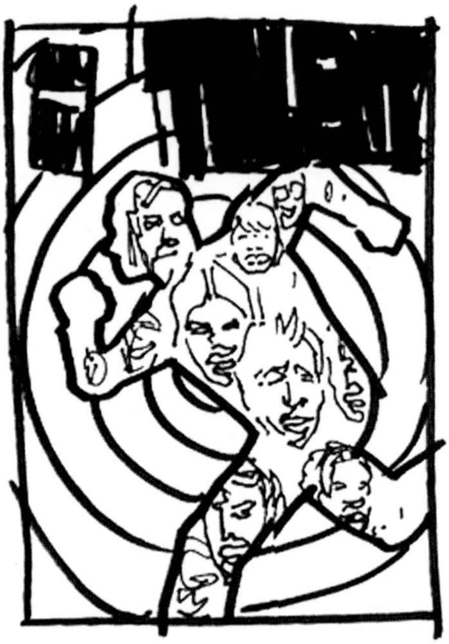

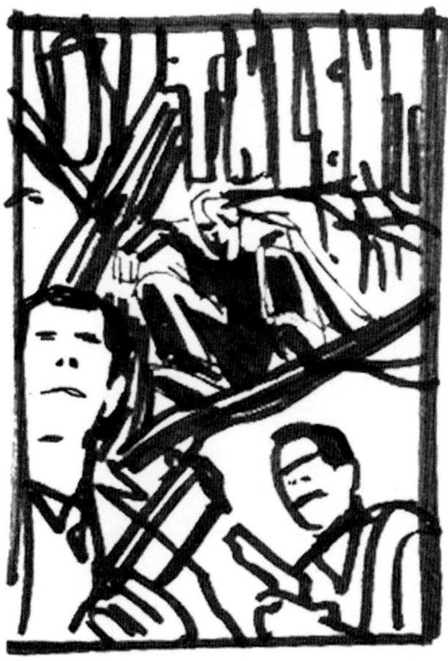

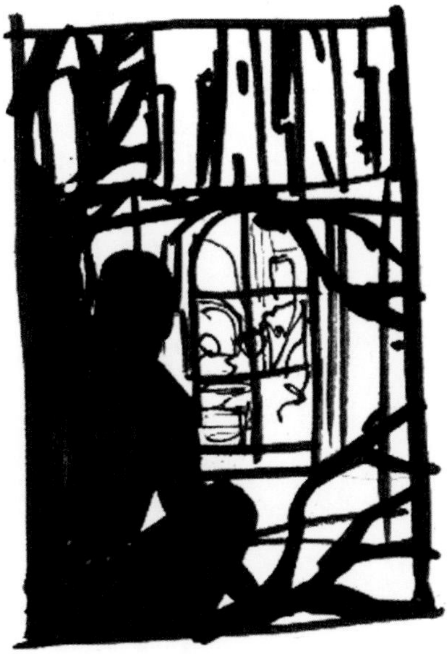

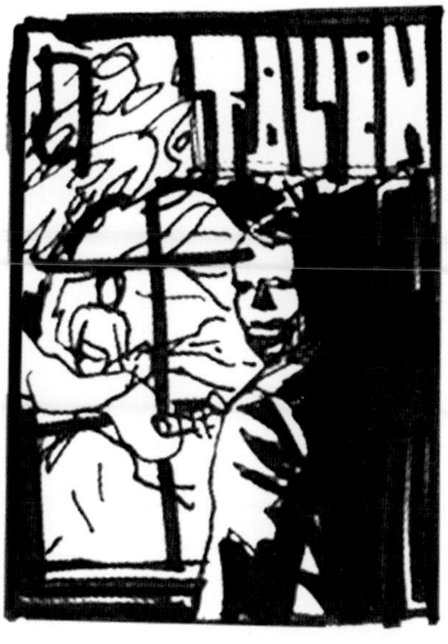

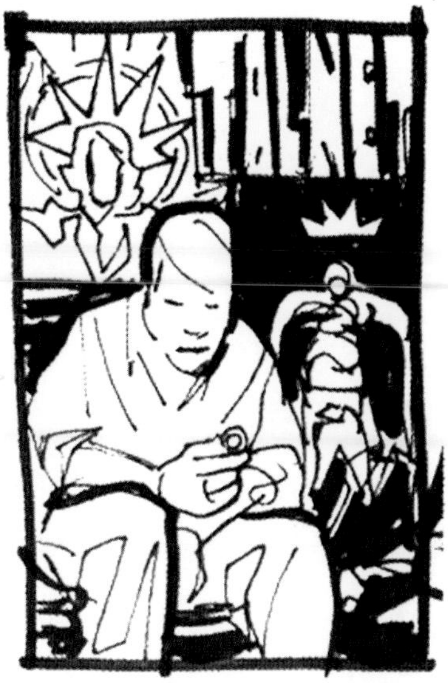

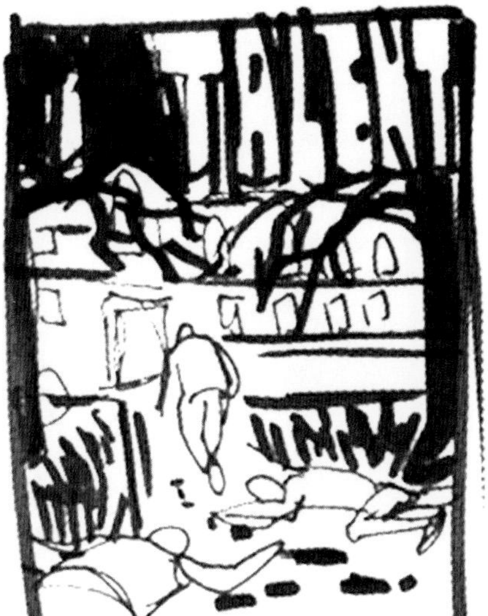
TALENT

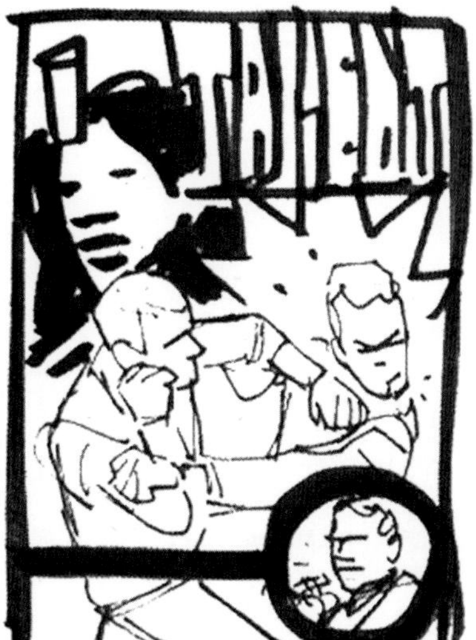

1

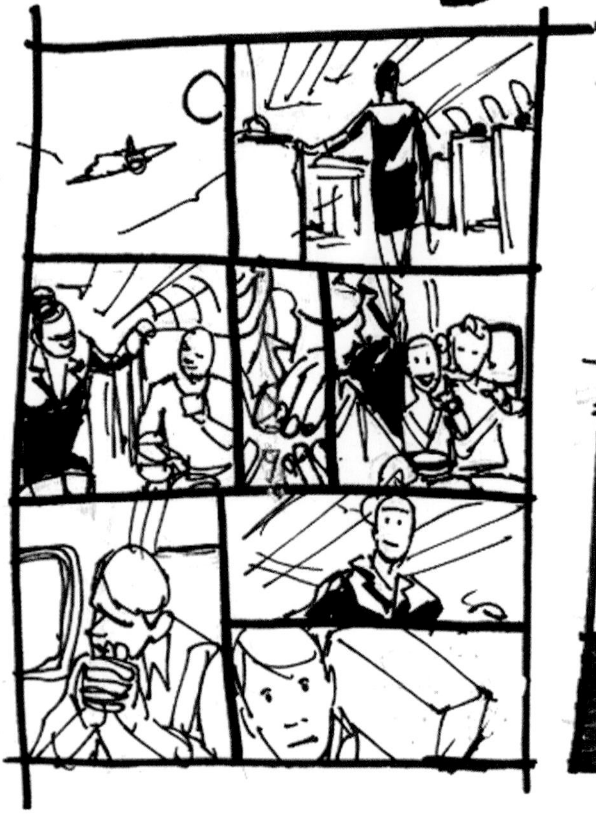

2

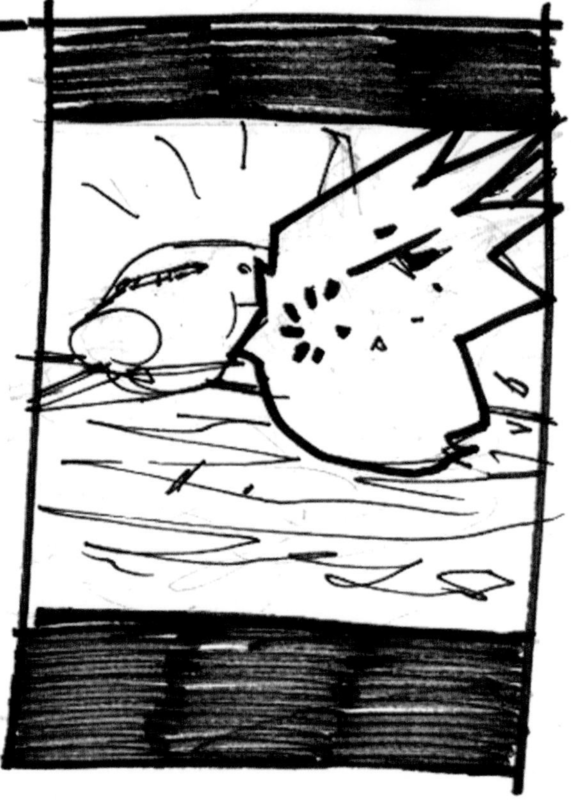

3

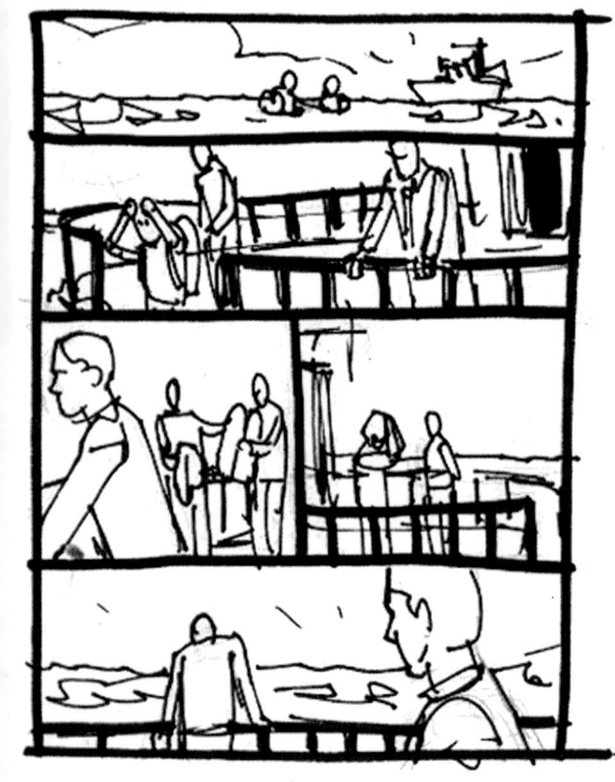

4

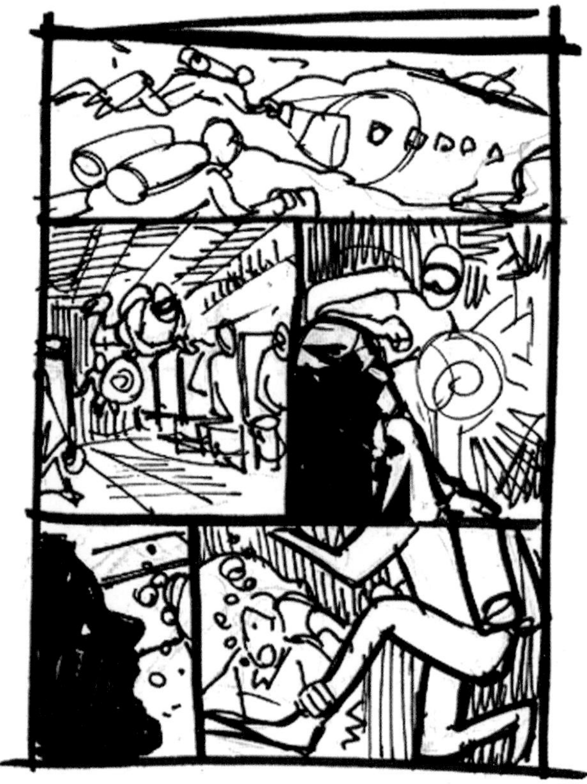

5

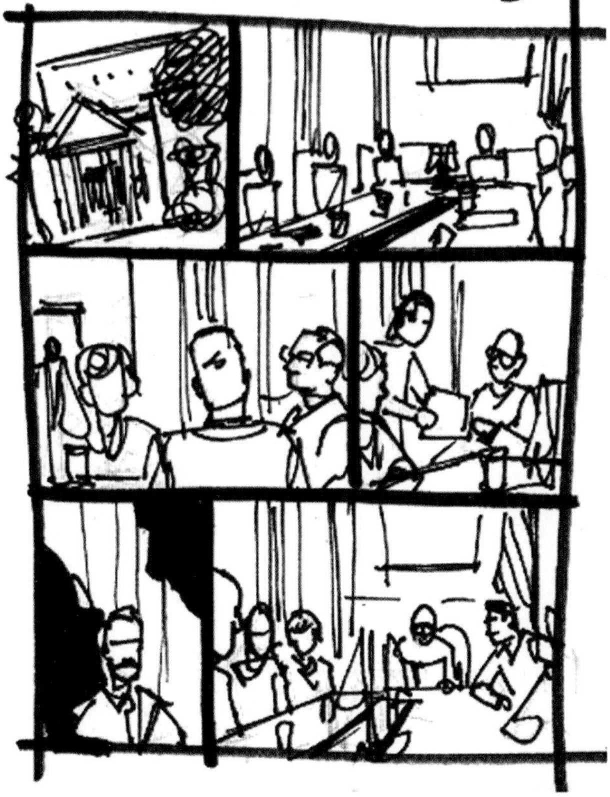

6

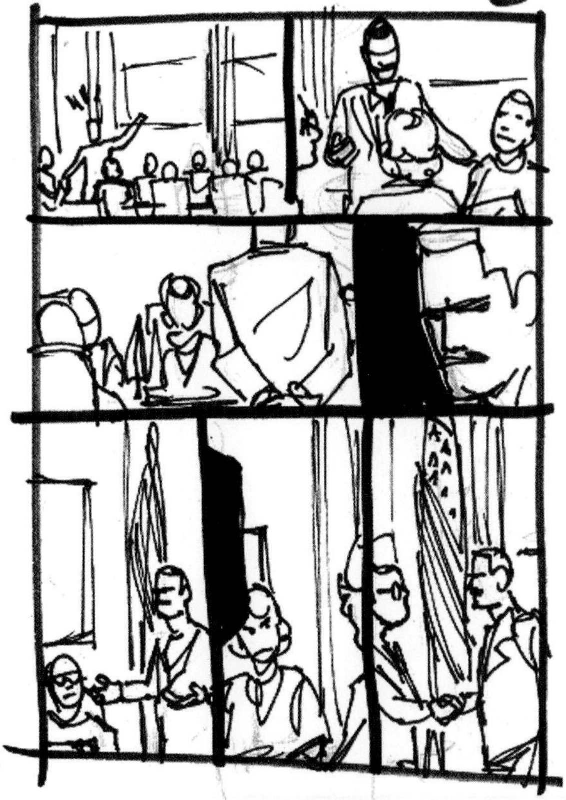

7

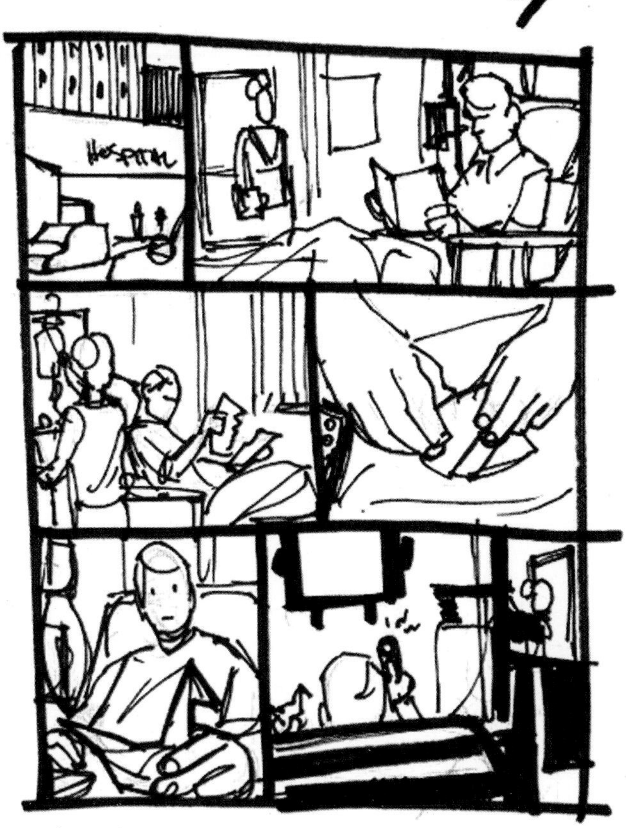
HOSPITAL

8

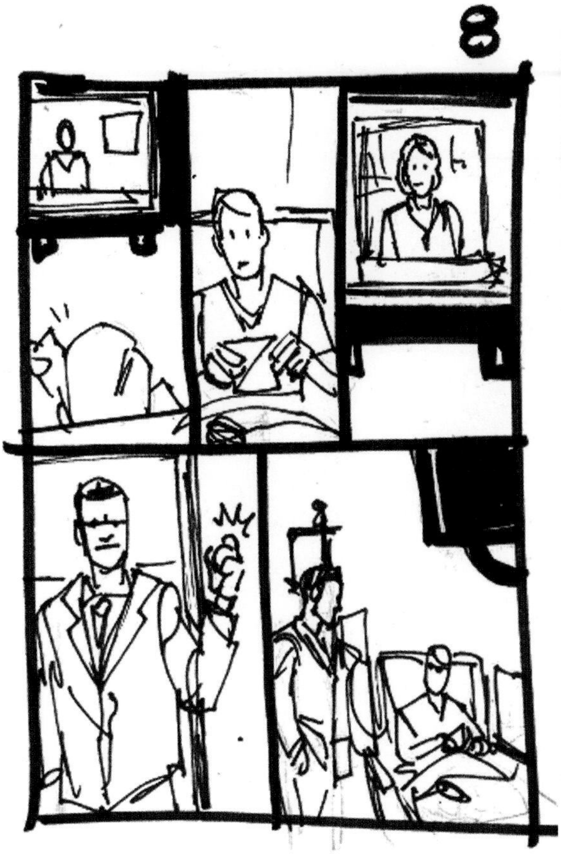

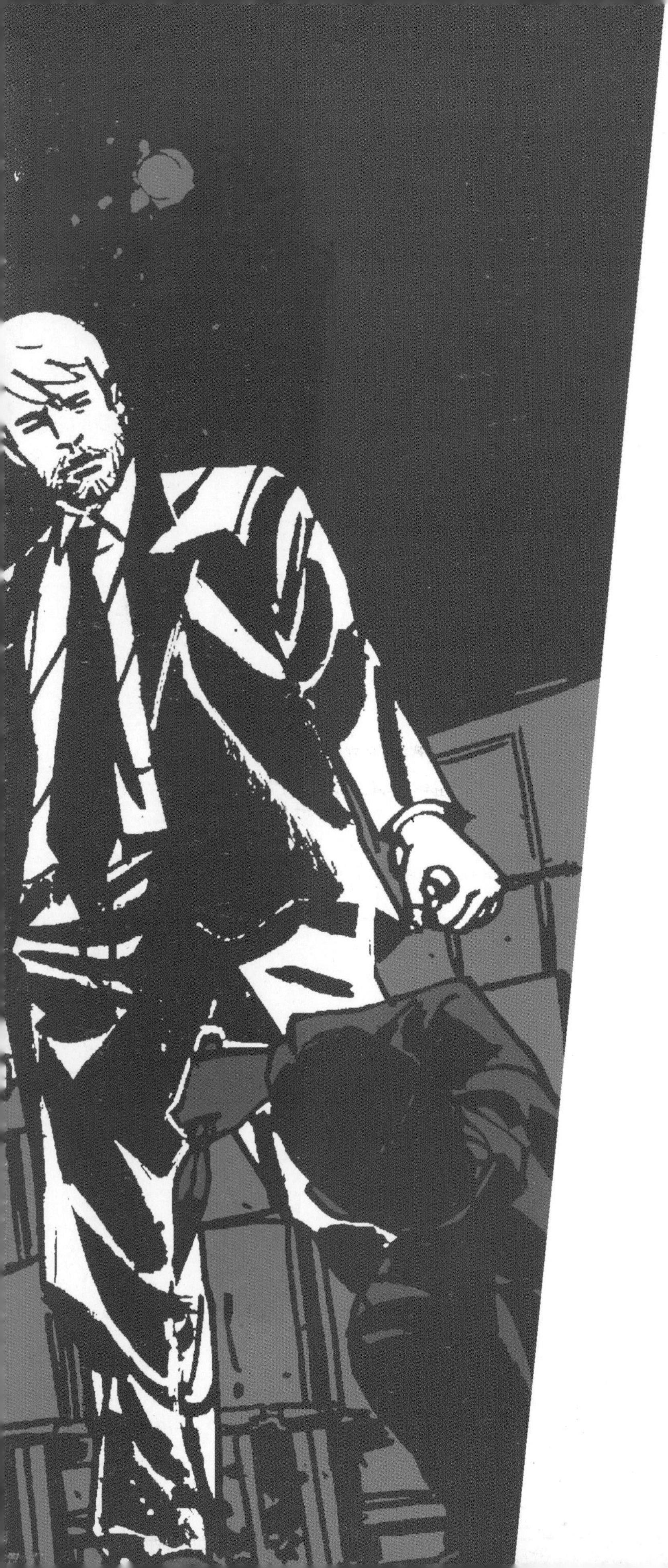

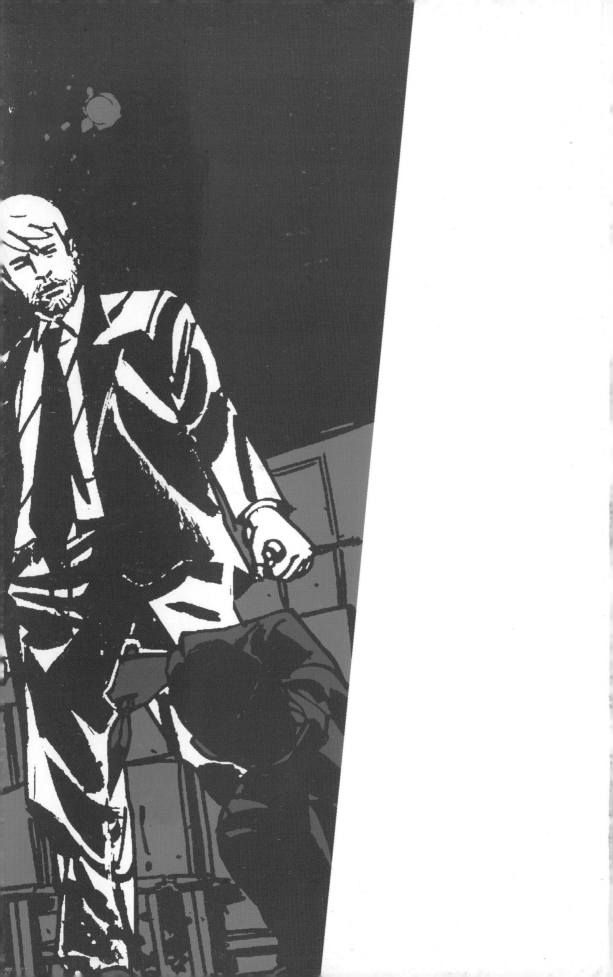